Straight science?

NO LONGER PROPERTY OF
SEATTLE PUBLIC LIBRARY

Homosexuality is a problem for evolutionary theory. How does a non-reproductive sexual preference survive? There is increasing evidence for a biological basis to homosexuality, not least the discovery in 1993 of markers for a gay gene. Yet Darwinism, the most widely accepted evolutionary theory, emphasises successful reproduction and the 'survival of the fittest'. How do we explain a lifetime preference for non-reproductive sex? What does evolutionary theory make of a behaviour that seems to be positively selected yet produces fewer children? Surely homosexuality defies evolutionary explanation? Is there an evolutionary advantage to homosexuality? *Straight Science?* examines the latest research and considers these questions from an evolutionary perspective.

While social constructivism offers explanations in terms of social learning and cultural preferences, the body of evidence for a genetic predisposition to homosexuality grows. The implication of adopting the social constructivist view of homosexual sex is that such sex is merely misdirected and therefore futile, but far from dying out it continues through the ages and across cultures.

Jim McKnight provides a comprehensive summary of the research on the biology of homosexuality, including twin studies; hormonal assays; anatomical, functional and molecular biology differences; and the search for a gay gene. The book considers biological and social evolutionary theories of the causation of homosexuality, and puts forward a model of the most likely causes. It concludes with an overview of the adequacy of social constructivist challenges to a biosocial perspective on homosexuality.

Jim McKnight is Chair of the Psychology Department at the University of Western Sydney, Macarthur, and author of six books including *Social Psychology* (1994) (with J.E. Sutton).

D1005203

Straight science?

Homosexuality, evolution and adaptation

Jim McKnight

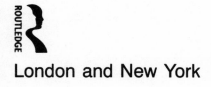

London and New York

First published 1997
by Routledge
11 New Fetter Lane, London EC4P 4EE

Simultaneously published in the USA and Canada
by Routledge
29 West 35th Street, New York, NY 10001

© 1997 Jim McKnight

Phototypeset in Times by Intype London Ltd
Printed and bound in Great Britain by
TJ International Ltd, Padstow, Cornwall

All rights reserved. No part of this book may be reprinted
or reproduced or utilised in any form or by any electronic,
mechanical, or other means, now known or hereafter
invented, including photocopying and recording, or in any
information storage or retrieval system, without
permission in writing from the publishers.

British Library Cataloguing in Publication Data
A catalogue record for this book is available from the British Library

Library of Congress Cataloging in Publication Data
A catalogue record for this book has been requested

ISBN 0–415–15772–2 (hbk)
ISBN 0–415–15773–0 (pbk)

For Des Crawley, who defended this work, *ad utrumque paratus*

Contents

List of figures and tables   ix
Preface   x

1 Is male homosexuality adaptive?   1
Homosexuality, futile sex?   3
Orientation or preference?   5
How many gay men and just what is homosexuality anyway?   6
What do we know and what do we want to know about   7
   homosexuality?
Explaining homosexuality?   8
Is evolution social?   14
Where to from here?   17

2 A biology of homosexuality   18
Homosexuality, a sexual inversion?   21
Does genetic inversion model homosexuality?   23
A chemical imbalance: the de-androgenised foetus theories   26
An anatomical difference?   38
Functional differences?   41
A genetic variation?   43
Discovering a difference: familial studies   44
A world of difference? Xq28   53
A typology of homosexuality   59
So where are we now?   62

3 Homosexuality as physical evolution   64
Is homosexuality really adaptive?   64
Models of balance polymorphism: a balanced superior   76
   heterozygotic fitness
Models of balance polymorphism: sperm competition   92
Models of balance polymorphism: density and frequency-   97
   dependent selection

Models of balance polymorphism: frequency-dependent sexual   101
    selection
Homosexuality as an evolutionary byproduct   115
Models of evolutionary futility: an overloving effect   116
Models of evolutionary futility: homosexuality – a continuously   120
    occurring mutation?

4 Homosexuality as social evolution   124
Kin selection   127
Kin selection for a homosexuality gene   129
Kin selection for genes other than homosexuality   135
Kin selection and a social preference for homosexuality   140
Parental manipulation   144
A social adjustment   149
The central theoretical problem of sociobiology   156

5 The seven deadly sins of sociobiology   163
The first deadly sin: we are animals   164
The second deadly sin: explaining homosexuality is   168
    unnecessary and misguided
The third deadly sin: trivial pursuits   170
The fourth deadly sin: a creeping reductionism   173
The fifth deadly sin: sly determinism   177
The sixth deadly sin: sociobiology is morally bankrupt   179
The seventh deadly sin: sociobiology is sexist   181
Conclusions   185

Glossary   188
Bibliography   194
Author index   210
Subject index   214

Figures and Tables

FIGURES

2.1 Changes in LH in response to a single injection of Premarin   34
3.1 Types of natural selection   70
3.2 Proportion of 1881 generation in subsequent generation   85
3.3 Mean values for lowest acceptable intelligence and involvement level   110
3.4 Double-matings, contraceptive use, and fertility   111
4.1 Population penetrance of direct versus indirect inclusive fitness   133
4.2 Reproductive success of bisexual and heterosexual women   151

TABLES

2.1 Maternal and paternal line gay relatives of homosexual men   55
3.1 Comparative content of fantasy material: frequency of occurrence   79
3.2 Equilibrium in simulated selection experiment due to rare-male advantage in *Drosophila pseudoobscura*   99
4.1 Reproductive success and descendants via kin selection and direct reproduction   132

Preface

At the risk of entirely blowing my credibility at the outset, let me start this speculative look at male homosexuality by saying that it is written by a straight researcher who is less interested in explaining homosexuality, or in passing comment on it as a lifestyle, than in the perspective of a theorist confronted with an enormous difficulty threatening the tidy order of his theoretical universe. Homosexuality is a major problem for those like myself who believe that Darwinism is the great unifying force which social theory, particularly psychology, so desperately needs for internal coherence. Unfortunately, few would agree and there are many challenges to a Darwinistic view of the social order. Perhaps one of the cleverest challenges to confront evolutionary theory is homosexuality. Homosexuality seems to be a tailor-made rebuttal of the great evolutionary credo – survival of the fittest. How do we explain what is often a lifelong preference for non-reproductive sex? Surely homosexuality defies evolutionary explanation?

This *is* a clever criticism. While far from being a life against nature, homosexuality seems to contradict the Darwinian logic of individual reproductive success. Yet any number of surveys tell us that there are many homosexuals, and history attests to homosexuality's antiquity. If homosexuality is 'futile' sex, why are gay men still with us? Despite the weight of a historical bad press, which sees homosexuality as a pathological inversion of normal heterosexuality, its continuance suggests it is an adaptive feature of evolution. What selective advantages might homosexuals enjoy? How is such a widespread social behaviour to be explained? In this book we set out to answer these and other questions from an evolutionary perspective. While many would argue that Darwinism adds little to our understanding of homosexuality, nevertheless, causation is an intriguing puzzle and, if a diverse gay literature is any guide, is often a source of confusion for homosexuals themselves. Apart from being a purely intellectual puzzle, these questions also touch on much broader issues about the nature of biosocial research.

If the genesis of a book arises from dissatisfaction, mine was professional. Whatever the truth about homosexuality, as a social psychologist I came to see that *social constructivism*, my profession's dominant paradigm, had virtually monopolised theorising about homosexuality. At its crudest level, social constructivists see behaviour as culture bound, so they are inevitably less interested in evolutionary theory than in explaining social behaviour from a subjective or perceptual viewpoint. While I am sympathetic to this approach, it leaves an incomplete feeling, as if social explanation is ultimately *ad hoc*. Homosexuality from this perspective is just the product of a chain of accidents which are ultimately gladly or sadly embraced. Without revisiting the nature/nurture debate, recent advances in the biological sciences have made such a one-sided account of homosexuality inadequate. Since the late 1980s we have been caught up in an explosive growth of biological knowledge which has revolutionised our understanding of genetics and brain function and given new urgency to an evolutionary analysis of social behaviour. Recent research suggests a genetic basis for some forms of homosexuality and it is against this backdrop that an evolutionary explanation is long overdue.

Immediately we face the difficulty that few people feel a pressing need to explain homosexuality and it was a novel experience for me to face opposition from peers who thought the project misguided, trivial and unnecessary. To echo a voice of yesteryear, why is this so? Is it merely that many automatically reject Darwinian explanations of social behaviour, or are there more fundamental doubts? Perhaps such explanations threaten the very core of social science, starting it on the slippery slope of biological reductionism. I had hoped this would be a rather uncontroversial review of the current state of biological research into the causes of homosexuality and a speculative look at its evolutionary origins. Such a task would seem simple enough but one has only to put a toe in the literature to see that an evolutionary analysis of homosexuality is a deadly sin just fractionally less wicked than bothering to explain it at all, and marginally more wicked than asserting that homosexuality may well have a biological substrate. Those interested in biosocial explanations seem to get short shrift. The dominance of the social constructivist paradigm became apparent when I started this manuscript. One gay academic friend read an early draft and was disturbed enough to write an allegory on the seven deadly sins of sociobiology for my benefit. The debate, suitably engaged, I hope this book is as much a rebuttal of these sins as it is an attempt to broaden the debate. After examining the more substantive issues, we shall consider these deadly sins in the hope that this will clear the intellectual undergrowth of some of the spurious challenges that might otherwise obscure more considered replies to a sociobiology of homosexuality.

So what you have before you is a long speculative look at the possible reasons for homosexuality from an evolutionary perspective, the product of three years of reading everything I could find on homosexuality and rigorously doubting everything I read in teasing out this puzzle. It is a book which does not pretend to rigorous empiricism but rather constructs selective scenarios which might explain why homosexuality happened and more importantly why it survives. What we have here is a series of how-possibly rather than how-actually explanations (Dray, 1957). The evolutionary philosopher Robert Brandon (1990) noted that unlike just-so stories, selective scenarios attempt to take a chaotic area and shake it into some semblance of order. As Jerome Barkow (1989), a noted evaluator of selective scenarios once wrote, selective scenarios provide a sense of closure, must agree with all the known data and be logically consistent. He also warns about never taking them too seriously given their unverifiable nature, but also notes they are fun for *aficionados*.

I would point out that there are two types of Darwinists writing selective scenarios. There are those who see a large gap between everyday life and ultimate evolutionary explanation and are not fazed by what seems to be maladaptive (non-fitness enhancing) behaviours. Then there are those who feel an obsessive need to make biophysical evolution square with culture. The former would probably doubt the necessity of this book as they would see no compelling isomorphism between what one does and an evolutionary reason for doing it. The latter are fascinated to see evolution at work in all human affairs and get agitated about things which do not fit this framework. There will be little doubt where I stand.

It might be wise to give some guidance about my approach. As a psychologist one of the first things I noticed when starting to read in this area was the absence of an empirical basis to most theorising, often by some quite revered commentators. As an evolutionary proof would take evolutionary time, this wasn't all that odd but I noticed that the alternative approach of assuming a set of values and modelling its outcomes was rarely followed outside the pages of the *Journal of Theoretical Biology*. When I tested some of these assertions against a set of assumed values quite a considerable number (particularly in the area of kin selection) did not stand up. Most of the assertions that I make in this book have been modelled on that sterling program *MathCad Plus*. I first wrote the book with the mathematics intact but was universally advised to desist. I've kept the book largely maths free but have written the logic out longhand. If anyone wants the numbers they can write to me.

As a final note, why restrict the book to male homosexuality? At present scientific studies of lesbianism are woefully inadequate. Not only are lesbians fewer in number than gay men but they are a less visible population, hard to target and harder to characterise. The lesbian press avoids the 'gay' label and sharply differentiates each community. My suspicions are that lesbianism and male homosexuality have very little in common at an evolutionary level but this is simply a guess, no more.

I'll end thanking those who helped along the way. First I would acknowledge Professor Des Crawley, my dean, to whom this book is affectionately dedicated. While it is proforma to thank one's superiors for their support and encouragement, Des *was* a support and more importantly knew its worth and backed his intuition with hard cash. I would also thank the Staff Development Leave Committee of my faculty for not giving me leave to write this manuscript and for providing me with written advice that they doubted my capacity to write it. As I had authored five books to that point, they in their wisdom knew this advice would act as an effective spur when I reached the inevitable blocks and despondency all authors face. It did. My longtime friend and colleague Jim Malcolm poured a gentle rain on my misguided attempts to 'biologise' anything as obviously social as homosexuality and shared his insights as a formerly married gay man who has crossed the great divide. My relatives Drs Tiina and Siiri Iismaa and Kieran Scott shared the wealth of their experience as molecular biologists in keeping me on the biological straight and narrow. I'd also thank those who read the work in whole or part: John Archer, John Buchner, Mark Dickerson, Sally Faedda, Michael Ruse, Kate Stevens and two anonymous reviewers. Just as important, I would thank Jon Reed and Vivien Ward from Routledge for obligingly making it happen. Last, I would also like to thank the many men, gay and straight, who have aided my research. I've sparingly sprinkled a few gems from their recorded conversations to illustrate my points. Where I've done this I've sourced them as 'Transcripts'.

Chapter 1

Is male homosexuality adaptive?

The law of evolution has a severe and oppressive countenance and those of limited or fearful mind dread it; but its principles are just, and those who study them become enlightened. Through its reason men are raised above themselves and can approach the sublime.

(Khalil Gibran, *The Prophet*)

Male homosexuality is a major puzzle for evolutionary theory, for if evolution has a purpose it is reproductive fitness, the passing of our genes to our children. This is our ultimate, if unconscious, reason for existence, as pawns in the grand evolutionary game. Sex that is not reproductive seems to make little sense within an evolutionary framework. Reproductive fitness is a simple and elegant theory. Successful species breed robustly. Natural selection weeds out the less fit and the species prospers. Within a species, if individuals who carry genes for a characteristic breed less, they gradually diminish their genetic representation and their special contribution is lost. Following this argument, over successive generations gay men, who presumably produce less offspring than straight men, should gradually be flushed from the gene pool. Unfortunately for such an elegant theory, this is not the case. Homosexuals were with us through antiquity and, if recent history is any guide, are a robust minority within society. So why hasn't male homosexuality died out as a less reproductive strain of humanity?

In the literature there are any number of responses to this question and most start by immediately rejecting evolutionary answers. Critics argue that homosexuality is not an innate but rather an acquired behaviour and that Darwinistic interpretations are spurious or ultimately misguided (Halperin, 1990). Other critics will allow the possibility of an innate disposition but argue that homosexuality is so culturally determined that any biological purpose is lost in the sheer variability of a socially constructed behaviour (Thorp, 1992). For these critics, what may have been true of our remote tribal ancestors has been overtaken by modern social realities. What was once homosexuality is not homosexuality now. Even those who allow that homosexuality is a problem for evolutionary theory, and who also assume that a gene for homosexuality exists, argue there is no compelling isomorphism between one's genes and one's behaviour. Perhaps these critics are right. Perhaps we choose to be homosexual and learn the right moves during adolescence. Perhaps homosexuality is developmental, a matter of too little testosterone at a critical period of prenatal growth. Perhaps it is just a part of our sexual repertoire and we are all at least a little gay. Clearly there are many ways of characterising homosexuality and the physical act is possibly the least important of these. But to the extent that one's orientation drives one's sexual desires the sex act does have profound consequences, so deciding between such alternatives is difficult but important.

Human sexual expression has a complex aetiology. Unfortunately, when our primate ancestors acquired self-consciousness as a survival strategy they also confused the issue by gaining an enhanced repertoire of sexual expressions. Beating the undergrowth for all the myriad ways we humans desire each other is a thankless task and enculturation and our own private experiences loom large in the pattern of our desires if not our orientation. We are also hampered by not having analogous models of homosexuality in our near relatives the great apes, whereby we might explore our own behaviour. To the extent that modern primates other than man are homosexual, such behaviour seems to serve ends only remotely connected with human homosexuality. So with a rising self-consciousness that took us far from our co-evolutionists came a capacity to tinker with the blind forces of evolution. The reasons for human sexual behaviour are now so diverse that it is not easy to tease out the relative contributions that various causative factors might play in one's sexuality.

While the social constructivist position is still the dominant view within sex research, in the last few years rapid advances in the biosciences have been providing solid evidence for a genetic basis for sexual orientation. Moreover, these advances have shaken complacent notions of homosexuality as a preference and strengthened arguments that it has a genetic substrate. If homosexuality has a genetic basis then we must see it as part of evolution rather than a simple phenotypic variation along the way. A biological basis that has genetic rather than environmental origins requires answers in evolutionary rather than social terms, and returns us to our starting question. For this reason the first task of those committed to a biosocial view of human behaviour is to establish a clear biological/genetic basis for the behaviour. This is the task of Chapter 2.

How then may we explain homosexuality? There are several biological accounts of homosexuality and its origins but unfortunately all have lumps. By way of introducing this fascinating puzzle we will briefly explore the nature of male homosexuality and the problems it poses.

HOMOSEXUALITY, FUTILE SEX?

Many would see homosexuals as poor, benighted individuals who are picking inappropriate sexual targets. A homosexual's apparent sexual confusion is God-given; an accident; or hormonal; a matter of poor parenting; or simply lack of real sexual outlets – it may even be genetic. Whatever it is, it does not produce children and so is simply futile sex. This view, which equates homosexuality with a sex act, is so simplistic it is nonsensical. Homosexuality is much more than just sex. However, the view's simplicity has a certain appeal to those who would like to see evolution in equally simple terms: evolution equals children; homosexuality does not equal children; therefore homosexuality is futile sex.

The rub of this argument is that even if we acknowledge a biological component to homosexuality we do not have to acknowledge its usefulness. It may be maladaptive. If for argument's sake we grant a genetic predisposition to homosexuality then we face several related questions: what is the purpose of a gay gene; how strong is its penetrance; is it adaptive; and most importantly – does it contribute to the reproductive success of the homosexual? We address the majority of these issues in later chapters but the issue of adaptive significance raises immediate problems for a biosocial theorist. To argue that a genetic predisposition exists is not to argue that it is adaptive. Genetic mutation throws up a multitude of deleterious changes for each successful adaptation and it has long been a view in biology that homosexuality is a sexual inversion, or merely a byproduct of evolution, even if genetic in origin. The futile sex view, then, sees homosexuality as misdirected sex. It acknowledges homosexuals are as sexually motivated as heterosexuals but simply choose inappropriate sexual targets. This comfortable assumption, while the dominant view this century, has several problems.

Perhaps the most immediate is that futile or misdirected sex theories of homosexuality say little about the reasons for such misdirection. Too many accounts simply stop with an assertion of futility.

A second problem with the futile sex theory is its constant use to reinforce morality and views of normality. Symons (1979) ruefully observed that with the death of organised religion the basis of morality died too and that Darwinism as its successor has always had to fight off attempts to make it the new morality (see, for examples, Midgley, 1985, 1994; Ruse, 1986). There is much truth in his statement. It is convenient to see heterosexuality as good sex and homosexuality as bad sex but at an evolutionary level such labels mean little. Behavioural geneticists and other interested parties are more concerned with questions of function than normality. 'Normality' means nothing in a process that has neither a blueprint nor an end. While this is a trivial difficulty in evolutionary theorising it is of immense importance to the social sciences. Much of the hostility to biological explanations of homosexuality seems a reaction to its moral neutrality, if not indifference to value judgements about sexual behaviour. Clearly, there is much confusion in the literature here. One may say that a behaviour does not lead to an efficient outcome while remaining silent on its worth.

At this point social science and biology sharply diverge. Biologists as scientists qua scientists are interested in the Pandora issue – what's inside the box? For the biologist science must be neutral even if its usages are questionable. That its usages are often questionable in practice is an entirely separate issue from knowing the facts, and facts must be pursued if for no other reason than intellectual curiosity – an old-fashioned view but one still dominant in the biological sciences. Social science with its less robust grasp of ultimate truth and a more immediate understanding of its own methodological limitations is warier of scientific theorising. Neither the process of knowledge generation nor its usage or dissemi- nation is seen as a morally neutral process. Social science practitioners are suspicious of scientific enquiry and more likely to equate truth, however conceived, with questions of usage. The what and why questions become awfully confused while biology pursues the much clearer how issue. Much of my dissatisfaction with the homosexuality debate flows from this dis- junction. Biosocial psychology straddles both the biological and social sciences and wishes to combine the rigour of biological proof with the freedom of social theorising. Much of the opposition to explanations of homosexuality is unhelpful. Surely it is more useful to question assump- tions about the futility of homosexuality than to protest against such theorising because it leads to discrimination against homosexuals or even reinforces the prejudices of the enquirers. We will return to these issues in Chapter 5.

Morality notwithstanding, there still remains the assertion that it is futile sex that does not produce children. Yet it is unlikely that homo- sexuality is just a misdirection of heterosexual impulse. Granted that recorded history is only a moment in evolutionary time and that homo- sexuality is not part of our fossil record, if a characteristic as seemingly pointless as nonreproductive sex survives for as long as homosexuality has, then it has some significant evolutionary function. If not it would have declined, to become a trivial part of the gene pool. If the incidence of such behaviour is as marked and regular as homosexuality, then it is unlikely that it is a random or spontaneous event. Sheer numbers of homosexuals, cross-cultural similarities, its early onset and its historicity, all argue that homosexuality is significant. Given increasing evidence, we may argue then that homosexuality is either a byproduct of some other adaptive process, or adaptive in its own right. Considering what this adaptive process might be is the major task of this book.

ORIENTATION OR PREFERENCE?

A more fundamental criticism of the futile sex view is the emerging consensus within sex research that we have considerable plasticity in our sexual orientation. Evidence from several studies we review suggests that rather than a bipolar homosexuality–heterosexuality we are all distributed on a continuum of several sexual orientations. In 1948 Kinsey wrote:

> Males do not represent two discrete populations, heterosexual and homosexual. The world is not divided into sheep and goats. Not all things are black nor all things white. It is a fundamental of taxonomy that nature rarely deals with discrete categories. Only the human mind invents categories and tries to force facts into separated pigeon-holes. The living world is a continuum in each and every one of its aspects. The sooner we learn this concerning human sexual behavior the sooner we shall reach a sound understanding of the realities of sex.
>
> (Kinsey et al., 1948: 639)

This perspective is not new and predates Kinsey. What is new is a growing recognition that our behaviour may be both categorical and continuous. It may well be that there are several discrete homosexualities and that they are all separately distributed on a Kinsey continuum from heterosexuality to homosexuality. There is also growing evidence that some of this variability may be inherited rather than simply a matter of learning or preference. While there are several types of homosexuality (we identify five) we will not consider them all here, rather concentrating on those for which an evolutionary logic is evident. We will return to this at the conclusion of Chapter 2.

Further, there is much confusion in the literature between sexual *orientation* and sexual *preference*. How we choose to express ourselves sexually may be quite different from the way nature has made us. A sorry history of gay men passing as straight men is indicative that one's preference or even how one wishes to be is often not how one is. From a biological perspective a genetic predisposition to homosexuality would be just that, a precursor, or orientation, and no more. Sexual preference on the other hand may well be learned or a matter of personal choice and may even go against one's nature. While a predisposition does not determine one's sexual preference it does affect it and when aggregated across a culture will show its influence. Yet for any number of reasons an individual may choose a sexual expression that is at odds with their heredity. In cultures where homosexuality is frowned upon, a homosexual may choose heterosexuality. Such plasticity is not strong evidence for either nature or nurture accounts of homosexuality, merely indicative of human behavioural flexibility. Unfortunately, one's culture and life experiences are obvious and immediate shapers of sexual expression and it is often easier to give proximate reasons for one's sexuality than to look for more fundamental reasons. It is part of our purpose here to redress this tendency.

The important point here is that this confusion is more than theoretical. It serves ideological ends. To show that one chooses one's sexual expression is not necessarily a sufficient explanation of one's sexuality. A substantial agenda has emerged that equates preference and orientation. This is often deliberate and only points to the shallowness of much theorising about homosexuality. The literature is full of accounts of men who have reluctantly abandoned fulfilling lives as fathers and husbands to acknowledge a driven need to express an orientation which is often confusing and sometimes repugnant to them (Ross, 1983; Malcolm, 1997). More importantly, the variability of sexual behaviour has always been seen as intuitive evidence for a constructivist view of sexuality but it may be argued that it reflects evolution just as well. If we have an innate predisposition to adopt a greater range of sexual expressions then it is relatively easy to argue several ways in which this flexibility is adaptive. Evidence for this view is only indicative at this stage and those in support of a biosocial perspective would not wish to argue nature provides more than a predisposition towards one's final preference. If it is the case that behavioural plasticity is both innate and adaptive, homosexuality can hardly be considered futile sex. We will return to this question in Chapter 3 but for our present purposes let us not confuse preference with orientation.

HOW MANY GAY MEN AND JUST WHAT IS HOMOSEXUALITY ANYWAY?

Part of the difficulty of accurately assessing homosexuality's aetiology is we still have little real idea of the extent of homosexuality in our communities. This is partly due to the stigmatisation which keeps a substantial proportion of gay men in the closet but more fundamentally a confusion about the nature and classification of the homosexual experience.

Just what is male homosexuality? As we have already seen homosexuality may be either a preference, or an orientation. It may be enacted or latent, a fantasy, a feeling, or a set of behaviours, or all of these. Would you classify a man of 55 happily married with grandchildren a homosexual if he reported no homosexual contacts but has had a lifelong erotic attraction to men? Kinsey reported that approximately 13 percent of males 'react erotically to other males without having overt homosexual contacts after the onset of adolescence' (Kinsey et al., 1948). Is a man who is happily married with children, yet cruises bars and beats for casual homosexual sex homosexual? Weinberg et al. (1994b) found that bisexual men typically experience an erotic attraction to the opposite sex two years before their first attraction to a male. However, they typically experience homosexual contacts a year *before* engaging in heterosexual sex and on the average first label themselves bisexual at age 27 (and it is worth noting that 25 percent of Weinberg's sample were still confused about their sexual identity!). Johnson et al. (1994) found in their cohort of 2,051 British men aged 35–44 that while 5.9 percent reported experiencing a homosexual attraction, 8.4 percent had had some homosexual contact, although less than 1 percent had had homosexual sex in the last five years. Johnson's study as with the others shows that the greatest proportion of homosexual contact occurs in adolescence and then declines as the sample ages. Are adolescents engaging in homosexual sex homosexual or just displaying developmental immaturity?

These and other illustrative examples drawn from the major surveys of sexual behaviour demonstrate the difficulties of defining homosexuality based on feelings, behaviour, or indeed fantasy life. This is further compounded by attempting extensional definitions based on typologies. Just how many gay men are there? How would you begin counting them? If we cannot decide just what is a gay male then we are unlikely to generate a typology with sufficiently discrete categories into which a diverse behaviour may be fitted. This difficulty becomes acute when you consider the sheer variability of any one person's behaviour – after all variety is the spice of life.

WHAT DO WE KNOW AND WHAT DO WE WANT TO KNOW ABOUT HOMOSEXUALITY?

The way ahead, and this is the only real possibility short of a DNA test for gayness, is to recognise that within the confusion there are similarities of experience and action that might act as medians. There are categories of homosexual behaviour that might be stratified by age, sex, developmental history, fantasies, and sexual behaviour. One of the least helpful approaches is to blur the boundaries of these medians. To do so is to render discussion between viewpoints meaningless. While remaining silent for a moment on its aetiology, much can be said in a short paragraph about homosexuality when adopting this approach: irrespective of type, homosexuality is four times more common in men than women; each seems to be distributed on a continuum from lifelong exclusive homosexuality towards heterosexuality; it is a relatively rare orientation with approximately 1–3 percent of men identifying as exclusively homosexual and having abstained from heterosexual sex over the last five years. Although the rate of homosexual behaviour is highly variable across cultures, 30–40 percent of men have had some homosexual experience; for the vast majority this ends at adulthood. For those whose homosexual experience continues past adolescence, as many men are bisexual as are exclusively homosexual, although the primary orientation of most of these men is heterosexual. While homosexuals and heterosexuals vary markedly in attitudes and behaviour, on the whole they are more characteristically male than female, that is, gayness is a male behaviour.

This brief and no doubt controversial overview will be discussed in glorious detail in this book. But even such a brief account raises many questions and the following list is designed to convince you that it is a topic worthy of exploration. What do we want to know about homosexuality? Perhaps the most important question is, is there a homosexuality or are there different homosexualities? Is homosexuality a preference or an orientation? If just one of these homosexualities has a biological basis what purposes does it serve? Is it adaptive or a byproduct of evolution? If we can find a genetic basis for homosexuality how did it arise and for what purposes? Even more importantly, what maintains this behaviour in the gene pool? Are all men potentially homosexual? Is homosexuality a discrete orientation or is it part of all our natures? Are there mechanisms which might allow us to identify gay foetuses and should we do so if it were possible? Is homosexuality something to be celebrated or remediated?

Clearly the concern with these questions is in the uses to which the answers may be put. One of the many criticisms of the evolutionary enterprise is that sociobiologists and particularly evolutionary psychologists are far too uninterested in the use of their research. Allied to this is a concern that evolutionary theory is a resurgent eugenics programme and many gay men and many commentators worry that the decision has been taken on homosexuality and we merely await a reliable means for its identification and eradication.

EXPLAINING HOMOSEXUALITY?

If we assume that homosexuality is adaptive and has a gene, what purpose does it serve? It may well be a mistake to assume that all homosexuals breed less than their heterosexual counterparts, but homosexuality still has curious purposes within evolution. Why do we need homosexual behaviour? This is a fascinating question of itself and of considerable interest to those who have an open mind as to the ultimate nature of human sexual orientation. It also poses a big problem for the biosocial perspective if gay men do breed less. Those who would argue that human social behaviour is lawful, and may be viewed as an expression of evolution at work, are seemingly confounded by a behaviour that is at odds with their theory. To assume that homosexuality should breed itself from the gene pool presupposes that it is maladaptive but we have already argued that it may well be adaptive. Where do we go from here?

The central thrust of this book is that exclusive male homosexuality is an evolutionary byproduct of an adaptive advantage which keeps it balanced in the gene pool against its diminished reproduction. As such, the homosexuality gene is part of our beneficial genetic variability. The synthetic theory of evolution which combines genetics and Darwinism argues that the greater the variation within a population the greater the opportunity for a species to evolve. The British geneticist R.A. Fisher noted in 1930 that 'the rate of increase in fitness of any organism at any time is equal to its genetic variance of fitness at that time' (Fisher, 1930). Fisher's theorem raises interesting questions for homosexuality and species adaptation. The basis of his theorem is the notion that the greater the range of genetic variability, the greater the flexibility of a species to adapt to its environment and to new challenges. If homosexuality is genetic then the incorporation of homosexual genes with the wider heterosexual gene pool may notionally increase an individual's adaptability if they carry both heterosexual and homosexual genes. This of course presupposes both that the gene is not deleterious and that there is some isomorphism between homosexual behaviour and its gene. We should also note that Fisher's theorem was ultimately aimed at explaining the rate of evolutionary change within populations. Increased genetic variability provides a greater range of responses to evolutionary crises than is possible for those species with a more limited message. While there is little evidence to show that homosexuality is the leading edge of human evolution, such genetic variability may be leading to greater plasticity in human sexual orientation. If this is the case, it raises interesting possibilities. These are both hotly debated issues and will be explored at length in Chapter 3.

It is interesting to see where we might go if we grant these assumptions. There are two main super-theories within the sociobiology of homosexuality which try to answer why the gene survives against its diminished reproduction. We will briefly introduce them here as stalking horses before considering them at length in later chapters.

Kin selection

Some theorists argue that homosexuals disqualify themselves from direct reproduction to assist kin who have closely related genes. The kin selection theory has two variants. One argues that a person in some way recognises they are going to be poor reproducers and withdraws from the game and sublimates their heterosexuality into same-sex contacts. The other variant takes a more positive view and argues that the homosexual-to-be has either superior opportunities or superior abilities to gather resources and that this capacity is enhanced if they withdraw from the reproductive stakes. Both variants assume that the homosexual altruistically passes on help and/or resources to near relatives who are reproductive, and as they share common genes, by that means maintain their genes within the population. Michael Ruse (1988), in his thorough-going review, notes that the first variant may well be true in tribal societies but hardly likely in developed nations where affluence ensures equal health for both homosexuals and heterosexuals.

So while it may well be adaptive for the diseased to abandon hetero-sexuality and to give whatever aid they can to close relatives, it is hardly likely to be an effective strategy in all cultures. Moreover, it assumes that the illness is a consequence of homosexuality, that there is a pool of individuals who are either genetically or otherwise predisposed to ill-health by being homosexual. The kin selection theory argues that homo-sexuality is:

> an adaptive manoeuvre to help a person become a better reproducer than he/she would otherwise be. The homosexuality stops the person vainly or inefficiently following heterosexual pursuits, and thus frees him/her to concentrate on aiding the reproduction of close relatives.
>
> (Ruse, 1988: 229)

As Ruse points out, the difficulty with this view is to see a nexus between the unhealthy individual and a homosexuality gene. If the homosexual gene was disabling it should gradually be eliminated from the gene pool, so homosexuality seems an after-the-fact recognition of some other dis-abling force, genetic or otherwise. Given this view it is hard to see homosexuality as a genetic process in its own right, as adaptive as it otherwise may be. Homosexuality is then simply a consequence, unless of course we all have a homosexual gene which acts as an antibody, springing to our reproductive defence if ill-health intervenes. Nor does this theory argue any compelling necessity to be homosexual. Why isn't the person simply neuter? This variant assumes that homosexuality is a consequence or byproduct of an adaptive process and implicitly that failed straight men sublimate their heterosexual drives into homosexual forms.

The second variant assumes a superior ability to aid reproduction of one's kin. Immediately a question arises. Why don't they reproduce them-selves? After all, in most cultures superior abilities equal greater resources and an enhanced ability to reproduce. If homosexuality is genetic then the answer must be that it is reproductively disabling and that homo-sexuality and kin selection are social adaptations to a debilitating genetic condition. If the homosexuality gene is not disabling then some environ-mental constraint must limit one's breeding potential.

While kin selection theory is one of the strongest models in evol-utionary psychology, it has the problem that reproductive fitness is a stronger one (Ruse, 1988). Whatever the merits of kin selection theory, it is easily demonstrable mathematically that direct reproduction is a superior method of ensuring reproductive fitness.

Balanced superior heterozygotic fitness

So we are left with a conundrum. The regularity and durability of homosexuality argues that it is not maladaptive and yet a simple chart of reproductive fitness argues that it is. How may we reconcile this paradox? G.E. Hutchinson in 1959 provided an elegant answer to the question of homosexuality – balance polymorphism, an intriguing solution drawn from population genetics, which has become the basis for a second family of related explanations. Population genetics had a similar puzzle first raised by Allison (1954). Why is the mutant gene for sickle-cell anaemia, a severe disturbance of blood haemoglobin, so prevalent in certain African and Asian populations? The sickle-cell mutation is a severe form of anaemia which if untreated kills the majority of sufferers in underdeveloped countries before they reproduce. One would expect it would decline in frequency within the gene pool. Yet its frequency has remained fairly constant. Why?

Before we can answer this we need to start with a refresher course in basic biology. Our physical characteristics are a combination of the messages (genes) we receive from each of our parents at conception. For each characteristic we have two sets of information (alleles), one set from each parent. If the gene is the same from each parent then this characteristic, eye colour or whatever, is said to be homozygous (the same). If different, then heterozygous (one of each). If our parents have different alleles then they may produce three types of offspring for this characteristic. Taking eye colour as an example, if there are alleles for blue eyes and brown eyes in the gene pool and if both parents carry messages for both colours, then they might produce a homozygous blue-eyed child by each contributing blue-eyed genes. They may also produce a homozygous brown-eyed child if both contribute brown-eyed genes. But what happens if one parent provides blue-eyed genes and the other brown-eyed genes? The heterozygote will have conflicting instructions for eye colour and the result will be a consequence of which allele is dominant, or capable of suppressing the conflicting information. In human populations the brown-eyed gene will suppress the blue-eyed gene and the child will have brown eyes. For other characteristics the situation is far more complicated than this, with many genes contributing their influence to a characteristic. Dominance of one set of information over others is usually far less overwhelming.

However, the critical point is that this child still has both sets of instructions and our interest is in the effect of the suppressed gene(s) within an individual. Returning to our sickle-cell anaemia example, epidemiologists working in equatorial Africa noticed that the frequency of the sickle-cell mutation was highest in regions where a particularly nasty form of malaria was endemic and caused far more fatalities before puberty than did sickle-cell anaemia. They hypothesised that possessing sickle-cell genes conferred a resistance to malaria and genetic surveys subsequently confirmed this. In this example, while the gene for abnormal haemoglobin is potentially lethal and is selected against (weeded out) in most human populations, to be without it in malarial regions may be fatal. The heterozygote has a superior chance of surviving to their reproductive years because of the immunity conferred by one sickle-cell gene. Heterozygotes, who have only one allele for sickle-cell anaemia, will be less affected by their abnormal condition and in addition gain a relative immunity to malaria. Homozygous children with two sickle-cell genes will rarely reach puberty, dying of severe anaemia. Homozygotes with no sickle-cell genes will die from malaria in greater numbers before puberty than heterozygotes with their relative immunity. Therefore more heterozygotes will reproduce and carry forward to future generations a gene for anaemia which on the face of it should have been bred out. In this sense there is a genetic balancing act at work. The heterozygotes have superior fitness to their homozygous peers and they carry lethal genes balanced against the benefits they provide, hence – balanced superior heterozygotic fitness.

The parallels with homosexuality are clear and this suggestion was first made by G.E. Hutchinson in 1959 but brought to prominence by Edward O. Wilson in 1975. Perhaps homosexual genes confer some advantage to heterosexuals and may directly advance their adaptiveness. Thus homosexual genes may benefit heterosexuals who carry a homosexual allele. Those members of a population who carry only homosexual genes are more likely to express themselves as homosexuals and to breed less. Note that this is a robust theory and readily accommodates one of the main challenges that social constructivists are wont to throw at explanations of homosexuality – that gay men are often married and, even if they are not, regularly have children anyway. This is not a problem for the balanced superior heterozygotic fitness scenario; all that is required is that gay men breed less than straight men. In terms of our conundrum the balanced superior heterozygotic fitness scenario would partly explain why the homosexual gene is carried forward from generation to generation without being removed from the gene pool. Because the gene confers some benefit to the heterosexual who carries it, it remains in the population.

This theory has fascinating implications. It supposes that heterosexuality is dominant over homosexual orientation yet the mix of these two orientations is somehow superior to those individuals who carry only heterosexual genes. That is, heterozygous straight men are super-fit and have a reproductive advantage compared to their homozygous straight peers. What this adaptive advantage is, is not clear and is the concern of our third chapter. It is little known that balance polymorphism, the short term for this genetic mechanism, may act in several ways. By way of introduction, another form of balance polymorphism argues that homosexuality is not directly adaptive as in our sickle-cell analogy but is a byproduct of some advantage to the heterosexual community and therefore of no direct advantage to homosexual offspring who are seen as 'maladaptive'.

The balanced superior heterozygotic fitness account is by far the dominant genetic explanation of homosexuality but it has its problems. It assumes that the homosexual gene is carried autosomally, that is, not on the sex chromosomes, or, put another way, has analogous copies (alleles), one from each parent. If the gene is autosomal then the balanced superior heterozygotic fitness scenario works well as a model of homosexuality, if not exactly explaining what advantage it provides that keeps it in the gene pool. Whatever the advantage the gay allele provides the heterosexual who carries it, it does so as a gift of the other parent's allele. Now on our sex chromosomes we have only one allele; the one we get from our other parent is non-homologous – if we are male, that is. Our mother provides the X and father the Y and although these do interact to control our development they do so separately. As it is likely that our sexual orientation is controlled by our sex chromosomes and the evidence clearly seems to be pointing this way, it is not possible for the balanced superior heterozygotic fitness model to work, unless of course you are a woman, and we are interested in male homosexuality.

So we are left with the main genetic explanation of homosexuality having a large conceptual difficulty. This brief explanation has massively oversimplified the issues of course and there are ways in which non-homologous alleles, or combinations of them, may generate a balanced superior heterozygotic fitness-like effect. Yet the explanation with the most empirical support suggests that male homosexuality is a consequence of something being passed from mothers to their daughters. How?

Dean Hamer, who identified markers for the gay gene, and located it on the maternal chromosome, speculates that women may have a gene for 'a desire to love men' (Hamer et al., 1993) or something similar that enhances their reproduction. In this case homozygous women who have two alleles for this trait will reproduce more than their heterozygous sisters. Their male offspring will inherit this desire-for-men gene and become homosexual. Because some mothers will have two copies of this gene and their sons only one, this differential in reproductive rates will keep this gene balanced in the population. This is the opposite to balanced superior heterozygotic fitness. In this case of balance polymorphism, the reproductive advantage is held by the homozygous mother. However, Hamer's model sees homosexuality as a byproduct of heightened female heterosexual desire. From this viewpoint homosexuality is not adaptive in its own right, rather it is a continuing spin-off of another adaptive process.

A less indirect view of balance polymorphism is to see homosexuality conferring some direct benefit to heterozygous straight men who carry the gene but then we are left with the difficulty we have just discussed. This problem does not seem to trouble those who construct balanced superior heterozygotic fitness accounts; their concern is to determine what advantage is being generated. There are a number of speculations as to the nature of this advantage but most suppose it to be sexual – increased fertility, potency, greater erectile strength, higher libido and the like. In this variant, homosexuality is directly advantageous to heightened male sexual functioning rather than a byproduct of female sexuality. What this advantage might be is one of the most exciting speculations in evolutionary theorising but the problem is that there are several scenarios and they seem contradictory, at least on the surface.

Of course this brief account oversimplifies the actual case enormously. The actual genetics of homosexual orientation are probably polygenetic and highly variable depending on the 'dose' one inherits. It opens the possibility that we might eventually model the degree of variability in homosexual identification within the gay population, the variability of gayness within the wider gene pool, and actual penetrance patterns.

IS EVOLUTION SOCIAL?

As a final comment it is not often appreciated that evolution is a biological *and* social process and that social evolution is the Cinderella of evolutionary theory. This is unfortunate. Charles Darwin, though lacking a mechanism for natural selection, was under no illusions about the importance of social forces in evolution. Half of his *The Descent of Man* (1871) is a thorough account of sexual selection in all its permutations, social and physical. So it would be unwise to ignore the possibility that homosexual orientation may have other than just biological origins.

Biosocial psychology as the intersection of social and biological worldviews tries to explore the nature of social evolution as a consequence of our biological nature. In this sense it is a hierarchical account of social behaviour in which the more fundamental and general directions are biological while the more immediate and individual are social. What we face here is the problem of what is the appropriate level of explanation we should use to characterise homosexuality? As Jerome Barkow (1989), in his magnificent book *Darwin, Sex and Status: Biological Approaches to Mind and Culture*, notes: 'Sociobiology is not and cannot be a theory of human nature – for that we need vertically integrated, multiple-level accounts'. There was never more immediate a case than homosexuality, in which any attempt at explanation is bedevilled by commentators who ignore this evident truth.

It is entirely likely that we are dealing with a human capacity which on one axis of explanation is genetically predisposed by our genes, biologically enacted in our uterine development and suppressed and/or embraced by social pressures and individual choices. That is, we might explain homosexuality as an irregular repeated DNA code; the interaction effects of the genes they encode; the hormonal chemistry they control; the physical structures these chemicals affect; and the developmental adjustments one makes; under the ultimate sway of what is acceptable in one's culture. On yet another axis, homosexuality might be characterised as an aspect of the grand evolutionary plan; dissected by its selective vectors; analysed in terms of mechanisms and processes; or discussed in terms of individual motivations. When one approaches the literature on homosexuality, this clash of levels and axes of meaning makes coherent argument difficult and critiques from partisan vantages relatively easy. While it is impossible to write a book such as this without trying to straddle all the levels, it is worth remembering that the ultimate truth of the matter will embrace this multi-layered texture. Our approach here is to explore homosexuality somewhere in the middle of this matrix. We are less concerned with individuals and motives and more concerned with mechanisms and processes. Yet even the mechanisms are less important than their purposes in the grand scheme of things and here we try to remember Barkow's advice:

> Whatever other properties they have, whatever algorithms they use, our evolved mechanisms should tend to generate behaviour likely to enhance the fitness of people living as our ancestors once did. Mistaking a theory of the selection pressures likely to have produced those mechanisms for a theory of the mechanisms themselves, that is, for a theory of human nature, is an error that sociobiologists and readers of sociobiologists often make.
>
> (Barkow, 1989: 47)

So it is worth remembering that what we have here is an enquiry into the selective scenarios which may have generated homosexuality and, more importantly, sustain it. Explanation then is less a matter of whether homosexuality is physically or socially determined (it is probably determined by both) but rather, it is a matter of what evolutionary logic it serves.

If the many-textured nature of homosexuality was not enough of a complication, man is a thinking animal and, as Sir Julian Huxley noted as long ago as 1942, the mechanism of evolution in man has been transferred to the social or conscious level, and slower methods of variation and natural selection are giving way to speedier processes of acquiring and transferring information. Germ-line genetic engineering, in which social decisions directly shape our physical evolution, clearly makes this point. This type of evolution is often seen by social constructivists as evidence of the inherently social nature of homosexuality but in so doing they ignore the biological base from which it arises. To restate the obvious, evolution is both a biological and social process. There are two possible types of social evolution at work here: directed and undirected social evolution. Directed social evolution is akin to the controversial position taken by Campbell in his presidential address to the American Psychological Association in 1975. This recognises that certain behaviours are so successful that they are purposively retained from generation to generation across all cultures. Reciprocal altruism may be such an example. People help each other because it pays to belong and we expect to be helped in return. Such social evolution mimics physical evolution and is often mistaken for it because it obeys the same ultimate logic – what works helps us to survive and helps us to reproduce. Such behaviours may evolve as conditions change but on the whole are quite stable. We tend to repeat that which works. The important notion here is that this level of social evolution is fairly conscious. Not only is it coded for in cultural mores but individuals when forced to defend their actions are usually capable of a sophisticated defence. Nevertheless, these idiosyncratic actions sum across a species to most effective ways of behaving and they in turn reflect the selective pressures to which they are a response. Even conscious directed evolution is still subject to the blind impersonal laws of survival.

There is also the environmental side of Darwin's natural selection equation. White moths are more obvious and are eaten more often when trees turn black with soot (Plomin et al., 1980). But why do the trees become sooty? Undirected social evolution is a consequence of our social organisation but incidental or accidental to our purposes. For example, if homosexuality is a consequence of a mother's stress hormones blocking the masculinisation of her unborn child, this may alter his reproductive fitness. Such physical stressors are environmental and a consequence of the evolution of our cultures. That they are accidental byproducts and unlike directed evolution, are unstable, does not lessen their importance. From this view homosexuality may be a melange of environmental factors which change over time but obey the same laws of natural selection. That which works survives. This is a crucial point because we psychologists have a curious blindness and tend to see environmental causes as non-biological and external to ourselves. Yet our bodies are as much an environment as our families. Dean Hamer summed this up precisely:

> To geneticists the word 'environment' means anything and everything that is not inherited, including some factors which are purely biological. So from our point of view, undergoing prenatal development in a womb swimming with male hormones is as much an environmental factor as growing up in a devoutly religious household.
>
> (Hamer and Copeland, 1994: 82)

It may well be that homosexuality's evolution is as much a result of the byproducts of social evolution as it is of accident and uncertainty. If homosexuality is a result of imbalanced prenatal hormones then this liability may be entirely environmental even if the causes are physical. Labelling these causes *evolutionary* is a recognition that they too follow the same logic – those less fit do not reproduce as well as they might. Labelling these causes *social* is not entirely a misnomer because it recognises we are a gregarious species and that much of what happens to us at a purely physical level is a consequence of our social nature. The highly-stressed single mother's homosexual son is as much a consequence of her status as a single parent, and of a culture that has many single-parent families, as it is of a chemical imbalance.

Social explanation therefore is necessarily biological when it addresses issues of sexuality. Human beings are conscious and they may influence the directions of evolution but they do so within the parameters that biology and evolution set. It is highly unlikely that genetics would set more than a predisposition to homosexuality and many forms of homosexual expression may well be learned. Homosexuality is contained within a biological envelope of reproductive preference but why do we choose one form of sexual expression over another? Exploring this question is the task of Chapter 4.

WHERE TO FROM HERE?

So there are many fascinating questions in trying to understand homosexuality from an evolutionary perspective. Perhaps homosexuality is more than just a biological accident. Indeed it may be a wonderful advantage that enjoys both biological and social selective pressures and is remoulding our species into newer, more adaptive forms. Whatever, our task here is to see if a gene for homosexuality exists and, if so, what its purposes might be. With the steady emergence of a more biological basis to homosexuality has come a steady increase in speculation as to its purposes. That some explanations are more fanciful than others is the nature of scientific enquiry but one wishes there was a greater knowledge of biology. For example, to suggest as some do that a homosexual gene has evolved as nature's way of curing overpopulation is abysmally ignorant of basic biology. Other evolutionary accounts are elegant and warrant close attention. And so, having complained about a lack of biological knowledge we turn now to a consideration of homosexuality's biological bases.

Chapter 2

A biology of homosexuality

I grew up in an ordinary family, went to a State school and brawled with the rest of the kids on the block. I want to stress that – I had a completely heterosexual upbringing in a very homophobic culture. I didn't know anyone who was queer, I didn't know much about queers and certainly didn't know I was queer. All I know is that my adolescent dreams were about blokes. When we went out, my mates eyed off girls, but I eyed off my mates. They'd have been horrified! ... It was not on to be queer in the 1960s so I went underground. I married and had children but dreamed about fucking rough blokes in leather. Eventually my masquerade as a straight ended. You can't imagine the sheer driven-ness of needing to express your gayness. I don't understand it but I can say that I've read a lot of rubbish that tried to explain it as crook parenting, or even more ludicrously as a lifestyle choice. I didn't decide to be this way, it's just the way I am.

(Transcripts)

To argue that homosexuality is a spoke in the great wheel of human evolution is to assert that its origins are ultimately biological. Unfortunately, this assertion immediately plunges us into bitter controversy. While there are many theories, a great and unfortunate chasm lies between biological and social accounts of homosexuality and theorising is polarised into two antagonistic camps. On one side are social constructivists who see homosexuality as an acquired or constructed behaviour, part of our repertoire of sexual roles. On the other are essentialists who feel homosexuality is genetically programmed. It is useless to note, as Symons (1979) does, that the evolutionary theorist deliberately avoids taking sides in the nature/nurture debate, which is about *how* behaviour develops rather than *why* it does; the debate is too bitter and polarised. This classic divide lies at the heart of much social theorising but unlike other topics there are few integrationist theories of homosexual causation in the middle ground. Evolutionary social theorists try to cross this chasm by arguing that human evolution is both a social and biological process.

Ultimately they would see social behaviour and cultural evolution as reflections of our nature, arising within the bounds set by evolutionary biology. Therefore, the first task of a sociobiology of homosexuality is to establish its biological credentials. In subsequent chapters we consider how homosexuality fits into the evolutionary scheme of things as a biologically and socially determined behaviour.

Why is evolutionary psychology so concerned with finding biological precursors for social behaviour? Evolutionary psychologists see social traits as either adaptive or maladaptive and inexorably shaped by natural selection. As we have seen, if a behaviour persists across diverse cultures over millennia, then it must be adaptive, or a byproduct of some other adaptive process, otherwise it would have ceased long ago. It does not matter how social or voluntary an act is, if it is maladaptive, it is gradually overwhelmed and replaced by more appropriate behaviour. While this seems a nonsense to those who argue that social behaviour is voluntary (we choose to act as we do) this ignores the timescale involved. Biosocial theorists think in terms of hundreds of thousands of years. It is the relative sum of the consequences of such acts that will determine which social behaviour is more, or less, adaptive. Those who are better suited to their environment (and their behaviour plays a large part in determining this) will have greater reproductive fitness even if this is only an infinitesimally small margin of advantage. Over millennia this small margin is overwhelming.

Now we come to the chicken and egg part of the argument. Some might argue this advantage just arises from continuing correct choices but others see it as a consequence of genetic predispositions underlying the behaviour. In either case, adaptive behaviour has a transmission mechanism that places it squarely in the main thrust of evolution and explains seemingly inherited behaviour. Put another way, evolutionary theorists would argue that genetic variation occasionally throws up advantageous predispositions and those who capitalise on these advantages gradually replace those who do not. As homosexuality has proven such a durable part of human culture it must provide such an adaptive advantage, otherwise homosexuals would have bred themselves out of existence long ago. Alternatively, it may be a way of disqualifying those less suited to reproduction, part of nature's weeding out the less fit. Either way, it is ultimately a biological process for it expresses itself in differential reproduction. It does not matter whether homosexuality is itself adaptive, or a byproduct of human evolution, for the evolutionary theorist, a behaviour so ubiquitous and durable must have some biological substrate, however social it first appears.

So for a sustainable biosocial theory of homosexuality, the first challenge is to demonstrate a clear and unambiguous biological basis for the behaviour. Ideally, we might find that this is genetic rather than a result of environmental factors which otherwise affect our physical development. Before we can say that homosexuality is driven by evolution we need to identify its causal processes. This is done in one of two ways. An open and shut view of evolutionary biology would require that homosexuality be genetically programmed and that its markers and sites be identified. Many biosocial theorists would not accept less than this. However, as we saw in our introduction, human natural selection is also a social process, so, alternatively, we may find that some environmental factor leads to a biological difference which regulates sexual orientation. In the latter case we then need to explore how, in the absence of a genetic basis, the behaviour endures. In either case we are still left with the question of why homosexuality persists, but this is the work of later chapters; it is sufficient here to establish a biology of homosexuality.

As far as theory goes, social constructivists have certainly commanded the high ground until fairly recently. Only in the last decade has solid evidence for a biology of homosexuality started to accumulate. Biological accounts fall into two types. The oldest explanation asserts that homosexuality is a sexual inversion, or an interruption of normal heterosexual development. For over 100 years developmental theorists have argued that something happens to the foetus which alters sexual orientation for life. In reaction to this rather unpalatable view which sees heterosexuality as normality and homosexuality as a developmental aberration, recent research has tried to discover a genetic basis for homosexuality which may establish it as part of normal (expected) human variability. Those persuaded by this view argue that if a genetic locus for homosexual orientation could be found it would be no more an aberration than left-handedness. While this view optimistically ignores the point that many genetic influences are clearly detrimental, proponents rest on a fundamental proposition that if a behaviour is durable it must be paying dividends in the evolutionary stakes. So on to a biology of homosexuality.

Proofs for homosexuality's biological nature fall into discrete types. Even though the earliest researchers were sure that homosexuality was genetically programmed, in the absence of elaborate neurobiological or genetic techniques, they relied on familial and case studies to tease out the genetic penetrance of homosexuality within families. In the 1960s and 1970s morphological studies started to identify differences in the structure of the brain and its chemical messengers and attempted to tie these to sexual orientation. At the same time several genetic conditions were identified which seemed to support earlier views of homosexuality as a sexual inversion. In all of these testosterone seemed to be the villain.

HOMOSEXUALITY, A SEXUAL INVERSION?

A colleague wandered down the corridor and enquired about my latest book. When I had explained, he said something like: 'But every one knows why some men are gay. Their brains get mucked up before birth and they end up with too much female hormones, turn into effeminate boys who aren't into sports and things and then turn into homosexuals. Extreme cases have sex change operations.' This view of homosexuality has the widest popular currency and several assumptions underpin it. First, homosexuality is an inversion of normal development. Second, it suggests that this is a result of prenatal developmental abnormalities. Although this is often assumed to be genetic – to quote my friend, 'The poor buggers were made that way' – some would see it as an environ-mental insult in the uterine environment. Third, it sees hormones, specifically sex hormones, as the culprit. Fourth, it assumes that homo-sexual men are an intermediate sex somewhere between men and women, although inclining towards the feminine with increasing doses of hormonal aggravation. Finally, it assumes that gay men are victims of their biology. Let us start with the first assumption.

Since ancient times views of homosexuality have swung from con-demning it as a perversion, to seeing it as faulty libidinal development. Biological research into the causes of homosexuality started with the German jurist Karl Heinrich Ulrichs, who between 1864 and 1879 pub-lished instalments of his monumental *Researches on the Riddle of Love Between Men* (Ulrichs, 1975). Ulrichs was impressed by reports of the undifferentiated state of embryonic sex organs in early stages of develop-ment. He felt their plasticity suggested we might develop into either sex, or perhaps gain a sexual orientation not tied to one's genetic sex (Kennedy, 1980/81). His theory of a third sex, 'a female soul trapped within a male body', set the tone of research for the next century, where homosexuality came to be seen as a sexual inversion caused by hormonal imbalance (Wingfield, 1995).

This point was not lost on Baron Richard von Kraft-Ebbing (1886), who, building on Ulrichs' work and his own clinical investigations, rejected a growing view that learning was a plausible explanation of homosexuality and insisted that it must be innate. Both theorists, and those first researchers who followed in the early 20th century (Ellis, 1915; Hirschfeld, 1920; Forel, 1924), saw homosexuality as an inversion of normal hetero-sexuality, unless it was mere 'perverted experimentation'. Unlike Freud and other psychosocial theorists, they argued that homosexuality must have an innate trigger because homosexual socialisation was not demon-strably different from that of heterosexuals (Ellis and Ames, 1987). Further support for an innate sexual inversion theory came from their observations that homosexual orientation came early in life, seemed to parody heterosexual lifestyles, and was unusually resistant to therapy. From the 1920s researchers started to use newly identified hormonal differences between the sexes as a model for homosexual orientation (Hirschfeld, 1920; Forel, 1924). They argued that: 'certain unspecified imbalances could result in a homosexual orientation' (Ellis and Ames, 1987). Such suppositions went nowhere given the limited molecular biology of the day and in the absence of any definitive hormonal differ- ence investigators turned their attention to rare genetic inversions to model homosexuality.

There are clear cases of human developmental inversion and they are often used to demonstrate brain-based effects, although the link to homosexuality is often less demonstrable. Before we consider the pros and cons of sex hormones in sexual inversions we need to understand normal development. The basics are as follows.

We, like most mammalian species, are female in design. At conception we are all female but by the end of the first trimester of pregnancy those of us who have a male genetic message are exposed to small doses of two triggering hormones, chorionic gonadotropin and luteinising hormone (LH). These are secreted by our mother's pituitary gland and enter her bloodstream, cross the placenta and start the differentiation of the gonads into testes. The rapidly developing testes then take over the job of con- tinuing male differentiation and secrete male sex hormones (androgens) which regulate the growth of male characteristics.

These hormones have two jobs – controlling our sexual development and differentiation, and regulating their function. These so-called organis- ational and activational hypotheses (Arnold, 1980) are linked in hormonal theorising about homosexuality. From an evolutionary perspective, differ- entiation of the genitals and secondary sex characteristics is less interesting than changes in brain mechanisms controlling sexual behaviour. It is assumed that a demonstrable inversion in one's sexual development means corresponding changes in its neural function and control:

> Normal differentiation of genital morphology entails a dimorphic sex difference in the arrangement of peripheral nerves of sex which, in turn, entails some degree of dimorphism in the representation of the periphery at the centrum of the central nervous system, that is to say, in the structures and pathways of the brain.
>
> (Money and Ehrhardt, 1972: 8)

The brain is a sexual organ and part of the differentiation into maleness is an appropriate androgenisation of the brain. Yet unlike other gross sexual characteristics, androgenisation of the brain does not require defeminisation of the basic female pathways. Whereas the undifferen- tiated gonad becomes either a testis or an ovary, in the brain differentiation seems to lay down independent pathways towards maleness and femaleness. Thus, acquiring masculine brain characteristics, and the loss of feminine brain characteristics, are separate processes occurring at different times (Goy and McEwen, 1980) and involve quite 'different neural substrates as well as different hormonal metabolites' (Byne and Parsons, 1993). Homosexuality is seen as an interruption of this process, an altering of the relative balance between the two systems, leading to a change in sexual orientation which is at odds with one's genetic predisposition.

This theory hypothesises a diverse sexual orientation. The quantity and types of hormones one's brain is exposed to in the prenatal period determine your sexual orientation. 'Male heterosexuality and female homosexuality result from prenatal exposure to high levels of testicular hormones, while homosexual males and heterosexual females are exposed to lower levels and thus retain a female pattern of brain organization' (Byne and Parsons, 1993). In practice, two models of hormonal irregularity are proposed to account for these changes: the first suggests a genetic predisposition most clearly demonstrated by relatively rare instances of pseudohermaphroditism; the second suggests environmental causes. We will take the first, first.

DOES GENETIC INVERSION MODEL HOMOSEXUALITY?

Pseudohermaphroditism is an autosomal recessive genetic condition which leads to characteristics inappropriate to one's genetic sex. At birth, the genitals are usually ambiguous and gender assignment starts shortly thereafter with corrective surgery. There are several of these relatively rare conditions and we will consider just two – the 5-alpha reductase, and 21-hydroxylase deficiencies as causal models of male homosexuality. These rare genetic conditions are of considerable interest to homosexuality researchers because they provide extreme-case models of sexual inversion. More importantly, they allow researchers to assess the relative contributions of genetics versus gender-role socialisation.

5-Alpha reductase deficiency

One of the more media-worthy examples of sexual inversion is 5-alpha reductase deficiency. Julianne Imperato-McGinley and her colleagues in 1974 reported a pool of natural transsexuals who started life as girls but later became boys. For at least three generations several families in the central Dominican Republic have had sufficient numbers of girls turn into boys to suspend a final gender assignment until puberty settles the matter (Imperato-McGinley et al., 1974, 1979). These *guevedoces*, (eggs (testes) at 12) children, are born with female genitalia. At puberty, under the influence of testosterone, some girls make a complete transformation to boys, developing full male genitalia. For others the physical changes are less complete with only partial fusion of the vagina, requiring reconstructive surgery. While the incidence of 5-alpha reductase deficiency seems concentrated in these Dominican villages, it has been noted in many other communities (e.g. Money and Ehrhardt, 1972).

The process is relatively straightforward even if the causes are still obscure. It appears an autosomal genetic deficiency inactivates the enzyme 5-alpha reductase which normally converts testosterone into dihydrotestosterone (DHT). DHT, which is present in both genetic sexes, has a primary role in masculinising male external genitalia (Savage et al., 1980). Genetic males who have this deficiency produce normal amounts of testosterone but this is not converted into DHT and the child's genitals develop according to our species' female default.

While this is a clear case of sexual inversion, it does not model homosexuality, or at least not a recognisable male homosexuality. As a natural experiment, it fails to be convincing as this culture has a high tolerance of sexual ambiguity but nevertheless does assign a gender at birth. Photographs of the infants' genitalia are ambiguous (Breedlove, 1994) and this is a sign to parents to be cautious about the child's eventual gender (Imperato-McGinley et al., 1991). If the child's gender assignment is female, they might be considered lesbians as, at puberty, these children prefer female sex partners, irrespective of how complete their subsequent masculinisation is (Rubin et al., 1981). However, if their assignment is masculine or intermediate (raised as girls waiting to become boys) they have quite clear masculine identity and heterosexual orientation at puberty (Breedlove, 1994). What is important in this research is the question of desire. These children, first raised as either girls or boys or an intermediate gender, desire women and this is unlikely to change even if their gender does. One explanation of such results is that: 'fetal testosterone masculinized the brain so that, social rearing notwithstanding, the individuals were inclined to think and therefore behave like men' (Breedlove, 1994). That they prefer other women and that this is a fixed preference despite gender reassignment suggests other than a learned role for sexual orientation.

Accounts of 5-alpha reductase deficiency which link it with homosexuality usually suggest a hormonal influence on the brain of those with the deficiency. These rather striking effects on primary and secondary sex characteristics are presumed also to affect the brain and hence orientation. However, in the case of this rare disorder, DHT has little influence on brain differentiation, which proceeds normally. Perinatal serum testosterone is unaffected by this deficiency and, as we will see, has a rather more direct effect on the brain in the development of appropriate receptor sites, which become functional at puberty. The leap which ties this pseudohermaphroditism to homosexuality is an assumed link between these brain receptors and an innate behavioural masculinity. The argument goes that, as the brain is masculine, so then is one's sexual orientation regardless of one's gender. Unfortunately, the evidence is far from complete and studies have only demonstrated such effects in rats (Hull et al., 1980, 1984). To assume that such genetic inversions directly affect homosexual sexual orientation is ahead of the evidence at present.

21-Hydroxylase deficiency (congenital adrenal hyperplasia (CAH) syndrome)

A look at another genetic inversion will reinforce this point. Both sexes produce testosterone. In a small number of genetic females the adrenal gland which normally synthesises stress hormones produces large amounts of testosterone due to a genetic deficiency which controls cortisol production. This leads to masculinisation of the foetus and to children who appear male to varying degrees. As masculinisation is rarely complete, the majority of these girls are surgically corrected shortly after birth and raised in their genetic sex. However, the literature shows that such gender assignment is often ambiguous, with some considerable ongoing masculinisation (Berenbaum and Snyder, 1995). Longitudinal studies show that many of these girls have a much wider sexual repertoire than their peers and often prefer partners of the same-sex (Ehrhardt, 1978; Money et al., 1984). Indeed they display high levels of lesbianism, bisexuality and sexual ambiguity (Money and Russo, 1979; Money et al., 1984; Dittmann et al., 1992).

At this point you are probably wondering about a seeming contradiction. Surely this later syndrome seems to have a direct link to homosexual orientation despite a gender reassignment towards heterosexuality. However, several points call this genetic inversion into doubt as a model for homosexual orientation. First these are genetic females who, if raised as men, should prefer male partners if this models homosexuality. While it is true that fewer of these children are raised as males, the majority that are, remain heterosexual (Money and Ehrhardt, 1972). Second, there is strong evidence that one's gender assignment is an important determinant of sexual preference. These adults experience high levels of ambiguous sexual identity (Money et al., 1984). These are very atypical adults who, given such factors as needing to take lifelong hormonal supplements, are more conscious of the whims of sexual identity. So it is less surprising that their sexual identity is diverse. Money, Ehrhardt and others build a careful case for masculinisation of behaviour, fantasies and erotic ideation of these women, but does this point to preference or orientation? More importantly, no study has found evidence of genetic pseudohermaphroditism in the mainstream gay population.

Still, pseudohermaphroditism has been an influential model in the homosexuality debate and we would be unwise to dismiss it too readily. The two genetic inversions we have discussed are instances of homozygous autosomal recessive penetrance, the result of two parents passing the gene to their offspring. However, such genes are also passed on in a heterozygous mating where only one gene passes to the child. It may well be that the recessive gene is not completely masked and partially expresses itself in the heterozygous condition. While these children are not demonstrably pseudohermaphrodites, it may be that they have a genetic liability to hormonal feminisation of their brain pathways. The suggestion remains that a hormonal deficiency, genetic or otherwise, has a role in one's sexual orientation.

A CHEMICAL IMBALANCE? THE DE-ANDROGENISED FOETUS THEORIES

Several theories argue that a relative insensitivity to testosterone leads to demasculinisation of the foetal brain, altering the balance between masculine and feminine pathways. Homosexuality is then a function of the degree of feminisation of the adult brain, with most homosexualities distributed between masculine and feminine orientations. These theories account for the wide variability in gay behaviour and assume that homosexuality is an intermediate form of heterosexual orientation. While such theories promote proximate environmental causes for this demasculinisation, most argue that an ultimate genetic vulnerability predisposes some foetuses to an inverted orientation. Another form of pseudohermaphroditism serves as a model.

Androgen insensitivity syndrome

A little closer to the mark is the androgen insensitivity syndrome, another genetic autosomal recessive condition in which genetic males vary in their sensitivity to testosterone. In the few cases of complete insensitivity, these children appear female at birth and usually go undetected until puberty when they fail to menstruate. Longitudinal studies show a complete identification with their feminine gender and, unlike the other two conditions, do not seem to have an inverted sexuality, being completely at home in their feminine role (Ehrhardt, 1975). This is usually interpreted as powerful support for the social nature of sexual orientation (Money, 1969).

What is interesting about the androgen insensitivity syndrome is the far more plentiful cases of partial insensitivity to testosterone (Aiman and Griffin, 1982). Theorists such as Dorner argue that androgen insensitivity is on a continuum and that male homosexuality is a mild, subclinical case of the androgen insensitivity syndrome (Dorner et al., 1991). This model suffers fewer theoretical problems than other recessive conditions and was influential in suggesting that a relative insensitivity to androgens leads to degrees of brain feminisation short of actual inversion. Most such theories posit a genetic predisposition and an environmental trigger. They see male homosexuality occupying an intermediate position between masculinity and femininity. While the androgen insensitivity syndrome is genetic, with well characterised genetic markers (McPhaul et al., 1993), the de-androgenisation theory of male homosexuality is essentially developmental. It argues that, irrespective of a genetic inversional system or uterine developmental insult, the gay brain is left with androgen receptor sites that are less sensitive to testosterone than they would otherwise be. The de-androgenised foetus theory argues that, as the intrinsic pattern of mammalian development is female, in the absence of the appropriate sex hormones a male foetus is demasculinised and continues to develop as a female to a greater or lesser extent. Male homosexuality is then an intermediate position between genital demasculinisation and normal development. As sexual orientation is brain-based, the theory argues that homosexuality results from a demasculinisation of those parts of the hypothalamus which are influential in sexual orientation, even if the boy's outward appearance is masculine at birth.

Several mechanisms mediate appropriate levels of androgens in the sexes.

Many animal studies show that interrupting testosterone production produces marked effects on rodent sexual behaviour. The most direct manipulation is to remove the testes within the first week after birth (Ford, 1983). Given their short gestation period, rats are born physically and neurologically underdeveloped and interrupting testosterone supply by castration at birth markedly affects neuronal organisation. Castration of primates after birth has no sexually inverting consequences, although it may affect drive after puberty (Feder, 1984). Rats castrated at birth display reduced sex drive, little interest in receptive female rats and inverted behaviours towards their own sex (Dorner and Hinz, 1968). As the testes are critical to the sex drive, homosexual behaviour has to be switched on by injections of testosterone, or its derivative estradiol, after puberty. Estradiol appears to be the main activator and organiser of sexual behaviour, regardless of the animal's sex or sexual orientation (Ellis and Ames, 1987; Breedlove, 1994).

The differentiation mechanism, at least in lower mammalian species, is fairly clear. Testosterone is the main sex hormone involved in organising male orientation and activity. From a basically female mammalian blueprint, genes on the Y chromosome begin to switch on the production of Leydig cells in the tissue which will become the testes. Before the Leydig cells begin to operate, they must be switched on by triggering hormones secreted by the mother. These allow the Leydig cells to synthesise testosterone and its derivative, dihydrotestosterone, which controls the process of masculinising external genitalia. At the same time, Sertoli cells are formed in the developing male gonadal tissue and these act to block the development of the uterus and fallopian tubes. As women do not have a Y chromosome, Leydig and Sertoli cells do not form and the female foetus develops to the basic mammalian default position.

The effects of masculinising hormones during pregnancy are direct in producing the primary sex characteristics, the penis and testes, but also lay down potentials for the development of secondary sex characteristics which are acquired at puberty. The main vehicle seems to be the development of a large amount of androgen receptor protein, which is not synthesised until triggered by further high levels of testosterone occurring at puberty. It is the alteration of these pathways which is suggested as the cause for homosexuality.

Such a theory should be relatively easy to test. While numerous speculations abound, three tests seem evident. If testosterone causes differences between homosexual and heterosexual brains, then these should react differently to inputs of sex hormones. Similarly, it would not be unreasonable to expect that homosexual men have differing testosterone levels from heterosexual men or, alternatively, differences in androgen receptor sites in their brains. Then, given that synthetic sex hormones have been available since the 1940s, it is also likely that inappropriate or accidental administration of these drugs to pregnant women should lead to homosexuality in their offspring, along lines similar to a genetic predisposition.

Unfortunately, the evidence is far from clear and, for that reason, research has waned over the last decade. Several studies show no differences between homosexual and heterosexual men in freely circulating testosterone levels (see Meyer-Bahlburg (1984) for a review). Testosterone varies in men to the point that even tests of statistical significance are confounded (Birke, 1982). Equally, as we have noted in the pseudohermaphroditism studies, the administration of sex hormones to children may play a role in developing the physique appropriate to one's assumed gender but socialisation and cognitive variables play a much larger role in determining one's sexual identity. What of administering sex hormones to foetuses to gauge the effects at puberty?

The effect of sex hormones on infants

As hesitant as I am to suggest that administering sex hormones might materially advance the debate (given the many charges that biosocial theorising leads down the slippery slope to cruel and unusual experimentation), natural tests of the de-androgenisation theory are modelled by chemical insult. Maternal progestins rise rapidly shortly after conception and play an important part in maintaining pregnancy (Ellis and Ames, 1987). In the 1960s, a wide variety of progestins were given to assist mothers in difficulties with their pregnancies, to help them carry to term, and several of these were later implicated in interrupting foetal androgen production. Although the great majority of children whose mothers took these drugs show no sex inversional behaviour (Ehrhardt and Meyer-Bahlburg, 1981), there were reports that overdoses of synthetic progestins such as medroxyprogesterone acetate may have demasculinising effects on male genitalia and behaviour (Aarskog, 1971; Yalom et al., 1973) and analogous effects were observed with prenatal exposure to the synthetic oestrogen diethylstilbestrol (DES) in young girls (Meyer-Bahlburg et al., 1995).

In 1973, Yalom, Green and Fisk reported a natural experiment on boys exposed to progestins and the synthetic oestrogen DES. Two groups of children, 6- and 16-year-olds, were compared on a number of measures to controls. The results were inconclusive. The 6-year-olds were not markedly different from controls and the only real difference was in teachers' evaluations that they were 'less masculine' on assertiveness and athletic coordination. The 16-year-olds were less masculine on several measures and the authors reported a slight effect for these anti-androgen drugs. However, critics savaged their study. Hoult (1984), for example, notes that their sample was composed of chronically ill mothers at risk of losing a child and who may have been overprotective in later life as a consequence. He also suggests that 'if important aspects of psychosexual development stem from prenatal hormone exposure . . . such development should have been more evident among younger boys who have had less time to be socialized in terms of gender norms'. A reply might well note the importance of puberty in cementing a gender identity but Hoult and other critics' observations are based on a number of analogous studies, which in sum say more about their methodological difficulties than their experimental effects.

The maternal stress hypothesis

In 1975, Gunter Dorner, Director of the Institute of Experimental Endocrinology in Berlin, published an article in the *Archives of Sexual Behaviour*, at that stage a relatively new scientific journal (Dorner et al., 1975). His report was quite media-worthy and it remains a mystery why it was not instantly picked up by science writers and made much of by the popular press. Dorner claimed that male homosexuality was a consequence of insufficient male androgens during pregnancy, and identified maternal stress as the culprit that blocked an adequate supply of this masculinising hormone. Neither idea was particularly new, but Dorner released details of a study of hormonal manipulation in human males that represented a significant advance in the homosexuality debate, which we will review below. The maternal stress hypothesis had, until then, been a purely infra-human research project. Several studies by Dorner, and by Ingebord Ward and her associates, showed that pregnant rats confined to small spaces and subjected to intense sensory stimulation had markedly elevated levels of the blood-borne stressors adrenaline, corticosteroids and adrenocorticotrophic (ACTH) hormones (Dorner and Docke, 1964; Ward and Weisz, 1980; Ward, 1984).

These stress hormones freely cross the placenta and block the synthesis of foetal testosterone, leading to inverted sexual behaviour or bisexuality in their offspring (Ward, 1977). The timing of the stress event is important. Several studies stressed mothers within a week of parturition and showed marked elevations of stress hormones and lowered plasma testosterone in new-born kits compared to controls (Dorner, 1979). Earlier stress had less marked results. This suggests that stressing the foetus interferes with the development of androgen receptor sites that influence masculine behaviours, rather than gross feminisation of the brain itself, although this is inferential at the moment and awaits a direct anatomical comparison. What is clear from these and other rat studies is that, although maternal stress may block foetal testosterone and cause sexual inversions in otherwise quite rigid and stereotypical sexual behaviour, it is far from a complete behaviour change. While such rats display inverted behaviours such as lordosis (presenting) to other males and a decreased interest in females, their sex drive is not impaired and other sex-typical behaviours are not inverted (Dahlof et al., 1977).

The evidence for the maternal stress theory was, until Dorner's 1975 paper, largely comparative and based on animal models. In the 1970s, as a result of his work, interest revived in the impact of hormones on the brain. Dorner's work on the role of androgens in rodent brain differentiation and sexuality really came to prominence in 1980, when he released findings that men born during the war years in Germany had a much higher incidence of homosexuality than in a twenty-year period from 1934 (Dorner et al., 1980). Dorner speculated that the high stress that pregnant women experienced during the war years and its aftermath led to an overproduction of stress hormones which blocked the formation of masculine pathways in the male foetus, leading to a relative feminisation of the brain. The central assumption of his theory was that distinct masculine and feminine sex roles and behaviour exist and are innate. Dorner moved centre-stage in 1987, when his work was featured in the magazine *Omni*, with such bold claims as 'Homosexuals are born, not made . . . [Dorner] has proof positive that sexual orientation is sealed in the womb' (quoted by De Cecco and Parker, 1995).

Dorner et al. (1983) followed up with a second study which asked mothers of homosexuals, bisexuals and heterosexuals to recall stressful events in their pregnancies. The researchers assumed that very stressful events would lead to clear and more reliable recall of circumstances affecting their pregnancy. This is an important assumption, given the barrage of criticism which followed this study, casting doubt on mothers' ability to recall events some thirty years in the past. However, Dorner and his colleagues found that two-thirds of the mothers of male homosexuals easily recalled severe stressors such as the death of a close friend or relative, interpersonal difficulties such as divorce or separation, or severe financial difficulties. In contrast, only one-third of the bisexual and less than 10 percent of the heterosexual sample reported such instances.

However, such *post hoc* explanation has been severely criticised on methodological grounds, with several studies partially supporting or failing to confirm these results. For example, Bailey et al. (1991) examined the maternal stress theory by taking stress-proneness and reports of stress during pregnancy from 215 mothers of male and female heterosexuals, bisexuals, and homosexuals. For the men in their sample, neither between-family nor within-family analyses revealed a maternal stress effect for either sexual orientation or childhood gender nonconformity. However, male homosexuality was strongly familial, suggesting either genetic and/or familial environmental causes.

What mechanisms support this effect? Dorner mounts the following argument (Dorner et al., 1991). The relative levels of blood androgens in the perinatal environment dictate brain organisation into male or female sexual orientations. This is most easily established by observing post-pubertal sexual preference. The higher androgen levels are during the brain organisation period, the higher will be male-type, and the lower female-type, sexual orientation and behaviour, irrespective of genetic sex. Given foetal developmental plasticity, foetuses are more vulnerable to alterations of androgen levels than in later life. This argues that sexual orientation is innate and irreversible.

What support does Dorner provide for this argument? In his review article (Dorner et al., 1991) Dorner summarises thirty years of his and others' research. In male foetuses, inhibition of testicular androgen secretions may produce female hormonal levels approaching those of female foetuses. His research has identified two mechanisms with similar effects. A 21-hydroxylase deficiency, or a partial 3-beta-ol steroid dehydrogenase deficiency, when combined with stressful events, leads to an overproduction of androstenedione, an adrenal precursor of oestrogen in the placenta.

There, androstenedione is aromatized to estrone and conjugated to estrone sulphate. Estrone sulphate, as demonstrated in animal experiments, is able to inhibit significantly testicular androgen production during brain organization, resulting in more or less feminization of the brain and hence more female-type gender role behavior and sexual orientation in males. Thus, low-dose administration of estrone sulphate in new-born male rats gave rise to androgen deficiency during brain organization, followed by complete or at least partial feminization of gender role behavior (play-fighting) in prepubertal and sexual orientation in postpubertal life.

(Dorner et al., 1991: 146)

Dorner argues that the incidence of 21-hydroxylase deficiency in mothers and homosexual offspring demonstrates that it is carried heterozygously. As we saw in our discussion of sexual inversions, this may provide a predisposition to homosexuality and maternal stress, both psychological and physiological, that then acts to trigger a modified orientation. Dorner (1989) and Dorner et al. (1991) report experiments with adrenocorticotrophic hormone, which controls the release of corticosteriod hormones from the adrenal gland. These stress hormones act antagonistically to ACTH, blocking its further secretion by the pituitary gland. The mode of action of ACTH is to directly stimulate the testis to produce testosterone, blocking the release of ACTH and its tributary hormones, acting as a negative feedback loop. Given that both males and females produce both sex hormones the relative balance of the two is important here. Blocking ACTH increases the relative levels of oestrogen and its precursors. The ratio of 21-deoxycortisol (21-DOF), an oestrogen precursor, to cortisol (F), gave a 21-DOF/F ratio which was markedly elevated in male homosexuals. The significance of this finding is that elevated 21-DOF levels are excellent markers for the genetic 21-hydroxylase deficiency (Fiet et al., 1989).

Dorner et al. (1991) found that eight of nine mothers of homosexual men, and their homosexual offspring, who were administered ACTH had significantly increased levels of 21-DOF, and 21-DOF/F ratios at least one standard deviation greater than the mean of their heterosexual controls. They also reported similar elevated androstenedione levels and cortisol ratios for their homosexual subjects when compared to their heterosexual controls. In their sole deviant case Dorner found that a three-fold increase of plasma dehydroepiandrosterone sulphate, and a dehydroepiandrosterone sulphate/androstenedione ratio, suggested a partial 3-beta-ol steroid dehydrogenase deficiency in this homosexual man. Dorner notes that Pang et al. (1985) found this a probable cause of male homosexuality. Dorner notes: 'Our findings suggest that most homosexual men and/or their mothers display heterozygous forms of 21-hydroxylase deficiency' (Dorner et al., 1991).

The maternal stress theory may be tested experimentally. Dorner (1976) notes that if the male homosexual's pathways have been feminised then they should be more reactive to surges in cyclic female sex hormones accompanying ovulation. This (o)estrogen feedback effect (EFE) is part of the ovulation cycle and high oestrogen levels stimulate a surge of luteinising hormone from the anterior pituitary prompting ovulation. In 1962, Barraclough and Gorski noted that in early embryonic development, androgens switch off parts of the anterior hypothalamus in the male brain, which are responsible for cyclic hormonal regulation. In women, the hypothalamus remains: 'cyclical and capable of triggering a surge of LH in response to high plasma levels of estrogen' (Birke, 1982). Dorner argues that due to insufficient masculinisation of the foetal brain, male homosexuals should demonstrate this effect.

Dorner et al. (1975) tested this effect with twenty-one homosexual men hospitalised for sexually transmitted diseases and other problems. His sample, as he predicted, was intermediate for the positive oestrogen effect, falling between the non-reactive heterosexual men and reactive heterosexual women.

Dorner's maternal stress hypothesis and his tests of it have been severely criticised on several grounds, mainly social constructivist in nature. Apart from the difficulties of post-hoc explanation and other procedural problems, several biologically-minded critics also question his interpretation of his findings. For example, to take the oestrogen feedback hypothesis, Dorner explicitly accepts that bisexuality is an intermediate form of sexual orientation between homosexuality and heterosexual. This notion, implicit in older conceptions such as the Kinsey Scale, has been severely challenged since Bell and Weinberg's *Homosexualities: A Study of Diversity among Men and Women* (1978). In a re-analysis of Dorner's 1975 study Thomas Hoult noted that responses of bisexual men were quite discrepant: 'the average negative result achieved with bisexual men was far larger than the average achieved with heterosexual men' (Hoult, 1984). This is quite contrary to expectations based on a continuum approach to sexual orientation.

Then again, the results of this study were problematic, as not only did Dorner have a very small sample, but the variance within groups was troubling. Only about a third of his gay sample had a strong positive effect and half had no discernible differences from heterosexual controls. The scale of the surges was also small, approximately 3 percent of the peak female ovulation surge. Dorner explained this small response as being due to serum testosterone blocking luteinising hormone release and to the differential demasculinisation of his homosexual sample. Yet, as Birke (1982) notes, this does not account for the failure of response in half of his homosexual sample. She also cites studies that demonstrate a normal luteinising hormone surge in some primate species.

There have been several such studies that have attempted to remedy some of the more problematic aspects of Dorner's work. For example,

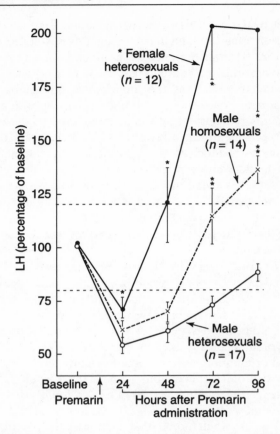

Figure 2.1 Changes in luteinising hormone in response to a single injection of Premarin

Note: Values are means ± standard errors (vertical bars). Dashed lines indicate the 95 percent confidence interval for baseline values for all groups. Group comparisons: (*) female heterosexuals significantly different from male heterosexuals and homosexuals at all times (*P* < 0.05, Newman–Keuls multiple comparison test) and (**) male homosexuals significantly different from male heterosexuals at 72 and 96 hours (*P* < 0.05, SNK). All groups show a decrease from baseline at 24 hours.
Source: Gladue et al., 1984: 1496

Gladue et al. (1984) reported in *Science* a thoughtful and carefully controlled study of fifty-five healthy, drug and oral contraceptive free, and relatively stress-free adults. Twelve heterosexual females, 17 heterosexual males and 14 homosexual males were given an injection of Premarin, an oestrogen preparation, and blood samples were taken over the next four days to measure both luteinising hormone and testosterone levels. Results are shown in Figure 2.1 and confirm Dorner's findings, with the gay men at 96 hours being significantly different from both heterosexual groups and intermediate for the positive oestrogen effect, falling between the non-reactive heterosexual men and reactive heterosexual women. Although baseline values were the same for all three groups, the magnitude of the luteinising hormone surge in homosexual men was much greater than in the Dorner study, approaching two-thirds of the peak female values at 96 hours after administration of Premarin.

As you will see from Figure 2.1 all three groups initially dropped from their luteinising hormone baseline and at the 96-hour mark heterosexual men had yet to recover baseline values. Examination of the individual response patterns showed a greater variability among homosexual than heterosexual men and reflected Dorner's findings. Similarly, testosterone levels were initially the same for both groups but homosexual men had a significantly lower baseline from 72 hours than heterosexual men, which argues a differential 'down regulation' of testosterone receptors. Both these findings may shed some light on the difficulties of Dorner's study. The initial drop from baseline of both the luteinising hormone and testosterone level would explain some of the variability of Dorner's homosexual sample's responses. Similarly the amplitude of response in this later study was much closer to heterosexual female values and an independent confirmation of the variability of homosexual responsiveness would go some way to meeting Birke's difficulties with Dorner's study.

The authors caution that while these results may reflect an *adult* hormonal correlate of sexual orientation independent of perinatal sexual differentiation, their results: 'invite the idea that there may be physiological developmental components in the sexual orientation of some men' and that these responses might: 'constitute a biological marker of their orientation' (Gladue et al., 1984).

However, Louis Gooren, who is professor of transsexiology at the Free University Hospital of Amsterdam, is entirely critical of the work of Dorner and dismissive of Gladue et al.'s replication (Gooren, 1986b). Gooren (1995) notes the almost impossible task of deciding the matter on the basis of free circulating blood serum hormone levels due to three confounding variables:

(1) Hormones are produced in bursts of secretion and, as a consequence, fluctuate within certain margins. (2) Another fluctuation, called circadian rhythm, occurs naturally throughout the day. Hormonal levels in the morning are approximately 25 percent higher than in the late afternoon. (3) Aging has a profound effect on testosterone production; with advancing age testosterone levels decline and estrogen levels rise in men.

(Gooren, 1995: 240)

Given individual male variability as a further confounding variable, Gooren doubts the value of assaying blood and urine to measure testosterone levels between groups of men. As for the oestrogen feedback effect, Gooren doubts the science and possibly the results too. In two replication studies (Gooren 1986a, 1986b), he reported tests of Dorner and Gladue's work starting with their assumption that the sexual orientation was fixed in the perinatal period. In his first study he measured the oestrogen feedback effect in male-to-female and female-to-male transsexuals before and after they had received any hormone therapy or surgery (Gooren, 1986a). He reported that they had EFEs similar to their sex before treatment, and after hormonal therapy and reassignment surgery had EFEs appropriate to their new gender. Gooren chose to interpret this as evidence for the plasticity of sexual orientation and evidence against an intermediate EFE (his transsexual subjects had EFEs similar to heterosexual baselines). That this may be an effect of the reassignment procedures was addressed in his second study. In this study Gooren replicated the work of Dorner and Gladue with a larger sample of homosexual and heterosexual men (Gooren, 1986b) and failed to find an EFE or subsequent luteinising hormone increase that reliably differentiated the two orientations.

Gooren (1995) cautions that this may be a result of sampling differences between his and Dorner's and Gladue's studies, but thinks this unlikely. As there was some variability in his sample, to test this possibility he administered: 'a powerful endocrine stimulus (human chorionic gonadotropin) . . . to those men who had the highest (female like) LH responses to estrogen' (Gooren, 1995). His results showed that those men who had the closest results to those of Dorner and Gladue's studies had the weakest production of testosterone following human chorionic gonadotropin administration. Gooren concludes that an EFE is more likely a result of variable testicular function than of sexual orientation.

Gooren also notes that studies supporting an EFE as a determinant of sexual orientation had ignored the obvious in not administering the synthetic hypothalamic hormone which directly controls luteinising hormone secretion – luteinising hormone releasing hormone (LHRH). Those of their homosexual subjects who had a positive EFE should, if administered LHRH, have a much stronger luteinising hormone response following oestrogen exposure than controls. Gooren (1995) argues that 'Since they omitted the latter test, there is technically no reason to accept their claim that they encountered a positive EFE in homosexual men.' Gooren administered LHRH to all of his sample, including men who had a luteinising hormone response to oestrogen and found that 'in all cases . . . the LH responses to LHRH decreased following estrogen exposure'. Gooren (1995) concludes: 'Therefore the responses of LH to estrogen found by Dorner and Gladue et al. in homosexual men can be viewed as a response of LH to falling testosterone levels and not as an expression of a positive EFE.'

A receptor site?

A direct test of the androgen insensitivity hypothesis was conducted by Macke et al. (1993). Operating on the assumption that a DNA sequence variation in the androgen receptor gene plays a causal role in the development of male sexual orientation, they set out to test whether there were alterations in the receptor gene. The androgen receptor had been previously fairly well characterised, as had a large number of its mutations which underlie the androgen insensitivity syndrome (see McPhaul et al. (1993) for a review). Perhaps sexual orientation is not so much a matter of alterations of blood serum testosterone and other hormones, but in the relative sensitivity of the neural sites which are activated by them?

To test this hypothesis, Jennifer Macke and her colleagues first: 'measured the genetic linkage between the androgen receptor locus and sexual orientation in 36 families in which there are two or more homosexual brothers'. Linkage analysis will be discussed below when we consider Dean Hamer's search for the gay gene, but consists of looking for variable DNA markers which should be shared in common by people who share traits such as homosexuality. If they found that gay brothers shared one form of the gene in common then the next experiment would be to see if this differed from their heterosexual brothers. If so, then they would have established a linkage between this site on the genome and sexual orientation. They also 'compared the lengths of two polymorphic amino acid repeats in the amino-terminal domain of the androgen receptor in a sample of 197 homosexual males and 213 unselected subjects'. This region has been implicated in certain degenerative motor diseases in which the androgen insensitivity syndrome plays a role in expanding the polyglutamine tract in the androgen receptor: 'from a normal range of 15–30 amino acids to greater than 40 amino acids'. Comparing repeat sequences in this area between gay men and unselected controls should indicate if expansion of the glutamine tract was the mechanism for androgen receptor insensitivity. To be sure that they were not neglecting other sites that might be implicated in the androgen insensitivity syndrome they: 'screened the entire androgen receptor coding region for sequence variation . . . in 20 homosexual males with homosexual or bisexual brothers', and to be thorough 'screened the amino-terminal domain of the androgen receptor for sequence variation in an additional 44 homosexual males'. By looking for sequence variation in these areas they were trying to decide if one genetic sequence was common in their samples, or if variability throughout the sample made this unlikely.

Macke's research was uniformly disappointing for the androgen insensitivity hypothesis. They did not find a common sequence in gay men across their studies and what concordance there was, was not significant. Their results suggest that DNA sequence variation in the androgen receptor gene does not play a major role in most of their homosexual subjects. However, it may be that DNA sequence variation in the androgen receptor gene plays a minor role in some gay men and a larger sample would be required to see if some of their non-significant concordance could reach a significant level. Alternatively, Macke and her colleagues may have missed differences in non-coding sequences that may alter levels of expression of the gene, rather than the faulty protein synthesis held responsible for the androgen insensitivity syndrome. This is unlikely given that it is a well characterised section of the genome.

So where are we with the de-androgenisation theory of sexual orientation? Dorner notes the variability of findings of a de-androgenisation effect but argues that the weight of evidence is clearly on his side (Dorner et al., 1991). Gooren (1995) in a review argues otherwise. While it is not yet possible to decide the mechanism on the evidence so far, one factor has emerged from this debate which needs to be acknowledged:

> The public debate about the ontogeny of sexual orientation seems especially misguided because there is profound agreement between scientists who favor psychosocial theories ... and those who favor biological theories ... that sexual orientation is determined very early in life and is not a matter of individual choice.
>
> (Breedlove, 1994: 413)

AN ANATOMICAL DIFFERENCE?

Now we come to the next major biological theory of homosexuality, that there are differences in the brains of gay men which make them homosexual. Usually this theory is a subset of the de-androgenised foetus theory as it assumes that hormonal upset has been the cause of these anatomical differences (LeVay, 1993). It is one thing to postulate that a hormonal difference *in utero* feminises the brains of males who subsequently become homosexual, but it is another to demonstrate that it does so. While testosterone therapy is indicative, it lacks the credentials of explicit sites at which the process operates. Perhaps the most interesting question to be answered in the search for explicit anatomical sites and functional differences in the brains of homosexuals and heterosexuals is the issue of feminisation versus difference. It is explicit in the work of Dorner and others that testosterone deprivation leads to a feminisation of the male brain. That is, sites and action of the brain become feminine. Therefore we would expect anatomical differences to lie intermediate between heterosexual men and women. Several studies have found anatomical and functional differences but these do not conclusively support the feminisation hypothesis. Indeed several suggest that homosexuality may be another type of orientation entirely. Before we consider this question we will review studies which support differences in the brains of homosexual men.

Nearly two decades have passed since the pioneering work of Roger Gorski and his colleagues (Gorski et al., 1978) first identified sexually dimorphic areas in rodent brains and studies which are just now starting to identify differences in the brains of homosexual men (Swaab and Hofman, 1995). The first such human study, by Swaab and Hofman (1990) of the Netherlands Institute for Brain Research in Amsterdam, found clear differences in the suprachiasmatic nucleus (SCN) of the hypo- thalamus, which was twice as large in homosexual, compared to heterosexual men. This pioneering study was controversial, not the least in that the SCN is involved in regulating sleep and activity cycles in the mammalian brain and would seem to have little to do with sexual orien- tation. Nevertheless, it pointed to a distinct biological difference between homosexual and heterosexual men and was ground-breaking for that reason alone.

In 1985, Swaab and Fliers reported that they had found a sexually dimorphic nucleus in one of the interstitial nuclei of the anterior hypo- thalamus (INAH), that was substantially larger in men than women. While subsequent studies questioned this sexual dimorphism (Allen et al., 1989), it was significant because the anterior hypothalamus is 'exactly where we would expect some nucleus that may control sexual orientation to be located' (Allen, quoted in Barinaga, 1991). This area has long been implicated with sexual functioning and Swaab and Fliers' (1985) finding suggested that larger dimorphic nuclei in this area were associated with masculine sexual behaviour.

These findings prompted the curiosity of Simon LeVay, then of the Salk Institute in San Diego, who speculated that a size dimorphism in the INAH area may reflect sexual orientation rather than sex differences. LeVay hypothesised that having larger nuclei in this area may reflect a sexual orientation towards women, irrespective of gender (LeVay, 1991). Therefore, heterosexual men and lesbians would show larger nuclei than heterosexual women and gay men. LeVay tested his hypothesis on brain tissue from forty-one subjects who had died in New York and Californian hospitals. While his sample included homosexual men and heterosexual men and women, he was unable to gain a lesbian sample and abandoned this part of his investigation. His results confirmed his predictions. There was an obvious heterosexual dimorphism, while homosexual male brains were anatomically no different from those of heterosexual women.

LeVay cautions that his findings do not imply that this area causes homosexuality (LeVay, 1993). Rather, it is in line with animal research that ties hypothalamic differences to sexual behaviour. Research with rats shows that INAH development is affected by testosterone levels before and immediately after birth. Reduced testosterone levels lead to a smaller sexually dimorphic nucleus and reductions in masculine sexual behaviour. Increasing testosterone levels show the opposite picture and cause female rats to mimic male sexual behaviour. However, altering testosterone levels only causes differences in this area 'during a perinatal sensitive period' (LeVay, 1991) and even: 'extreme interventions' such as castration show: 'little effect on the size of the nucleus' thereafter. LeVay suggests this points to a critical period in the development of sexual orientation and if differences in behaviour shown by these studies may be generalised to humans then it is likely that human sexual orientation is set around the perinatal period (LeVay, 1993).

LeVay's study is highly suggestive and has generated much research interest, all the more poignant because LeVay admits he began his project as a casual diversion from his research on the visual areas of the brain (Barinaga, 1991). Despite LeVay's impressive reputation as a meticulous worker, this result awaits confirmation. Nor should we assume that his results suggest that INAH dimorphism causes homosexuality, as sexual orientation might *cause* brain differences rather than the other way around. Then again it may prove to be a consequence of another related variable such as the greater promiscuity of homosexual men (Bell and Weinberg, 1978). However, in light of the human testosterone studies reported above, it fits the developing weight of evidence suggesting that the de-androgenisation of the foetal brain leads to homosexuality.

Cautious support for LeVay's work comes from the studies of the anterior commissure, a pathway connecting our right and left cerebral cortices. Laura Allen and Roger Gorski, in a series of studies, have demonstrated that the anterior commissure in gay men is larger than in heterosexual men, and is approximately the same size as that in women (Allen and Gorski, 1992). LeVay (1993) remarks that, although Allen and Gorski's findings do not necessarily relate to sexual functioning (it is more likely that they underlie differences in cognitive functioning), they do support his findings. Not only does this strengthen the notion that gay and straight brains differ but it also supports a biological causation of homosexuality:

> Finally, the very fact that the anterior commissure is *not* involved in the regulation of sexual behavior makes it highly unlikely that the size differences *result* from differences in sexual behavior.
>
> (LeVay, 1993: 123)

The question remains, though: are these differences the effects of intrauterine demasculinisation, or of a genetic orientation? On the whole, LeVay favours a developmental aetiology.

FUNCTIONAL DIFFERENCES?

Findings that homosexual men are anatomically different from hetero-sexual men and women are supported by electroencephalographic (EEG) studies by Alexander and Sufka (1993). Alexander started with the assumption that anatomical differences observed by LeVay, Gorski, Swaab and others should have electrophysiological correlates, but their search of the literature found no studies of sexual orientation research at the functional (working) level. A somewhat surprised Alexander set out to see if such correlates were evident.

Twenty-four undergraduates (five homosexual males, nine heterosexual males and ten heterosexual females) were given spatial, and facial emotion recognition, and verbal, and emotive word-pair judgement tasks. All subjects were screened to ensure right-handedness and that gay males' homosexual preferences were active, lifelong and at least of Kinsey 5 level. Performance during the two tasks was measured on a standard eight channel hookup using an electrode cap. Baseline and experimental readings were then obtained. Measuring behavioural task performance showed no significant difference between groups, indicating that all sub-jects were responding similarly. However, the EEG measures gave quite a different picture.

Alexander found there were quite distinct differences in activational patterns between homosexual males and heterosexual men and women.

> EEG activation exhibited by homosexual males was different than both male and female heterosexual groups during baseline recording and different than heterosexual males during affective judgment for verbal and spatial stimuli, but not significantly different from heterosexual females. This pattern of results, in which homosexual men differ from heterosexual men, but not heterosexual women during cognitive tasks, has been found in both biological . . . and behavioral studies.
>
> (Alexander and Sufka, 1993: 273)

We should note that there is no evident link between these findings and anatomical differences reported by LeVay, Gorski and others. Alexander's findings are merely suggestive of such a link but do fall in the direction anatomical studies suggest. Homosexual men a have significantly larger anterior commissure, a neural pathway connecting the cerebral hemi-spheres than do heterosexual men and Alexander notes that this brain region is implicated in transferring visual information during cognitive tasks (Hooper, 1992). Heterosexual women tend to fall between these two groups (Allen and Gorski, 1992). The affective judgements required in Alexander's study may lead to greater communication between the two hemispheres via the anterior commissure in homosexual men compared to heterosexual men and women. While this study is one of cognitive performance rather than sexual behaviour it does make the point that observable differences in sexual orientation parallel distinct differences in neural anatomy. This should give us confidence that studies such as LeVay's which report distinct differences in brain areas which are more likely to influence sexual orientation have similar functional correlates.

Critics may argue that this is simply argument by analogy and that Alexander's study is silent on whether these differences are causal or merely the effects of socialisation or the environment. Nevertheless they are indicative and, when taken with the developing evidence for anatomical differences, give weight to a biological predisposition. Further clarification of this point awaits a larger scale investigation which has been underway since 1994. Joel Alexander (personal communication, 1996) reports preliminary findings supporting his original study and that: 'these EEG patterns are dynamic and change with the degree of homosexuality reported in the individual. It isn't just an on/off switch.'

Further confirmatory evidence comes from the work of Martin Reite and his colleagues at the Neuromagnetism Laboratory of the University of Colorado (Reite et al., 1995). Using a group of homosexual and heterosexual men they took magnetoencephalographic (MEG) estimates between the two groups. The MEG is an improved technology for measuring activity in the brain. Because the skull is 'electrically resistant but magnetically transparent' (Beatty, 1995) the distortions which so bedevil EEG recordings are minimised by the MEG process, which measures magnetic rather than electrical fields. However, the MEG process is still in its infancy, posing formidable technical problems of application and interpretation. Nonetheless, it is yielding valuable information, not the least at the M100 source location in the superior temporal gyri. Although this part of the cerebral cortex has no evident role in regulating sexuality as far as we know, it does show strong gender differences when stimulated. Auditory evoked potentials, measures of brain activity in response to auditory stimulation in this region, had shown significant asymmetry between the two hemispheres of men's brains, being more anterior (further to the front of the brain) in the right compared to the left hemisphere. The M100 site (the location that responds to the auditory stimulus) tends to be more symmetrical in women, and left and right hemisphere locations 'are generally not significantly different' (Beatty, 1995).

Reite and his colleagues thought this would be a good test of anatomical differences in gay and straight men.

Since this MEG-based metric appears to be a robust index of sex-based cerebral laterality, suggesting the male brain is more lateralised than the female brain, we thought it important to assess the possible influence of sexual orientation on this measure.

(Reite et al., 1995: 586)

Eight homosexual men and nine heterosexual men had their brain's responses to an auditory stimulus measured at the M100 source location. The results showed that gay men did not demonstrate significant differences between right and left hemispheres. But, as expected, straight men had significantly more anterior reactions in the right hemisphere compared to the left one. Additionally, heterosexual males demonstrated significant laterality (to the sides) of the hemispheres whereas gay men were not significantly lateral. Reite et al. note that this source is positively correlated with spatial performance measures and McCormick and Witelson (1991) had shown that homosexual men do less well at this task than heterosexual men. Women do less well at these tasks (block designs and figure shape reversals) than men and perhaps Reite's study indicates an intermediate position between straight men and women. However, as they did not have any psychological performance measures, whether they are intermediate or similar is still speculative. What their study did show is yet another anatomical difference in sexual orientation and, as with Alexander and Sufka's study, demonstrates that these differences lie in a consistent direction.

One of the key debates to emerge from the anatomical and functional studies is not so much that male and female brains are different and that gay brains are different yet again but rather what is the nature of that difference? It is still premature to suggest, as Dorner does, that gay brains become more or less feminised by a process of demasculinisation. Rather, the debate is now one of feminisation versus difference. Still, a direction is clear. Gorski finds a sexual difference between men and women. Swaab and Fliers report a sexually dimorphic nucleus in the anterior hypothalamus (INAH) substantially larger in men than women. LeVay speculates that these differences reflect sexual orientation and that homosexual males' brains are anatomically similar to those of heterosexual women. Allen and Gorski find that the anterior commissure in gay men is about the same size as that of heterosexual women and Alexander and Sufka provide supporting evidence in their EEG studies. Reite and his colleagues find a cortical difference which discriminates gay men and straight men on a cognitive task that favours men over women. Clearly, the evidence is pointing towards a biological predisposition for homosexuality. What is behind this difference, intrauterine demasculinisation or genetic difference?

A GENETIC VARIATION?

There is a vast difference between finding that a behaviour has biological predispositions and asserting that it is part of our genetic code. Many examples of evident difference may have non-genetic origins. As we have seen, the androgenised foetus theory does not require a genetic basis. It may well be that homosexuality is a consequence of biological processes within the intrauterine environment but these processes are environmental in origin nonetheless. To assert that homosexuality, as a biological process, is environmentally based, does not invalidate an evolutionary rationale, but as we have seen it would be more comforting to find that it is part of our genetic message and so indisputably part of our evolutionary history.

Unlike the foetal hormone and structural difference theories, genetic research proceeds on a very different set of assumptions. Geneticists are less concerned with difference as such but rather whether the observed differences are genetic in origin. While this sounds obvious, such determinations are unusually difficult to make. Correlation does not equal causation, and discovering that a certain combination of genes is linked with a behaviour does not provide a causal link. As we will see, even discovering a genetic difference in the right place on the right chromosome still leaves us guessing whether it is causal. Given the complexities of social behaviour, identifying genetic bases are often more matters of inference than certainty. The obvious next step would be systematically to vary the genes to observe the results but, as with homosexuality, ethical considerations rule out such experiments, even if we had the techniques to engage in the complex polygenic manipulations that would be required. So we are left with social research to strengthen genetic theories. If the difference is observed early enough we may predict that, all other things being equal, the direction and degree of genetic difference will predict sexual orientation.

Nor are geneticists all that concerned with issues of normality and abnormality but rather of function. In the absence of delineation of the complete human genome we are uncertain of the bounds of the human genetic message, nor are we certain of what is expected and what is unusual in human variability. Given human diversity, genetic drift and the complexity of the genome, it is unlikely that we will ever arrive at a complete correspondence between genes and behaviour, even without considering added complications of environmental influence. For these reasons, geneticists think more in terms of adequate functioning than abnormality. If a genetic difference does not inhibit functioning then that is the end of the story. This limits geneticists' interest in the area.

DISCOVERING A DIFFERENCE: FAMILIAL STUDIES

Before we start reviewing proband studies it would be well to consider where discovering a familial concordance may lead us. In the biosocial scheme of things, heredity is the final proof of homosexuality's biological origins but it is much more. If we can establish higher concordance rates among relatives of homosexuals then we are well on the way to demonstrating that homosexuality is a positive human adaptation selected for in the evolutionary stakes rather than an inversion. Given the considerations raised in the last chapter, if there is a significant hereditary component in homosexuality, we may then argue that these genes are contributing to an individual's reproductive fitness. While there are many genes which are deleterious, in evolutionary theory these are either rare, lethal, or carried forward safely in a latent heterozygous condition. In any case they are eventually selected from the genome, *unless they contribute some advantage to the species*. That they are occurring in greater numbers within gay men's families may be a result of a reoccurring deleterious mutation but this is unlikely given that the incidence of exclusive male homosexuality far exceeds any expected mutation rate. While we are entering a controversial area of human genetics, establishing a familial basis for male homosexuality advances the possibilities of a Darwinian explanation, whatever the reasons. We will return to this at length in the next chapter.

How do we establish a genetic basis using familial studies? There are many approaches but four main lines of enquiry are pursued. A simple test of the proposition is to measure the sexual orientation of gay men's family members to see if they have another gay relative. The assumption here is that such familial studies indicate a shared genetic background and would have higher concordance rates than for a heterosexual control group. The problem with such an approach is that the higher concordance found in gay families may well be environmental, growing up in the same home. This approach has been fruitful (Pillard and Weinrich, 1986; Bailey and Bell, 1993) but there is always the doubt. A refinement is to use monozygotic (MZ) co-twins and assess how often homosexuality occurs and their degree of shared sexual orientation on the Kinsey Scale, or similar measure (concordance rate). The higher the concordance, the more likely a genetic (familial) factor is at work. At its most simple, this approach uses only a few case studies of twins, often just one pair, to make detailed analyses of concordance (Klintworth, 1962; Green and Stoller, 1971; Zuger, 1976; McConaghy and Blaszczynski, 1980; Green, 1987). While the elegance of this approach is the detailed description possible, it suffers from a lack of generalisability: just how typical is the pair being studied and we still have possible influences arising from a shared upbringing. For this reason we will not pursue these two types of study in any depth here.

Another approach contrasts the incidence of homosexuality in MZ and dizygotic (DZ) twins where one twin is gay. With the increasing sophistication of twin registries and sampling techniques it is possible to find enough gay men who are also twins to make a sufficiently powerful study. If a genetic trait is at work, then the concordance of sexual orientation should be much greater in identical than in fraternal twins, given their identical genes (Kallmann, 1952; Heston and Shields, 1968; Bailey and Pillard, 1991; Buhrich, Bailey and Martin, 1991). However, critics argue that these studies do not address possible confounding environmental influences (McGuire, 1995). For example, identical twins may have more common experiences or be treated differently from fraternal twins. The two other types of study address these possible confounding variables. Despite their rarity, some studies have identified a gay MZ twin reared apart from their co-twin and then assessed their concordance for homosexuality (Eckert et al., 1986). Given the astronomical odds of finding such twins, these studies have a very small sample and are merely indicative. Another, and perhaps the most difficult, approach is to directly measure the relative influence of environmental and hereditary components. We will return to this method as our final analysis of familial studies.

Although at present twin studies are the best evidence we have for a widespread genetic effect for homosexuality it is wise to be a bit cautious about their validity. Farber (1981), in her widely cited book, sounded a warning about the reliance placed on MZ studies and, while noting their use, also pointed out that most commentators assume that 'concordance of traits is linked to genetic factors while discordance is linked to environmental influences' (Haynes, 1995). Clearly this is not the case, and the widely held belief that genetic similarity will express similar traits ignores the many influences that may modify the expression of otherwise identical genetic information. Farber sets up five criteria which are necessary in her view for MZ studies to be experimentally sound. None of the studies we review met all of her conditions for the reasons we consider below:

1 Selection of genetically identical individuals (MZ twins).
2 Random selection of subjects.
3 Random assignment to rearing conditions.
4 Selection of pairs that are reared separately as single individuals.
5 No organic and non-genetic features (such as prematurity) should exist within pairs which might artificially inflate or deflate hereditability estimates.

(Farber, quoted in Haynes, 1995: 103)

While there were several earlier studies of the familial components of homosexuality (Lang, 1940; Darke, 1948) it is fairly traditional to start with Franz Kallmann's 1952 study which had a sample large enough to be meaningful. Kallmann (and his colleagues) investigated the concordance rates in 85 pairs of twins in which at least one twin was homosexual. To the disbelief of many commentators he found an absolute concordance in his sample of 40 MZ (identical) twins, all of which were gay. In stark contrast, his results for the 45 DZ (fraternal twins) was non-significant. Kallmann concluded that the chances that one's brother was also likely to be homosexual were least when they were ordinary siblings; slightly more when DZ; and greatest when MZ (Hoult, 1984). He concluded that there was a strong hereditary basis to homosexuality.

While this study captured the imagination of the popular press it drew strong criticism from Kallmann's peers, who were fairly unanimous in finding his methodology flawed. The inadequacies of Kallmann's scientific reporting were such as to make his findings neither replicable, nor easy to interpret. Kallmann himself eventually acknowledged some methodological limitations (Kallmann cited in Rainer et al., 1960) and suggested that his 100 percent concordance was probably an artefact of having drawn most of his gay sample from correctional institutions and the mentally ill. It is also clear in Kallmann's initial study that notions of sexual inversion were an implicit subtext and his sample, while convenient, reveals this. However, more basic critiques were mounted. Kallmann failed to separate genetic and environmental influences by not taking into account that most, if not all, of his twins shared a common family environment. Even if his results were valid, he had not controlled for the effects of the twins' socialisation; however, this is a problem that virtually all successive studies face and we will return to it. A more profound criticism was that given Kallmann's conclusions, you would expect DZ twins would show some significant concordance as they do share common genes. Kallmann failed adequately to account for this unusual result. Other studies we review below did find such concordance, but well below that of MZ twins.

Kallmann's study was a call to battle and the literature was flooded with many studies that set out to confirm or refute his findings. These ranged from clinical case notes of identical twins where one brother was not homosexual (Klintworth, 1962) to more elaborate replications of his study (Heston and Shields, 1968). Nevertheless, the general trend of proband studies has been to support a genetic component to male homosexuality. Three major studies have addressed this question in recent years.

Bailey and Pillard

The largest twin study yet reported in the literature is by Michael Bailey and Richard Pillard (1991). With considerable ingenuity they obtained, through gay publications and newspapers, a sample of 115 twin pairs, where one partner was gay. The significance of Bailey and Pillard's study was that they also found forty-six gay men with adopted brothers, allowing a test of environmental versus genetic effects for brothers raised in the same environment, although these were from different families from the twins. The researchers assessed zygosity by self-report and degree of sexual preference by questionnaires. Their homosexuality was assessed by personal and phone interviews, ratings by relatives and co-twins and their questionnaire responses. The concordance rate for identical twins was 50 percent, 25 gay co-twins from 50 cases. The rate for fraternal twins was 24 percent, 11 gay co-twins from 46 cases. Interestingly, the rate for adoptive brothers (11 percent) was not significantly different from that for the DZ twins, and was similar to the rate for non-twin brothers (9.2 percent).

This careful study is not without its critics. Lidz (1993) notes that one would have expected higher rates for DZ twins and natural brothers, than for adoptive brothers. Simple genetics would lead us to expect fraternal twins and their non-twin natural brothers to share similar genetic endowments and concordances. Bailey and Pillard (1993) in reply note that this was indeed what was found: 24 versus 9.2 percent, even if not a significant difference, was anomalous compared to their previous study (Pillard and Weinrich, 1986) which found a rate of 22 percent for non-twin probands of homosexual brothers. Bailey and Pillard (1991) account for this discrepancy as a possible sampling artefact as they were unable to contact all the heterosexual adoptive brothers. McGuire (1995) suggests this demonstrates that homosexuality is: 'entirely environmental in origin', which conveniently ignores the study's main finding of significantly higher MZ concordance. Bailey and Pillard tackle the issue of environment and familiality head-on in their reply to critics.

> We close with an empirical challenge. Following publication of our article, we performed the following additional analysis on our data: if genetic factors contribute to twin concordance for male homosexuality, then the MZ twins from concordant pairs should have a higher genetic loading than those from discordant pairs. If so, then MZ probands from concordant pairs should have a higher proportion of homosexual nontwin brothers than should MZ probands from discordant pairs. This was confirmed.
>
> (Bailey and Pillard, 1993: 241)

Bailey and Pillard (1993) also note that in their original study they had two pairs of MZ twins who had been reared apart and both were concordant for homosexuality.

Whitam, Diamond and Martin

Frederick Whitam, Milton Diamond and James Martin in 1993 released a paper summarising the results of over twelve years of soliciting for gay men who were twins through newspapers, gay venues and through personal contacts. This carefully controlled study assessed all index cases and their co-twins on an eighteen-page questionnaire, completed at a personal interview where possible. Zygosity was measured using the Nichols and

Bilbro (1966) instrument which correlates highly with zygosity and, where possible, childhood and current photographs of the co-twins were obtained. Whitam's study had a lower number of cases of male homosexuality than Bailey and Pillard's (MZ 34, DZ 14) and reported on concordance rates for female twins as well. Of interest, they reported on the concordance of three sets of triplets. Concordance rates were similar to those of Bailey and Pillard. Concordance for MZ twins was 64.7 percent (23 of 34 co-twins) and for DZ twins it was 28.6 percent (4 of 14 co-twins).

Of the triplets, the first set was an MZ pair of brothers and a DZ sister. Aged 33, the brothers were homosexual and the sister heterosexual. Both brothers are heavily involved in the arts and reported that their sister was more athletic than either of them. The second set comprised three 24-year-old sisters: two MZ twins were homosexual and the third DZ sister heterosexual, a similar pattern to the first set. The third set comprised three MZ homosexual brothers who were not only concordant but shared a remarkably similar history: 'All three married heterosexually early in life, all had a single daughter, and all at age 40 divorced, self-defined themselves as gay, and presently report very strong same-sex attractions' (Whitam et al., 1993). A less complex study than Bailey and Pillard's, it has attracted less criticism.

King and McDonald

We end our discussion of twin studies with a report widely cited as disproving genetic concordance for homosexuality. In 1992, two British clinical psychiatrists, Michael King and Elizabeth McDonald, reported a study of forty-six homosexual male and female twins. Their survey found no differences in concordance between MZ (2 of 15) and DZ (2 of 22) twins. To use this study, as critics such as McGuire do, to contest the findings of Kallmann; Heston and Shields; Bailey and Pillard; and Whitam et al., is very unwise. King and McDonald's study did not separate men and women in their analyses, although they report that their sample was of 'predominantly young men (38 males, 8 females)' and that: 'In 33 pairs the co-twins were of the same-sex as the respondents'. Such imprecision completely ignores the major debate surrounding the co-familiality of lesbian and gay genetics (see, for example, Plomin et al., 1980; Bailey and Bell, 1993). Further, they did not question co-twins about their own and twin's sexual orientation '[d]ue to the sensitive nature of our inquiries'. Other concerns with their sample size, recruitment and methods of ascertainment, render this study not particularly valuable for comparative purposes.

Evaluating twin studies

Most of these studies described above suffer the same deficiencies which taxed Kallmann's study, that of not being able to control for the effects of the environment. The most obvious way of doing this is to find a sample of MZ twins who have been reared apart since birth *and* where one twin is homosexual. If the other twin is homosexual, then their homosexuality is more likely to be genetic than environmental. Doing such research raises enormous difficulties. The deficiencies of twin studies are more a result of sample and ethical constraints than flawed research. For example, given that the incidence of twinning in Western populations; and taking a conservative estimate of the incidence of male homosexuality in the West as about 2 percent (Hamer and Copeland, 1994), the expected incidence of at least one identical gay twin is less than 1:100,000 and here we are assuming the incidence of homosexuality in twins is the same as the general gay population, it may well be smaller. Even given the 'rubberiness' of these figures, gay identical twins are rare and the percentage of those pairs that were separated at birth is vanishingly small.

Hence, the difficulties of such a study are enormous. Nevertheless, Eckert et al. (1986) managed to find a sample. As one aspect of the ongoing Minnesota Study of Twins Reared Apart, they interviewed fifty-five pairs of identical twins separated since infancy and identified five pairs of MZ twins where one twin was homosexual and a sixth pair where one twin was bisexual. This small sample yielded one male pair where both twins were homosexual, and another male pair where one co-twin was homosexual and his twin had had a 'homosexual affair with an older man between ages 15–18' but now regards himself as 'exclusively heterosexual'. In none of the four female pairs, was more than one co-twin lesbian. No co-twins in the sixteen DZ pairs reared apart were homosexual. While their study has a minuscule sample and Eckert and colleagues note 'that the twins are highly selected cannot be doubted; they are not representative of twins or homosexuals', nevertheless, it is the best such study to date. Whitam et al. (1993), the only other source on record, report that their ongoing project has only thrown up two sets of twins reared apart where one co-twin was gay. Both MZ and male, one set was separated at birth and raised in different countries, only discovering they had a homosexual brother when they accidentally met in a Canadian gay bar. The other set was discordant.

These findings are indicative. While it is impossible to infer a genetic basis for homosexuality from such small numbers, this study when viewed against the backdrop of twins reared together is suggestive. Clearly, the incidence of gayness in male MZ twins is in line with the studies we have discussed and the concordance rate for homosexual orientation in male MZ pairs is 'consistently above that of DZ pairs and despite all problems of ascertainment and diagnosis, it is hard to deny genetic factors and aetiological role' (Eckert et al., 1986). In the pair of homosexual twins reared apart, their development of a homosexual identity was quite strikingly similar, providing a further indication of a biological predisposition.

While suggestive of a genetic predisposition in the male homosexual, Eckert's study does not support a similar view of lesbianism. This is much more controversial and is beyond the scope of this book. All four MZ co-twins were discordant and while three of the four pairs shared similar environments, their physical development was quite different. Eckert et al. noted that the lesbian co-twin was taller and heavier than their sister but despite this reached menarche later. The mean difference in onset of menarche was two years, whereas with their sample of heterosexual MZ twin pairs it was 0.9 of a year and normative data suggest a difference of only 0.3 years. They conclude that these findings: 'suggest that female homosexuality is a trait acquired after conception, most likely after birth, but before menarche'. These findings are not supported by wider studies of co-twins reared together. For example, Whitam et al. (1993) specifically comment on Eckert et al.'s findings in their own report of four twin pairs reared together. Three of the twins whose co-twin was homosexual were also lesbian, a concordance rate of 75 percent compared to Eckert's zero percent. Whitam and his colleagues suggest this is an artefact of the small numbers and propose several reasons for smaller lesbian samples. These variations reinforce our hesitancy to equate lesbianism with male homosexuality.

Eckert et al.'s 1986 study also reinforces difficulties of deciding just what 'homosexuality' means. In one of the four pairs of women, the homosexual co-twin had only limited homosexual experience and now identifies as a heterosexual. The woman was divorced and had her first homosexual contact at age 25 and over the next three years lived with two other female partners. While she is now remarried with children and regards herself as heterosexual with an active sex life, she still feels sexually attracted to both males and females and her orientation may well be bisexual rather than heterosexual. In one of the two male pairs, the heterosexual co-twin had an older homosexual lover in the same town in mid- to late adolescence. It is likely that this was developmental homosexuality as described by Kinsey, rather than an adult homosexual orientation, as the twin also had heterosexual dating and petting experiences while still in secondary school. In both cases, the twins' identification is heterosexual but their ultimate predisposition is not definite, given the social pressures to conform to a heterosexual lifestyle.

What do all these familial studies sum to? Clearly there is a strong genetic element in MZ homosexuality but this is not the total story. Several telling critiques have been raised against even strong studies such as that of Bailey and Pillard.

Twin research is fraught with methodological difficulties and virtually all the studies we have reviewed are open to sampling or ascertainment bias critiques. Given the difficulty of identifying and recruiting twins, the most balanced sample available is through twin registers. Unfortunately, the demands on those formally enrolled in twin registers are such that most researchers would wait years to gain a sample, and most twins are so pressured that they are reluctant to be involved in any but the most pressing of medical research. Most social researchers perforce have to rely on samples of convenience in their twin studies.

This ascertainment bias is a real problem to overcome and provides a convenient flail for critics. Advertising for participants in gay periodicals or similar strategies pursued in studies such as we have reviewed is seen as an invitation for participants to self-select. Critics such as Lidz (1993) and Byne and Parsons (1993) assume the motivation of those responding may differ from those who do not. It is hard to see how this impacts on the heredity issue. These studies aim to determine genetic concordance rates. Presumably, life experience would determine whether one chooses to participate or not, but it is hard to see a connection between one's heredity and a decision to participate. If indeed one's prior experiences influenced a decision, it would probably confound the genetic component of the study rather than the environmental, unless of course you are assuming a genetic urge to participate! Without wishing to take an 'us and them' stance, this critique seems trivial and ignores the care that researchers take to avoid demand characteristics. Of more importance is the worry that such methods may only be reaching a certain group of homosexuals, a point made by Byne and Parsons. However, the ongoing projects of the Minnesota group and of Whitam and Diamond do include a broad sample of homosexual lifestyles and a more definitive resolution of this question awaits a better definition of homosexuality and a better recruitment strategy.

In summary, several familial studies do show a concordance for identical twins of about 60–70 percent but our greatest concern is a question of similar environments for the probands. Considerable comment has been made that MZ twins share a unique environmental similarity that may lead to similar sexual orientation (Turner, 1994; De Cecco and Parker, 1995; McGuire, 1995). Critics argue that environmental similarity may well account for the high concordance rates found in the above studies. Put simply, people expect identical twins to be identical and so treat them identically. Presumably MZ twins would also share more interests in common than DZ twins and they, in turn, more than other siblings. It may also be that this environmental similarity is a consequence of genetic factors unrelated to homosexuality (similar personalities may lead to similar life experiences) or that similarity may just ensure similar familial rearing practices and expectations. Whatever the reasons, if the treatment of MZ twins was more alike than that of DZ twins or other siblings, then environment rather than genetics may lead to higher concordance rates. Further, unless we are able to specify those variables which influence orientation in families, their utility is ultimately problematic.

A WORLD OF DIFFERENCE? Xq28

On 16th July 1993 an article titled 'A linkage between DNA markers on the X chromosome and male sexual orientation' appeared in *Science*. Dean Hamer, Chief of the Section on Gene Structure and Regulation at the National Cancer Institute at Bethesda, Maryland, and his colleagues Stella Hu, Victoria Magnuson, Nan Hu and Angela Pattatucci reported their linkage and proband analysis of 114 families of homosexual men. This innocuous-sounding article reported the discovery of markers for a probable polygene at the tip of the long arm of the X chromosome in homosexual brothers. To say that this paper was controversial is a gross understatement. As its implications were understood by the popular media, an enormous wave of speculation arose and gay groups felt vindicated, while fundamentalists damned its findings. On a more exalted level, senior churchmen struggled with the idea that God may well have designed a gene for homosexuality and wondered aloud why he (she?) would do something quite that odd. The theology of sexuality was dusted off and re-examined yet again (Hastie, 1994). The Vatican woke up, expressed concern but in the end simply restated their advice to 'love the sinner but not the sin'. On a more secular level the public and sections of the scientific community were either alarmed or quietly happy about the possibility of developing a test for homosexuality so that unsatisfactory foetuses might be aborted. Even Hamer, who had a fair idea of the potential of his paper, was surprised at the scale of reaction (Hamer and Copeland, 1994).

Hamer's search for the homosexual gene started from scientific curiosity and an initial interest in the familial research of Michael Bailey. As we have already seen, Bailey had carefully measured the concordance rates of gay twins recruited through gay newspapers and was interested in measuring concordance rates *between* MZ and DZ twins, finding predictable differences. Hamer as a molecular biologist was more interested in concordance rates *within* the families of gay twins, as this would provide clues to the mechanism underlying concordance. Hamer asked Bailey to re-analyse his findings to establish the rates between gay/gay co-twins and gay/straight co-twins and their brothers, predicting that families of gay/gay co-twins would have a higher homosexual penetrance than those of discordant co-twins. When Bailey re-analysed his data he found that 'brothers of gay twins had a 22 percent chance of being gay compared with a 4 percent chance for brothers of gay/straight twins' (Hamer and

Copeland, 1994). These penetrance rates were identical to those found by Pillard and Weinrich in 1986, who measured the differences in concordance rates between straight and gay men and their non-twin brothers. This gave Hamer the confidence that whatever was causing homosexuality ran within certain families at a higher rate than within the wider population.

In consultation with Michael Bailey, Hamer and his colleagues started their search by mapping pedigrees within families of 114 homosexual men. This sample was recruited from several sources and only required that their respondents be gay. Hamer's pedigrees did not show any clear Mendelian patterns of inheritance, suggesting that homosexuality was polygenic, as might be expected from previous familial studies. Further, the rates of penetrance echoed those found in earlier studies and this suggested that genetic causes set a predisposition towards homosexuality rather than the lockstep switching that a single dominant gene would entail. Hamer's sample gave fairly conservative penetrance rates for male homosexuals having homosexual brothers (13.5 percent), roughly half that found by Bailey, and Weinrich and Pillard. Overall penetrance rates were also far lower than familial studies would have suggested. This was partly an artefact of Hamer's conservative categorisation of orientation when questioning gay males about their relatives' sexuality but it also pointed to other than genetic factors playing a role in sexual orientation. At first glance, Hamer's pedigrees suggested a polygenic predisposition towards homosexuality, which was triggered by both nature and nurture.

Further analysis found that male homosexual orientation seemed to follow the maternal line in families (Table 2.1). The first clue was a much higher frequency of gay uncles on the maternal side than the father's. This suggested an X-linked trait. Yet several other mechanisms might account for this other than an X-linked trait. Perhaps the simplest alternative explanation is that gay men have few children compared to women who carried the gene in a recessive condition. Gay men therefore were less likely to have inherited genes from their fathers, not because of an X-linkage but rather because fewer fathers were carriers. This would concentrate male homosexuality in the maternal line. More analysis was required.

Hamer re-analysed his results looking for the impact of maternal inheritance through the female line. Because sisters share up to 75 percent of the same genetic message on the X chromosome, it would be reasonable to suspect that rates of gay uncles on the maternal side would be equal to that of male cousins through maternal aunts. As can be seen from the bold type in Table 2.1, gay maternal uncles and maternal cousins through aunts were clearly more numerous than other gay relatives and in similar numbers. This supported the existence of an X-linked gene underlying

Table 2.1 The percentages of maternal and paternal line gay relatives of homosexual men

Relative	Gay/total	Percent gay
Fathers	0/76	0.0
Brothers	**14/104**	**13.5**
Maternal uncles	**7/96**	**7.3**
Paternal uncles	2/119	1.7
Maternal uncles thru aunt	**4/52**	**7.7**
Maternal cousins thru uncle	2/51	3.9
Paternal cousins thru aunt	3/84	3.6
Paternal cousins thru uncle	3/56	5.4

Source: Hamer and Copeland, 1994: 96

the trait but the frequency patterns did not suggest simple Mendelian inheritance.

The next step was identifying markers for the gene. Hamer used a technique called linkage analysis to look for concordant and discordant markers in a sample of forty pairs of gay brothers and a control group of 314 sets of random brothers. Linkage analysis relies on two aspects. First, that genes located close to one another on any one chromosome are regularly transferred together (linked) through the generations so that two close relatives such as brothers are likely to inherit the same genes. Second, if a gene influences a trait there is a good chance that if people share the same form of the predisposing genes then they are likely to share the same form of the trait – there is linkage between the forms of the genes and forms of the traits they express. From these two linkages comes the corollary that if a trait is inherited, close relatives should share common DNA markers located close to the gene underlying the trait (Hamer and Copeland, 1994). A marker is not a gene, but a region of a chromosome in which there is some observable characteristic, a mapped gene or a repeat sequence, that allows it to be readily identified. The basis of Hamer's study was to test known variable markers which should show concordance for his gay population sample but would show discordance in the wider population.

The next question was where to start looking for markers. Having identified a maternal line effect, the next step was to examine the X chromosome for variable markers. This was still a daunting task and Hamer chose to do a test run on the long arm of the X chromosome at a marker called DXS52 because he was trialling a new method of making DNA and this was a known convenient marker. As he compared the sequences at this marker he discovered that they were concordant for gay brothers but not for their mothers. In Hamer's words he was somewhat surprised to get a result so quickly and 'It wasn't until a few months later that I realised how phenomenally, blessedly lucky I had been ...

somehow I had managed to throw a dart at a map of three billion base pairs and hit very near the bullseye' (Hamer and Copeland, 1994). The DXS52 marker lies near the tip of the long arm of the maternal chromosome at the region Xq28. The Xq region is well explored and many researchers had already identified it as a hypervariable site connected to many debilitating illnesses (Turner, 1995). Hamer tested for known markers at this point, and:

> The complete experiment tested 40 pairs of gay brothers for 22 different markers along the X chromosome. The major finding was that 33 out of these 40 pairs were concordant, or the same, for a series of 5 markers in chromosome region Xq28. Thirty-three out of forty is 83 percent, which is considerably more than the 50 percent chance that a marker would be shared without having a connection to the brothers' homosexuality.
>
> (Hamer and Copeland, 1994: 138)

These results indicate that in the Xq28 region, at least thirty-three pairs of gay brothers shared five markers which were linked to their sexual orientation. Hamer is at pains to stress that he has not discovered a gay gene but that he has given a fair indication that there is one and where it resides for at least one type of homosexuality. He also found this concordance was tightly linked to the Xq28 region and testing downstream at Xq27 failed to find more than a chance result. On the basis of this study he was unable to say what the gene's penetrance is other than it could not exceed 67 (the most conservative estimate of concordance in his sample) and that his best guesstimate is that this gene 'plays some role in about 5 to 30 percent of gay men'. Similarly his study says nothing about lesbianism or ambisexuals although his lab has since reported further work (Hu et al., 1995) in which these groups show no sign of a link to Xq28.

That the gene might be female-linked was a bit of a surprise, given a long literature that suggested variability on the male sex chromosome – after all, male homosexuality is a male behaviour. Yet the X chromosome is a likely site for such a gene given that it is three-quarters of our species' sexual inheritance and that if it were Y-linked then gay men would be less likely to become fathers and pass it on to succeeding generations. How likely are Hamer's findings? The intense media debate obscures the fact that Hamer et al.'s study is a tentative, preliminary foray into a new area. The scientific community would normally have expressed cautious interest if the work had been in a less contentious area and simply considered it an interesting but unproven idea until the findings were replicated. Given the media's elevation of Hamer's tentative conclusions to immutable fact, several biting critiques have challenged his recruitment and sampling techniques, his testing of relatives, his statistical analysis, his laboratory methodology and his conclusions (Hubbard and Wald, 1993b; Maddox, 1993; Byne, 1994; McGuire, 1995). Many critiques were charges of omission which, in fairness, reflect more on the preliminary nature of his study, than on errors of method. However, several difficulties remained.

Replication is the surest path to scientific credibility. On 16th June 1995, *Science* gave advance notice of a follow-up study on a new group of thirty-three pairs of homosexual brothers which supported Hamer's original findings. Hamer's second study of thirty-three gay brothers was reported in *Nature Genetics* (Hu et al., 1995). It had three aims: to test the linkage observed at Xq28 with a new sample; answer criticisms of the first study that they had not tested heterosexual brothers of gay male sib-pairs to assess penetrance rates and control for segregation distortion; and to determine if the Xq28 locus was correlated with sexual orientation in women. Their study found a significant level of haplotype sharing at 67 percent, a lower level concordance than the first study's 83 percent but significantly greater than the expected rate of chance concordance by descent of 50 percent. They found a predicted inverse relationship between gay male sibs' concordance at Xq28 and that of their hetero-sexual brothers at 22 percent shared haplotype, which again was less than the null hypothesis of 50 percent. This discordance strengthens evidence for linkage of Xq28 with homosexual orientation. As predicted, they did not find any significant correlation between lesbianism and Xq28 markers (Pattatucci and Hamer, 1995). Perhaps the most interesting finding of their replication study was using the technique of multipoint interval mapping to try to refine the location of the homosexuality gene. They feel this is close to the DXS52 marker, but still caution about the small sample on which they base this estimate.

So far so good, but two weeks later, on 30th June 1995, *Science* reported that George Ebers and George Rice of the University of Western Ontario, had independently been investigating forty pairs of gay brothers. They 'found no evidence that gayness is passed from mother to son – "not even a trend in favor of X-linkage" ' (Marshall, 1995). However, while not finding concordance at Xq28, they did report a significantly higher rate of gay maternal uncles of 13.4 percent, versus 6.9 percent for the paternal line. Ebers and Rice's studies, have not yet been published and several other replication studies including Elliot Gershon's at the National Institute of Mental Health, and Richard Pillard's of Boston University, are still in the early stages at the time of writing. Marshall's article also reported that the Office of Research Integrity was investigating Hamer's research after one of his co-authors on their original paper challenged his sampling methodology and was dismissed (Bone, 1995). This develop-ment gave greater credence to those critics such as Byne (1994) and

McGuire (1995), who contest Hamer's recruitment and sampling procedure.

Clearly, Hamer's two samples were quite atypical of the gay community and that Hamer made no real attempt to gain a stratified sample of what in Kinsey's words was 'a highly variable and non-dichotomous behavior' (Kinsey et al., 1948). The argument revolves around whether homosexuality is X-linked and if recruiting gay brothers with strong maternal line homosexuality is a valid reflection of male homosexuality. Hamer asserts that he is not trying to represent all types of homosexuality, and that his exclusions from the study were a legitimate tactic to concentrate the genetic influence and make it easier to identify. In this he is correct. The technique of genetic enrichment is a time-honoured method, but usually in the search for less variable genes than sexual orientation will inevitably be. Along these lines, Hamer argues that Ebers and Rice's study is inadequate to assess his own because 'they made no effort to select families that display maternal patterns of inheritance' (Marshall, 1995). Hamer is only interested in one type of homosexuality, that of the maternal line, and argues that population linkage studies are an inadequate test of his theory. As Marshall notes, this would dilute the critical genetic information in a sea of noise. However, as Michael Bailey (1995) notes, it is unlikely that the different exclusion criteria in Ebers and Rice's study could account for the different results. 'Even with plausible adjustments, its negative results differ reliably from combined results of the two studies from Hamer's lab' (Bailey, 1995).

Criticisms such as these obscure the fact that Hamer *has* found a genetic difference in his sample. Some of his gay males *do* have different genetic markers unlike those of his heterosexual sample and of the general population. As Mary-Claire King (1993) and Robert Pool (1993) note, Hamer's linkage analysis is good science, even if we may now doubt aspects of his sampling and statistics. The question remains, is Hamer's effect directly related to homosexuality or is there some other variable linking homosexuality with this region? Given that Hamer has performed a linkage analysis rather than identified a gene, the answer will remain tentative until a gene is characterised. The extent to which the question may be answered now returns us to populations and sampling. Hopefully, someone is doing a carefully chosen population study to see if maternal line homosexuals have greater frequencies of gay uncles and cousins than the paternal line.

Whether a maternal linkage is germane to a particular type of homosexuality, or for that matter all male homosexuals, is still undecided at this point. To discover a gene for homosexuality would certainly give an added emphasis to our quest for a satisfactory evolutionary answer for gay behaviour. So to summarise: Hamer and his colleagues have discovered markers, a linkage difference on the X chromosome between gay and straight males. This is not conclusive proof of a gene for homosexuality, rather an indication of its existence. Hamer's study was correlational, that is, he noted that 67 percent of his sample of homosexual brothers shared a difference between themselves compared to straight men. However, this is only a correlation; widespread reports that a gene for homosexuality had been found are incorrect. Genes are pieces of DNA which encode proteins that underlie and may switch on and off physical processes and behaviour. Hamer's work moved the search for the homosexual switch 'to a few million out of the several billion bits of information that make us human'. The switches, when characterised, will certainly be polygenic and at this stage their possible mechanisms are still entirely speculative.

A TYPOLOGY OF HOMOSEXUALITY

By now you are most likely puzzled by the research reviewed in this chapter. What does it add up to? How close are we to unravelling homosexual causation? Clearly, there is still a fair bit of conceptual confusion in a literature which comments on homosexualities as if it were homosexuality. As Mildred Dickemann (1995) cautions, there is little utility in seeing homosexuality as a monomorphic entity, it is anything but. At this stage of our understanding, virtually all theorists agree that there are several different types of male homosexuality. However, this does not stop theorists from defining homosexuality as monomorphic when it suits them and much of the confusion so evident in current research is caused by inappropriate 'apples and pears' comparisons of inconsistent data drawn from different definitions of populations or samples to be studied. At the very least theorists should be required to specify what type of homosexuality they are commenting on when making such comparisons but it is hard not to speak in the singular voice when making general remarks, so perhaps this is too much to ask.

As a general and fairly uncontroversial statement it is clear from the first and second Kinsey studies and from the recent work by Johnson and her colleagues (Johnson et al., 1994) that many (if not most) adolescent boys have a homosexual phase in their early adolescent development, but this is overtaken by their emerging adult heterosexual identity. Of the 3–5 percent of men who have some continuing homosexual attachment in adulthood there are several distinct patterns but, like all ideal types, these categorisations blend into each other. Other theorists have given typologies of male homosexuality, notably that of James Weinrich (Weinrich, 1977; Pillard and Weinrich, 1987; Weinrich, 1988), but to tease out differences in homosexual orientation or preference in light of the discussion presented in this chapter I propose the following typology.

The experimenters

Clearly for the vast majority of people who have a homosexual experience this was experimental and more a matter of curiosity than of orientation. Of these experimenters, most will have been adolescents with whom it is more a matter of developmental immaturity and 'safe sex' with a friend than homosexuality as such. However, in the nature of things, many who experiment like what they find and decide to stay. So their decision to be gay is just that, a decision. While the advantages of being gay are not so obvious to the heterosexual community, they are substantial. For many men, a homosexual lifestyle provides remarkable freedom from the constraints of culturally mandated heterosexual roles (Gallup and Suarez, 1983) and many men at adulthood decide to be gay. Homosexuality for these men is socially determined. They must live in a society which has sufficient flexibility to permit homosexual lifestyles; they must have exposure to impressive homosexual models and sufficient contact with a visible gay community to become enmeshed. In other words, choosing a homosexual lifestyle is a matter of cost–benefit analysis for these men. They are so impressed with the benefits of a gay lifestyle that the majority of their sexual and social outlets are gay. It must be noted that just because many men adopt gay lifestyles from choice it does not follow that all homosexuality is socially constructed.

Swingers

One of the big homosexual debates is whether ambisexuality is a mid-pole on a continuum from exclusive heterosexual to exclusively homo-sexual sexual orientation. This idea is firmly entrenched in the critical commentary and seems an unintended consequence of the Kinsey Scale's popularity. While Kinsey and subsequent researchers have always been clear that we are dealing with homosexualities rather than homosexuality, the presence of a group of men whose behaviour seems to lie intermediate between homosexuality and heterosexuality lends itself to notions of a sexuality continuum. This is unlikely for several reasons, not least of which is that one's sexual behaviour does not predicate one's orientation. However, it is clear that there is a small proportion of men who actively engage in homosexual and heterosexual sex, and from Weinberg et al.'s (1994b) review of dual attractions it seems that some do so from a heightened sex drive which does not discriminate targets. The question then is whether these men are intermediate in orientation, or heterosex-uals with a heightened and indiscriminate sex drive. At this stage we do not know.

The unwanted

Some men act in a homosexual manner because they are unable to gain heterosexual partners. Some of the least helpful commentary equates homosexuality with paedophilia or other pathological inversions and examines homosexual behaviour without regard to possible underlying heterosexual desires. Many men engage in homosexual sex as a second-best option to heterosexual sex – gaols are full of homosexuals by this definition – and some men turn to other men, or even children, from fear of being rejected by women. The literature is replete with reports which start with sexual inversion assumptions. Such research is of limited utility as a model of homosexuality. Using such behaviour to justify a social constructivist view of homosexual behaviour is not only intellectually dishonest but ultimately counterproductive, at least to the extent that such studies rarely grapple with the vexed issue of whether the label 'homosexual' is best applied on the basis of one's fantasy life, or one's behaviour. Such homosexual behaviour may be only incidentally indicative of homosexuality.

The predisposed

Despite a bad press in recent years, it is probably premature to dismiss hormonal causes of homosexuality. The de-androgenisation hypothesis would suggest an aetiology for 'effeminate' sissy-boy homosexuals whose recollections of their childhood show levels of gender nonconformity reminiscent of the subjects' experiences reported in Dorner's work. Many of these men recount that they knew they were different from early adolescence, had early homoerotic attachments and formed unshakable gay identities with no heterosexual involvement. As a subgroup of the gay community these men are so visible as to be a source of envy for less sure homosexuals. Whether these men are a more extreme form of a general de-androgenisation process remains to be seen but, as Michael Bailey noted, that some gay men recall gender nonconformity and some do not. This argues separate aetiologies for these homosexuals (Bailey, et al., 1993), and clearly, the hormonal argument is not over yet (LeVay, 1993; Breedlove, 1994).

The driven

To the extent that we have made a case here that homosexuality is genetically predisposed in part, researchers would be justified in assuming that those with a greater genetic dosage are those most likely to become actively identified as homosexual. Even though one's orientation may not determine one's actions, the probability increases with gene dosage. The literature is full of anecdotal accounts of formerly married gay men and erstwhile straight men who were driven to express their homosexuality (Ross, 1983), often against their own wishes and those of their families. That research on such men shows they feel so compelled even though displaying a high level of internalised homophobia and ambivalence about their behaviour (Malcolm, 1997) argues a certain innateness, in my view. It is likely that gay men who have a genetic predisposition are a general or undifferentiated type of homosexual, both passive and active by turn, not obviously effeminate and with a wide variability of sexual thoughts, feelings, and behaviours, ranging from homosexuality to heterosexual. Their homosexuality is a consequence of a dose-dependent mix of genes that is 'almost certainly incomplete in penetrance and variable in expressivity, meaning that which bearers of the genes develop the behavioral trait and to what degree depends on the presence of modifier genes and the influence of the environment' (Wilson, 1975). That these gay men may be distributed on a continuum of sexual thoughts, feelings, and behaviours from homosexuality to heterosexuality does not imply that this form of homosexuality is a part of a wider continuum of homosexual types, which in my view are more likely to be discretely different types with their own continua. It is with this *driven* category that we are concerned here.

SO WHERE ARE WE NOW?

We started this chapter with a goal, to prove that homosexuality has a genetic basis. The social constructivist challenge to an evolutionary view of homosexuality bluntly asks how close are we to finding a gene that controls homosexual behaviour and politely doubts the possibility. As we have already noted and will return to at length, the biosocial view of homosexual orientation does not have to find a gene to be convincing; its evolutionary mechanisms may well be biological but environmental in origin. However, to find a gene would bring the argument to a sharp focus – is homosexuality adaptive and how far along are we in discovering its purpose?

As we have seen in this chapter, the biology of homosexuality is distinctly different from that of straight males and females, seemingly occupying an intermediate position between the two. Studies of hypothalamic and other anatomical differences and characteristic patterns of electrical activity in the brain show a concordance that needs to be explained. However, such differences may well be an effect rather than a cause. Some environmental cause, even uterine, may predispose a homosexual orientation. These studies are at best indicative. Hormonal studies suffer the same problem and, in addition, there is considerable debate that foetal de-androgenisation is implicated in homosexual causation. Too little is known about the biology of homosexual type for this research yet to be rescued by a convincing theory. When we address familial studies, we move to firmer ground. It is clear from the work of Pillard and Bailey, and others, that there is a distinct homosexual penetrance in families. Twin studies show, further, that this orientation is stronger for identical than for fraternal twins.

The anatomical studies of Gorski, LeVay, Alexander and others add yet another level of plausibility for genetic differences in sexual orientation. Although hypothalamic and encephalographic differences may reflect adult correlates of sexual orientation, the greater weight of evidence suggests perinatal sexual differentiation as a developmental component in the sexual orientation of at least some homosexual men. Still we are left with the chicken and the egg problem. These differences may be effects of some environmental problem rather than biological markers for homosexual orientation. What weighs against an environmental cause is mounting evidence that homosexuality is intermediate between heterosexual men and women. Hormonal assays, stress responses, maternal recollections, anatomical and encephalographic differences all lie, as Dorner (1976) predicted, somewhere between what is recognisably male and female heterosexual behaviour. While it is premature to suggest that this is due to a feminisation of the homosexual mind, it is certainly indicative of a biological basis in some gay men. We need more research which examines how these differences are distributed for those whose orientation, or at least preference, is less than a lifelong commitment to either heterosexuality or homosexuality. Sexual diversity, or a continuum? That is the problem.

As fascinating as it may be, the genetic research of Dean Hamer is still an open question. As we have seen, his reported genetic assays were good science even if questions are now raised about his sampling methods. The one independent replication so far gave problematic results and is yet to be published. As Hamer suggests, his study looked for genetic difference in homosexual males with maternal line pedigrees. It may well be that Ebers and Rice's replication is taking a wider sample of gay men's submerged maternal line homosexuality to a non-significant degree of variation within their overall sample, as Hamer rejoins. Other replications are underway and the jury is still out.

We started this chapter with a challenge to demonstrate a biological and genetic basis for homosexuality. While the first task is clearly accomplished, the evidence is still indicative, rather than definitive of a genetic basis. Notwithstanding, the data are more persuasive than a constant barrage of social constructivist criticism would admit. Certainly, there is more than enough evidence to pose a serious problem for those of us who see the hand of evolution at work in human affairs. We turn now to consider homosexuality as an adaptive advantage.

Chapter 3

Homosexuality as physical evolution

Being gay is like being a believer in an ocean of doubt. You know your desires but everyone says they're perverted. I don't understand how you can know so completely, so certainly that you are as you should be, when everyone else is so certain you're sick. I do know that I was meant to be gay and that being gay is the best way for me to be. Although I don't understand why I love another man as deeply as I do, I know that whatever the reason, it works for us.

(Transcripts)

We are either born to be gay, or choose to be that way. This dichotomy neatly divides our argument into two parts. Having considered the need to explain male homosexuality in Chapter 1 and having explored its biological bases in Chapter 2, here we reach for explanations of homosexuality as a biological process, and in the next chapter we treat it as a matter of social evolution. So, turning to the task at hand, if we grant a biological predisposition, then what role does homosexuality play in our physical evolution? Such behaviours are either adaptive or maladaptive, and, as James Weinrich (1995) so eloquently observed in his defence of the biosocial perspective, those committed to this view are natural optimists and always look for the adaptive advantage first. So shall we. In this chapter we first explore the case for homosexuality as a gift of nature and then turn devil's advocate and argue that male homosexuality is a spent force, a byproduct of evolutionary processes.

IS HOMOSEXUALITY REALLY ADAPTIVE?

If we grant, for the sake of argument, that certain forms of male homosexuality have a genetic basis, then we immediately plough headlong through several of the great debates of population genetics and evolutionary psychology. In this chapter we consider several theories of male homosexuality's evolution: Hutchinson's 1959 theory of balanced superior heterozygotic fitness; MacIntyre and Estep's 1993 sperm competition theory; Getz's 1993 theory of density-dependent polymorphism; Hamer's 1994 overloving theory; and my own of frequency-dependent sexual selection. All these theories assume that homosexuality is maintained in our species as a balanced polymorphism – that at an individual level some advantage is conferred to straight men (or their mothers) by their one, or possibly many, homosexual alleles, which allow the survival of an otherwise deleterious gene. What keeps this balancing act going is the central concern of this chapter, yet such a brief explanation skims over a multitude of important and contentious issues, only some of which we will have the space to address here.

The paradox of polymorphism

Polymorphism is a paradox. To argue that homosexuality is a balance polymorphism immediately contradicts neo-Darwinian orthodoxy. Jacques Ruffie (1986) puts this succinctly:

> How does one explain why individuals freely interbreeding, living together at the same place and the same time, and therefore subject to the same selective pressures, do not have the same genetic background? Polymorphism . . . is contrary to the neo-Darwinian assumption that there should be one particular genetic combination, and one only, that corresponds best to a particular environmental condition: the 'optimal' genotype seen in a species' or race's characteristic holotype, the inevitable fruit of natural selection. Intrapopulational polymorphism is a paradox to neo-Darwinism.
>
> (Ruffie, 1986: 105)

So why do we need homosexuality as a variant sexuality, isn't heterosexuality good enough? In answering this question we cross two major debates: is there a direction to human evolution; and how to define genetic load. Let's start with the easier problem – how does the addition of homosexual genes aid straight men, if by definition polymorphism increases genetic load? To answer as we will that they confer a heterotic advantage, does not minimise the complex problems of defining loads. To elucidate this problem we have to introduce another shaky term – that of *optimal type*. For now, let us use a rough operational definition of optimal type as the best or optimal combination of alleles or genes for the job in the circumstances – not the best theoretical solution perhaps but a description of what has actually happened. Immediately we have a problem. Heterozygosity leads to a genetic advantage while at the same time the addition of extra homosexual alleles causes load in the population – by adding a substantial number of homozygously disabled gay men and by adding otherwise deleterious recessive alleles into the gene pool. These loads seem a direct challenge to the optimal type. Why?

Genetic load is a theoretical nicety and a hard reality. Every time a gene successfully mutates the optimum type is challenged: 'The occurrence of another allele at the same locus (or loci) by creating an overdominant system, creates also a load through the production of an average Darwinian fitness lower than 1' (Friere-Maia, 1975). Why is this a problem? If we start with a gene pool in which all individuals are homozygous for a locus and this represents the optimal response to various selective pressures, then by definition the homozygous condition must have a Darwinian fitness of 1 (the best you can get). Also by definition, in an entirely homozygous population there is no selection and so no load at all (Freire-Maia, 1975). Note that we are only speaking of a locus or a characteristic, not of the whole organism. So, whatever causes homosexuality at a genetic level represents, by definition, a reduction of fitness of the overall population carrying this gene. Now if this new allele is clearly inadequate it will be flushed from the gene pool sooner or later. However, if it survives in a heterozygous condition we have a genetic load and the problem of explaining its survival. Whatever homosexuality's cause, in as much as it continues to exist heterozygously, it necessarily reduces the fitness of those people who carry two good copies of heterosexuality. Putting this another way, the act of mutation, genetic drift, substitution, or whatever causes the polymorphism, calls into question the fitness of the optimum type. How do we resolve this?

Here we are at the crux of a major debate in population genetics, how to conceptualise genetic loads. While the addition of a differing allele logically causes load, doesn't diversity favour a species? The way ahead is to acknowledge that while selection favours an optimal type there may be more than one of these in any population. Optimum types by their nature imply ecological stability and such stability is not realistic. In a constantly changing environment a polymorphic genotype is at a distinct advantage. To imply otherwise is to see life as stable and unchanging and to imply a rigid constant selective pressure which leads to genotypes incapable of change (Ruffie, 1986). To give just one example in a monomorphic population:

all individuals are tied to the same genetic programs and tend to do the same things – such as choosing food or sexual partners – at the same place and time. This form of monomorphism creates fierce internal competitions – an obvious disadvantage. In a polymorphic population, on the other hand, the times and places of various activities are much more widely dispersed. Polymorphism reduces competition and increases resources. It is a favorable selective factor.

(Ruffie, 1986: 123)

While diversity provides important insights into the nature of heterotic advantage it still leaves us with the problem of genetic load. A homosexuality gene creates real problems – the loads defined mathematically represent real people with reduced reproductive fitness. Wallace (1968) partially resolved this problem when he theorised that heterozygotes do not have a permanent selective advantage over homozygotes because their advantage is dependent on an environment (or other set of selective circumstances) which is transitional. Homozygotic advantage is more likely as environments tend to stability. So, assuming an optimum type assumes humans live under one set of environmental and social constraints and clearly they do not. While differing types of sexuality may reflect a lack of an optimum environment, paradoxically, polymorphisms can lead to great stability. The more genotypic diversity a population has, the greater its adaptability. The more heterozygous individuals are, the more likely they are to show stable behaviour in the face of change. Their advantage relates to the conditions of change not the constraints of the environment (Ruffie, 1986). This leads to the fascinating question of what factors in our environment necessitate a good solid dose of homosexuality for heterosexuality to get its act together.

Whether these eminently logical theoretical niceties are reflected on the ground is another matter. Polymorphisms arise for a multiplicity of reasons and, as one example, may simply be neutral, or transitions gradually being flushed from the gene pool. Homosexuality may be such a transition, gradually succumbing to a superior heterosexuality gene but its perseverance and ubiquity argue against this. The point is made. A genetic load problem may be more apparent than real and we will see situations where a load may confer a direct benefit (Clarke, 1975b; Plomin et al., 1980; Getz 1993). I will leave you to read Newton Friere-Maia's fascinating paper which, despite its presentation over two decades ago, is still a superb read on adaptation and genetic load. For our purposes, remember when we are discussing homosexuality as if it were an adaptation and a liability, in any polymorphic situation tending towards stability it must by definition be both.

Now we turn to the problem of selection, another word used far too loosely in most accounts of homosexuality. Is homosexuality selective? Yes it is but is this good? Or is 'good' even a useful concept in understanding homosexuality? Selection is in essence a mathematical construct which is almost impossible to demonstrate in man (Barkow, 1989). In using 'adaptive' as 'adaptability' or 'Darwinian fitness' – not quite synonyms but close enough for the moment – we are implying a direction to selection and that it is positive. Neither is accurate in evolutionary theory and we have already said often enough that evolution is a process with no end and no goal. Yet having said that, even Darwin himself was mindful that natural selection in all its myriad forms often appeared purposeful and progressive.

The inhabitants of each successive period in the world's history have beaten their predecessors in the race for life, and are, in so far, higher in the scale of nature; and this may account for that vague yet ill-defined sentiment, felt by many paleontologists, that organisation on the whole has progressed.

(Darwin, 1859: 345)

So, even if the formal notion is that natural selection is directionless and purposeless, in the shorter run we may say that most adaptations are responses to specific conditions. That is not to say that they are *positive* adaptations as this implies a selection *for* a characteristic and Lamarchianism – but rather, that they have not been selected against. It is important to be precise with language here. When we talk of genes 'advantaging a homosexually-enabled straight man', as we do through this and subsequent chapters, we are really using shorthand to say that the straight man who carries homosexual genes has an increased reproductive potential, as he has not been as actively selected against as a straight man who does not carry these genes. Evolution as a purposeless process selects by chance not choice. 'Genetic advantage' should be understood in these terms. So, the more general advantage provided by improved designs lies in their cumulative effects through time and better designs on the whole are favoured by natural selection (Gould, 1976). What is important to note is that species encountering new evolutionary pressures are usually sub-optimal in design for the reasons specified above. Change usually leads to a reduction in Darwinian fitness until other genes or mutations in the species' genome are selected, or it declines. Given the absolute brevity of our knowledge of homosexuality's history, just as long as our written records (we have no fossilised homosexuals), we are not really in a position to decide if homosexuality is progressive, merely if it is fit in comparison to other phenotypes in the population. It is worth remembering, as our discussion proceeds, that we do not know what the overall prognosis is for homosexuality but we will argue here that it is more likely to be part of the solution than the problem.

But what advantage?

If you distil a complex literature there are several explanations advanced for how male homosexuality may persist from generation to generation as an adaptive advantage. These fall into two categories: one set asserts that homosexuality is a superior genotype, selected and leading to a reproductive advantage; another that it is a byproduct of some other enhancing process. What both explanations rely on in making their case are concepts of hybrid vigour and balancing selection. They argue that natural selection, which normally favours traits leading to direct reproductive advantage is, rather, selecting heterotypes (heterozygous phenotypes) which carry an indirect advantage conferred by homosexual genes. Why nature takes indirect routes in shaping species is one of the more interesting twists of population genetics. So before considering these possibilities we will take a short detour into this discipline the better to inform our discussion.

On the nature of natural selection

So far we have used natural selection as a general term for superior reproductive efficiency. However, using the term this way obscures several varieties of natural selection at work in a sexually reproducing population. Directional selection favours an optimum type and refers to a ratio between normal or wildtype genes and their mutant alleles (variant forms). In most species virtually all members of a population have many spontaneous and naturally occurring mutant genes acquired from one or both parents which are carried heterozygously. Most of these rogue copies have lesser adaptive, or selective value and weaken the capacity of the animal to reproduce, unless they are suppressed by a more dominant allele. Directional selection flushes these genes from a population over time. Their degree of selective value determines their rate of departure. A mutant gene which renders the offspring sterile will be lost in one generation, although it may reappear as a fresh mutation in subsequent generations. To the extent that we carry less viable genes, they reduce our fitness. This genetic load is constantly being reduced by directional selection, which generally favours those with a lesser load. Very occasionally a mutation or otherwise newly acquired gene is superior to the wildtype and will eventually replace it. While this is happening there will be many transitional combinations until the gene becomes the new wildtype.

Directional selection only selects the 'best' genes and as we will see the extinction of deleterious genes is a powerful assumption in the homosexuality debate. Two things argue against this idealised scenario. First, we never get to fixity, or a complete homozygosity for a gene – the ultimate aim of directional selection – because there is always some variation at a locus for many reasons including mutation. Second, there is always a strong element of inbreeding in any population and this skews us away from an optimum type despite directional selection, because it preserves (concentrates) recessive traits such as homosexuality. For example, the number of our ancestors doubles each generation. In a thousand years, given an average twenty-five years between generations, you would have had to have had 1,099,511,627,000 unrelated ancestors to avoid any hint of inbreeding. This is at least 220 times more people than are around at the moment and, on even the most generous estimate, ten

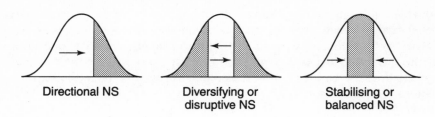

Figure 3.1 Types of natural selection (NS)
Note: The shaded area represents optimum types not selected against by natural selection. The directional arrows indicate how the gene pool is being shaped with unshaded phenotypes selected against.

times more people than have ever lived. In practice, other forms of selection work at the same time as directional selection and the makeup of any individual is an admixture of these selective forces.

Even so, much of the argument surrounding the genetics of homosexuality is based on an unconscious assumption of the virtues of directional selection – homosexuals have a lesser reproductive fitness; homosexuality is therefore part of our genetic load and should be gradually eliminated. While a straightforward model, it would seem to imply an optimum type best suited to survival and any deviation from this genotype will be deleterious. As we have seen, this concept has been extensively debated in population genetics. For our purposes, several other forms of natural selection offset or ameliorate this tendency to shed those with a higher genetic load (see Figure 3.1). Two in particular, diversifying, and stabilising or balancing selection, preserve genes which seem to increase genetic load and may account for a continuing homosexual presence.

The assumption that there is one optimum human genotype assumes we all live in the same environment. Further, it assumes the selective values of various genotypes operate independently of their rate of occurrence. Diversifying or disruptive natural selection argues otherwise. As Jacques Ruffie's quotation demonstrates, we live in differing environments, and what is an advantage in one may be a disadvantage in other settings. A species genome which carries a diverse range of genotypes is more adaptive in a differentiated environment than a notional optimum type. Nor are environmental constraints necessarily physical, as we also have to adapt to various social roles and expectations that have selective value. A diverse genome aids the adaptive potential of individuals and their species and it may be that homosexuality is one such socially adaptive variant. Such a notion is central to social evolution and we will return to this in Chapter 4.

Some species are quite polymorphic, having many differing forms. Ours is not as polymorphic as some but we do have several distinct heterotypes such as our sexes, races and sexual orientations. Clearly, polymorphism must pay dividends, even in the face of strong directional selection. For this and other reasons, population geneticists prefer to consider stabilising, or balance selection, as the dominant form of human selection. Stabilising selection selects for an optimum type that is an intermediate form, often phenotypically similar to the optimum type it replaces but genotypically more diverse. We are not sure how many genes appear in multiple forms but as an example we think that a minimum 30 percent of our genetic loci for serum proteins is heterozygotic and it is likely that most of our genome is of this order.

Another ready assumption of uncritical accounts of natural selection is that deleterious genes act deleteriously. While this is frequently the case, they are often suppressed by a more dominant allele, or may even confer an advantage, as we saw in our earlier discussions of the sickle-cell anaemia gene. In heterotic balancing selection, the fitness of the hetero-zygote is superior to both homozygous forms of the gene. The otherwise deleterious allele confers some benefit which provides an incremental reproductive advantage greater than that of the optimum type. That is, heterotic balancing selection selects for otherwise deleterious genes, leading to a new genetic equilibrium favouring a heterozygous optimum type. Unlike the balance struck between the reoccurring mutation rate and directional selection, the deleterious gene is carried forward to future generations as a gift of nature despite it being part of our genetic load. The important point here is that the heterozygote is genetically superior to both the normal optimum type and recessives with two copies of the deleterious gene. The nature of the advantage conferred is of crucial importance and the effects of heterotic balancing selection, which work in one setting, are often offset by diversifying natural selection in others. Returning to our sickle-cell example will make this clear.

West African tribes living in tropical wetlands in Sierra Leone have a much higher instance of the sickle-cell gene than their close genetic cousins who live in isolated but mosquito-free highlands 30 kilometres inland. In the highlands this gene provides no benefits and as part of the genetic load is all but flushed from the gene pool (directional selection), refreshed only very occasionally by importing brides from the coastal tribes. In the lowlands, the *falciparum* form of malaria was endemic and those who carried one sickle-cell allele have the benefit of an altered form of haemoglobin which is aversive to the malarial parasite. This genetic advantage was maintained or 'balanced' in the lowland population at the price of an aversive genetic load which caused a much higher death rate among those who carry two sickle-cell gene alleles. In the highlands, the genetic load, at least for this gene, was much lower. Therefore balan-cing selection in the lowland population was advantageous despite the load created, while directional selection deals with the load where it is not advantageous. Diversifying selection preserved the health of each group by maintaining two dissimilar genotypes in the human genome. Two points are important: this heterotic advantage favours only some; and the benefits conferred are context-dependent. In an era of insecticides eradicating mosquitoes in the lowlands, having sickle-cell genes is no longer an advantage.

In a similar way, homosexuality is balanced within our species' genome. That sexual orientation is phenotypically polymorphic argues that it is a product of balance selection favouring a heterozygous optimum type; that there are different sexual orientations of fixed proportions argues that diversifying selection is at work; while the deleterious nature of homosexual homozygotes argues that directional selection favours heterosexuality. So selection works on a trait in a number of directions at the same time. The equilibrium or balance polymorphism which results is a combination of genetic, biological, environmental, social and cultural factors, and is liable to change as these conditions alter. Throughout our following discussion we will sometimes use any of these selective vectors without fanfare, remembering that all contribute to homosexuality remaining within our species' gene pool.

On the nature of hybrid vigour

So most genetic theories of homosexuality rely on balancing selection to retain an otherwise disabling gay gene. What is interesting about these theories is an assumption of hybrid vigour. Hybrid vigour, or more formally heterosis, is a very useful but imprecise concept in classical genetics. Sometimes outbreeding produces bigger, stronger and more robust offspring than breeding close to one's kind. However, the actual mechanisms of this effect are even more complex than the vast number of genetic variations on which they depend. Although its mechanisms are numerous, geneticists argue the greater fitness of hybrid offspring stems from a higher probability 'that detrimental recessive genes are more likely to be masked by dominant wild-type genes because of heterozygosity at many loci' (Pai, 1985) and so the heterozygous offspring has the advantage of not having deleterious traits expressed. This is the first step in answering our puzzle. Heterozygous straights are more viable because they are minimising genetic load but this does not answer why the wildtype for heterosexuality has not pushed the homosexuality gene from the gene pool. How does it work?

Part of the answer is in noting that hybrid vigour comes in two forms: a heterotic effect is possible if genetic loads are masked (luxuriance) but also if an indirect reproductive advantage is somehow conferred (euheterosis), and both effects may work together (Dobzhansky, 1952). The form we are interested in here is probably euheterotic, where hybrid vigour is an incremental positive selective advantage over the balance struck between normalising natural selection and the genetic load or, put another way, a natural selection which favours other than one optimal type. Balance selection then favours the homosexual heterozygote for two reasons – first, because the deleterious gene confers an advantage in some instances and second, because it broadens the range of genotypes leading to species diversity. However, heterotypes do not always have superior fitness (the mule, for example) and all the balance accounts of homosexuality we review in this chapter assume it is part of the genetic load rather than a gene which is fit in its own right. That is, irrespective of whether the homosexuality gene is adaptive for, or a byproduct of, some other adaptive process advantaging heterosexuals, nature is still actively selecting against homosexuals.

So in summary, how does nature maintain an optimal response to a species' environment? As we noted, the neo-Darwinist position on directional or 'normalising' natural selection argues an optimal genotype as a response to a relatively fixed ecological niche. The balance theory of population structure argues otherwise and assumes a range of niches. To ensure species adaptability, natural selection may either favour a range of optimum genotypes within a species, or versatile individuals with a more heterogeneous genotype, or use both strategies. Using hybrid vigour in balance theories of homosexuality implicitly assumes a variable range of sexual orientations and a degree of versatility in forms of sexual expression as a positive evolutionary strategy. Adaptive accounts of homosexuality implicitly assume that homosexuality is latent within a heterosexual gene pool and of superior value under certain constraints. Note that these constraints are unlikely to be niche, or geographic, as most accounts of diversifying selection assume. It is likely that a homosexually-enabled straight man is more adapted to social rather than environmental demands placed on him.

And what is adaptive anyway?

We have thus far assumed that homosexuality is adaptive and have used this term rather loosely but what does *adaptive* really mean? Williams (1966) in his classic *Adaptation and Natural Selection: A Critique of Some Current Evolutionary Thought*, argued that 'adaptive' is one of the most abused terms in evolutionary reasoning: 'adaptation is a special and onerous concept that should be used only when really necessary' and that when used 'should be attributed no higher level of organization than is demanded by the evidence'. Williams was concerned that loose usage of the word would rob it of its technical meaning of 'functional significance', and argued that functional significance is ultimately not about whether a behaviour is currently beneficial or not but whether it has contributed to differential reproduction in ancestral populations. Yet such determinations are hard to make as we no longer live in those ancestral environments which gave rise to the behaviour. The difficulties of looking backwards to functional significance are compounded when you come to consider the present purposes of a behaviour. Evolution is an ongoing process and we cannot avoid questioning current adaptiveness. That evolution is a blind and indifferent process which has no goal makes 'adaptive' a matter of complete speculation. As Gallup and Suarez (1983) so eloquently observed:

> Evolution can be thought of as an unconscious existential game. Losing the game is defined as not leaving any descendants. Winning, on the other hand, is less tangible. Winning can be defined only as not having lost. The game is played according to cost/benefit ratios, and the objective is to maximize one's genetic representation in subsequent generations.
>
> (Gallup and Suarez, 1983: 316)

This leads to semantic difficulties. Are we talking about adaption as an adjustment to an environment, or adaptability, or adaptedness (Brandon, 1990)? The first assumes a reaction to our circumstances; the second an opportunistic variability of our genetic message that allows our species to handle change prospectively, or adaptedness which is a value judgement on the balance struck in the past between adaption and adaptability? This is not just semantics. When we say that a gene for homosexuality is adaptive are we commenting on its status, or making a value judgement, or being optimistic in our estimates? Let us explore this a little more deeply.

Natural selection is: 'opportunistic and blind and mechanical' and 'a dangerous balance of useful and harmful' forces (Huxley, 1942). Given the uncertainties of existence, to say that homosexuality is adaptive qua adaption is to comment on a past balance struck between viability and fertility rates; it says nothing of the future, or indeed the past. What is now adaptive is adaption, maybe. Newton Friere-Maia (1975) said this rather neatly when he commented that: 'natural selection uses the material at its disposal at a given moment' and, as it is 'blind and mechanical', it may lead to adaptional solutions that are: 'not the most efficient and economical among all those theoretically possible'. Note that Friere-Maia has introduced a new adaptive term – adaptional – and not by accident. Further, since we are dealing with a blind force, 'adaptive' takes no account of the wellbeing of particular populations, or has any direct relationship to their needs. Much of the literature which states that homosexuality is adaptive does so far too loosely to have much utility or meaning.

To the extent that we will use 'adaptive' in our discussion it will specify two related parameters, the first noted by J.B.S. Haldane in 1932: Darwinian fitness, or a genotype's relative contribution to future generation 'in comparison with other genotypes which are present in the same population' (Friere-Maia, 1975). The second, 'adaptedness', is from Sir Ronald Fisher, a biological statistician who noted in 1930 that for current populations 'adaptedness is an absolute parameter based on population size and the relative rate of resources against that of population growth'. While 'adaptive' bears some relation to 'adaptedness', it is using the present to double-guess the future and this is a risky business. To quote Newton Friere-Maia again: 'the average Darwinian fitness of a population is not a reliable indicator neither of its adaptiveness nor of its competitive ability'.

The purpose in raising these debates so early in the chapter is not to frighten you off evolutionary psychology or indeed population genetics but to demonstrate that we are dealing with complex problems whose nature is not easily amenable to empirical test even if we could get our experimental protocols through ethics committees. Proof in this area would take millennia to work itself out. For this reason, all scenarios are inferential and the hypotheses we generate are propositional rather than empirical in nature. In Chapter 2 we concluded that whatever homosexuality's biology was, it was a predisposition not a deterministic script to be slavishly followed. And note that we have not yet said anything about individual foibles, needs, or cultural prescriptions, all of which compound the problems of explanation. It is worth remembering, as we turn to review these selective scenarios, that they are just 'how-possibly explanations' (Brandon, 1990), and, as Jerome Barkow noted,

> An evolutionary scenario ... is a somewhat speculative theory in which the usual requirements for empirical verifiability are relaxed in favour of an emphasis on completeness, internal logic and plausibility ... Scenarios provide a sense of closure, but they must be consonant with known data and logically consistent. For human evolutionary scenarios, these 'known data' include the fossil record of human evolution, non-human primate behaviour, and the present behavioural and morphological characteristics of our species. Scenarios should never be taken too seriously, given their unverifiable nature. For *aficionados*, they are fun.
>
> (Barkow, 1989: 327)

And probably useful too. It only requires us to discover what these scenarios demand.

MODELS OF BALANCE POLYMORPHISM: A BALANCED
SUPERIOR HETEROZYGOTIC FITNESS

In Chapter 1 we considered how a variant of balance polymorphism might account for the continued survival of the homosexuality gene. Using the sickle-cell anaemia example we saw how a gene may confer a differential reproductive advantage despite its deleterious nature. And so it is with balanced superior heterozygotic fitness accounts of male homosexuality. Homosexuals holding two copies of this gene are byproducts of evolution with markedly reduced reproductive fitness. Yet unlike scenarios we will consider later, despite their personal liability, their homosexual genes confer a benefit to the species and this advantage keeps their genes preserved in the gene pool. In this sense, even if individual homosexuals are byproducts of evolution, their special contribution is not. What then is the benefit they give to their heterozygous peers?

It is likely that the most immediate benefit is sexual. As with the overloving effect we consider at the end of this chapter, it is probable that a gene for male homosexuality confers an immediate reproductive advantage by directly enhancing sex drive or some other aspect of sexual performance. The clearest examples of balance polymorphism are those which enhance hybrid vigour, particularly reproductive drive, and this has been implicitly assumed by commentators since Hutchinson first suggested a balanced superior heterozygotic fitness mechanism in 1959. Those straight men who have one homosexual gene (and here we are assuming a single gene for simplicity's sake; the actual situation is more likely polygenic) probably have an enhanced sex drive which leads to greater numbers of children and to a retention of the balanced homosexuality gene. These straight men are therefore genetically superior by virtue of having a dose of gayness – at least in this respect.

One note of caution must be sounded here. There may be a basic confusion in the literature between a gene for homosexuality and a gene for enhanced sex drive. Accounts from Hutchinson (1959) onwards have assumed that whatever causes homosexuality causes heterosis. In this view, if increased libido is genetically determined it is an effect of a gene which influences sexual orientation. However, it may not be the same gene. As we saw in Chapter 2, closely linked genetic material is more likely to be transposed together at meiosis than that more distant. Therefore, the balanced superior heterozygotic fitness effect may be a consequence of closely linked genes at a locus Xq28 or elsewhere, being constantly transferred together, rather than a consequence of a gene for homosexuality. That is, the gene for homosexuality may not cause increased sex drive but is regularly being passed along from generation to generation with a gene that does. The net effect may be to mistake increased libido for a consequence of a homosexual gene, rather than of closely linked genetic material, leading us into a correlational fallacy. If this is so, and we have no evidence either way, we are still left with the problem of explaining a gene for homosexuality. Something as complicated as sexual orientation is unlikely to be determined at a single locus and more than likely many loci working together govern our sexual predispositions. The important point is that homosexuality may be independent of, yet linked with, a balanced superior heterozygotic fitness effect that keeps it in the gene pool. What evidence is there for this effect?

Do homosexuals have elevated sexual drives compared to straight men?

If a gene for homosexuality or its closely linked genetic determinant increases sexual performance then this should be best observed in those who receive the largest dose. One of the most evident differences between gay and straight men is homosexuals' elevated sex drive:

> I'll pick up a bloke in a sauna and have sex with him two or three times and then cruise all night. I might have sex with two or three men, coming seven or eight times but when I get home I'm still so randy that I'll have to masturbate to get to sleep.
>
> (Transcripts)

This sort of sexual performance is at the far limits of heterosexual stamina (Masters and Johnson, 1966) but despite a large press that claims homosexuals are better lovers there is little hard evidence that homosexual sex drive is more potent than that of heterosexuals. The one clear piece of supporting evidence, homosexual promiscuity, is legendary and there are many studies pointing to an enormous differential between homosexual and heterosexual men's sexual contacts. By far the most comprehensive is the second Kinsey report (Bell and Weinberg, 1978) which found that in a sample of 685 men, over 90 percent had had more than twenty-five sexual partners, nearly half had more than 500 different partners, while 23 percent had over 1,000 partners. These findings have been echoed worldwide. Research still underway by Jim Malcolm and myself in Sydney in a carefully matched sample of eighty gay and eighty straight men found that over 90 percent of our heterosexual men had less than twenty-five partners; whereas over 90 percent of our gay respondents had at least that many sexual contacts, with one man claiming he had the names and addresses of over 700 men he had slept with over the past year. Such promiscuity is variously interpreted as evidence of depravity, or as desperate and futile sex with inappropriate reproductive targets, or evidence of a freer and less circumscribed lifestyle. Whatever the reasons, homosexual men clearly have markedly more sex partners than do heterosexual men.

While such studies usually provide support for an enhanced sex drive hypothesis there are methodological problems. Bell and Weinberg's Bay Area study was widely criticised for its failure to reach a broad spectrum of the homosexual community in San Francisco. Bell and Weinberg's sample was largely drawn from contact venues such as saunas and bars and perhaps reflected a younger and possibly more promiscuous community. San Francisco is the gay capital of North America and its relatively freer lifestyle permits wider contacts and more sexual exploration, biasing the sample. In our own research we were conscious that Sydney's gay scene is in many respects similar to that of San Francisco and we tried, with some success, to control for these biases. From our review of similar studies it is evident that many possibly more monogamous sectors of the gay community are quite hard to access, with many researchers regretting an inevitable skew towards a more swinging set. Still, Bell and Weinberg's research shows a quite promiscuous sample: 66 percent of their sample had more than ten homosexual partners in the previous year; 65 percent of these were strangers; 54 percent of which were one night stands; 53.5 percent of which were not seen socially again; and, perhaps even more tellingly, 68.5 percent of their sample only felt 'some' affection for less than half of their sexual contacts. The evidence such as it is strongly suggests a quite promiscuous lifestyle.

Apart from purely sampling considerations, an enhanced sex drive hypothesis is less likely to show itself in 'raw scores' than in measures of sexual potency. While sexual contact leads to reproduction it is a necessary but not sufficient condition. Contraception, frequency of sexual contact, and many other factors may be more influential. An increased sexual drive may manifest in a number of ways other than sexual partners: it may be that homosexual men have greater potency (erectile strength, or sperm counts); they may have a wider potency, being aroused by a wider range of partners; they may have a shorter refractory period, allowing a greater sexual responsiveness; the sex act may be more pleasurable; or it might simply arise from a heightened libido.

There are no comparative studies of the differential potency of homosexual and heterosexual men. The only credible work to date is Masters and Johnson's *Homosexuality in Perspective* (1979), which compared gender and preference differences for both men and women. Masters and Johnson's work may be summarised in this brief quotation:

Is there a a fundamental difference in sexual physiology if the respondents are homosexually rather than heterosexually oriented? Based upon more than four years of intensive observation of hundreds of completed sexual response cycles in homosexual men and women in response to a multiplicity of sexual stimulative techniques, the answer is an unequivocal *no*.

(Masters and Johnson, 1979: 124)

So as far as evidence for potency goes we are left with promiscuity and frequency of sexual encounters which strongly favour homosexual men (Kinsey et al., 1948; Bell and Weinberg, 1978), at best indirect measures of potency. Having several partners in one night suggests greater libido and erectile potency. It may be, however, that this is just partner novelty and an example of the Coolidge Effect, which we will describe below (Bermant, 1976; Buss, 1994). Further evidence from Masters and Johnson's study suggests this is so.

Comparative sexual fantasies were investigated by the Masters and Johnson study, both free-floating and short-term stimulative fantasies used as aids to sexual arousal. The comparative content of fantasy material is shown in Table 3.1. Homosexuals had a higher incidence of free-floating fantasy than heterosexual men and a distinctly different pattern of imagery. They were fixated on the penis and buttocks, although body imagery was rarely of anyone they knew. Homosexual male fantasies were more violent with the homosexual men, in all but one case dreaming

Table 3.1 Comparative content of fantasy material: ranked frequency of occurrence

Homosexual male (*n* = 30)
1 Imagery of sexual anatomy
2 Forced sexual encounters
3 Cross-preference encounters
4 Idyllic encounters with unknown men
5 Group sex experiences
Homosexual female (*n* = 30)
1 Forced sexual encounters
2 Idyllic encounter with established partner
3 Cross-preference encounters
4 Recall of past sexual experience
5 Sadistic imagery
Heterosexual male (*n* = 30)
1 Replacement of established partner
2 Forced sexual encounter
3 Observation of sexual activity
4 Cross-preference encounters
5 Group sex experiences
Heterosexual female (*n* = 30)
1 Replacement of established partner
2 Forced sexual encounter
3 Observation of sexual activity
4 Idyllic encounters with unknown men
5 Cross-preference encounters

Source: Masters and Johnson, 1979: 178

of forcibly raping men and women about equally. In contrast, heterosexual men fantasised as much about being raped by women as about raping. Of particular interest was the high incidence of cross-preference fantasies in the homosexual population. These usually had free-floating content of forced and forcing sexual participation with unknown partners, while cross-preference sex with known partners was usually with women from the homosexual's past and was more a matter of pleasurable anticipation and 'simple sexual curiosity' than forced sex. In contrast, heterosexual men's most common fantasy was substituting their current partner for some other known but idealised woman. Cross-preference sex was fourth on their list and was limited to physical attributes of their fantasised partner. Fellatio was the most fantasised act, with a curiosity about anal sex but containing few actual rectal penetrations.

Predictably, fantasy differences were those of orientation, with both groups showing common male patterns of imagery when compared with women's fantasies. Heterosexual men were more likely to use variety and novelty fantasies and this was supported by a strong Coolidge Effect in actual sexual performance in the laboratory. Although Masters and Johnson provide little quantitative detail, the picture emerges of homosexual and heterosexual men fantasising about fairly predictable male concerns, their fantasy life providing little on which to base a heterotic advantage.

By way of contrast, sexual inversion perspectives on homosexual promiscuity would see such research as suggesting a frantic and perverse tone to homosexual sexual activity: the misdirectedness of homosexuality showing a desperate attempt to obey the evolutionary imperative to procreate but with confused and ultimately unfulfilling sexual targets; promiscuity revealing the shallow pointlessness of an inverted sexuality. Such views, although neatly fitting a morality discouraging both extra-marital sex and homosexuality, may be a surface reading of the situation, confusing promiscuity with sexual drive. Male libido varies enormously and sexual appetites are often limited only by the availability of partners. The homosexual scene is quite different from that of straight society and the ready availability of casual sex and its taken-for-grantedness in sectors of the homosexual community lead to a seeming promiscuity of the whole. Differences in sexual response rates may just reflect a less constrained sexuality and a ready supply of partners.

To this point we have probably not stressed enough that the likely transmission of homosexuality is polygenic. Genetic influences on our behavioural traits identified thus far are a combination of many genes interacting (Cloninger et al., 1996; Ross and Pearson, 1996). Our discussions to this point have assumed a single gene with two variant alleles. The real situation is likely to be rather more complex, with many genes combining to produce an effect, and, even if a single locus, with many variant alleles. Even in simple Mendelian inheritance, the dominance and recessive relationships would be partial and complex. The net effect would be to have a range of possible sexual orientations and expressions – a fact fully in accordance with the literature. Homosexuality's probable polygenics also assumes a partial dominance or a combination of influences, leading to a balance effect. Although we incompletely understand the blocking effect of one gene on another, or of one allele on another, some genes are quite dominant and others less so. Often the phenotypic expression of a trait results from an averaging of a wide range of influences and triggers, the so-called: 'parliament of genes' (Ridley, 1994). What is important here is that even if the gene(s) for homosexuality lead to an increased sex drive, they are unlikely to set our sexual orientation completely. That is, homosexually-enabled straight men are unlikely to be completely suppressing their genetic heritage, and their 'homosexual dosage' would influence the degree of sexual activity and choice of sexual targets. It is likely that the heterosexual straight man would have a greater range of sexual expressions, would possibly be more sexually active and more promiscuous, would likely have a greater range of partners and so forth. Whether this partial dominance would lead to a change in sexual orientation, perhaps into ambisexuality, is also a moot point.

What follows from these assumptions is that the advantage the heterosexual heterotype enjoys is either a direct genetic endowment, or a consequence of some related process. This is an important consideration. If there is a direct effect, our genes directly controlling our sexual orientation, then we should see a stronger link between the degree of penetrance and sexual expression, a dose-dependent relationship. If, however, it is a consequence of a related process, then there is greater potential variability and less chance of observing a clear relationship. Returning to our sickle-cell gene example will make this plainer. The anaemia-causing gene is balanced in the population by altering blood haemoglobin chemistry making it unattractive to mosquitoes carrying malaria, a direct single-gene effect which makes the sickle-cell gene the textbook example of balance polymorphism at work. However, imagine if the sickle-cell gene's causing anaemia was moderated by an atmospheric effect which influenced haemoglobin's ability to bind oxygen, inducing serious hypoxia. Such an effect would be dependent on variable barometric pressure and would produce a much less mathematically elegant proof.

Whatever the case, if we grant an enhanced homosexual sex drive, what does it mean? From an evolutionary perspective male sexuality is designed for frequent sex with a range of partners. Donald Symons (1979) led the analysis of the implications of differential reproductive agendas between men and women, arguing that reproductive physiology favours male promiscuity and marital infidelity. Men have any number of opportunities to reproduce themselves, limited only by the availability of receptive partners. Women have fewer reproductive opportunities irrespective of the number of sexual partners they take. This provides men with two evolutionary strategies towards selective fitness. They may take a high risk R strategy, having any number of children and putting few resources into offspring, reducing the chances of their offspring reaching their own reproductive years. Alternatively, they may follow a K strategy, having fewer children but investing heavily in them to ensure their survival. Given that the end goal of sex is not reproduction but replication, virtually all human societies favour K strategies. This binds the men to the home and makes for a more stable society. More importantly, it reduces destructive competition for sexual partners. Women's limited reproductive capacity places an ultimate brake on R strategy, and species which allow open competition for mates encourage the more aggressive to survive but at the expense of narrowing contributions to the gene pool.

Irrespective of the institution of K-stable societies, male physiology still leaves the possibility of following an R strategy and this leads to different reproductive agendas between the sexes and no doubt to the disappointments both feel with each other. What we may be seeing in the promiscuity of homosexual society is an unfettered R strategy at work without the limits inherent in having a female partner who is following a different reproductive agenda. Two points flow from this proposition.

First, this assumes that homosexual sex is ultimately aimed at reproduction. Clearly it is not, and social constructivist critiques of the biosocial perspective make much of this. However, invoking the levels of analysis argument advanced in Chapter 1, while it may be entirely the case that homosexual men are not trying to reproduce themselves, nevertheless their sexual behaviour follows the patterns set by their reproductive biology which in turn follow the evolutionary imperatives which established them. Put another way, they are men first and homosexuals second. That this agenda is unconscious, while much heterosexual sex is consciously aimed at reproduction, is not an issue. That gay men may seek sex for personal gratification and social bonding does not detract from the reasons we all have a sexual capacity. Reproduction is sex's ultimate purpose.

Second, this assumes that homosexual sex is futile sex. Homosexual sex is not reproductive but we engage in sex for many purposes. What is important here is the strength of the desire, not its intention. The 'superiority' of the superior heterozygotic fitness of straight men with a dose of gayness would be best demonstrated by those carrying a larger measure of this advantage. This would be shown in a number of ways as we have already seen. What should not be confused here is the difference between quantum of sexual drive and sexual target. We have already noted that these two measures may be genetically independent, linked only in their transmission. Whatever the case, and even if a homosexual gene directly causes an enhanced sex drive, it is likely that this advantage is part of normal male sexual responsiveness simply heightened by the choice of a partner who is also following an R strategy. The test of this theory is not that homosexual men engage in more sex than their straight peers but rather that they enjoy an advantage in so doing. Thus, homosexuals with such an advantage would engage in sex more frequently than either group of straight men. Moreover, it is not in this instance a deviancy but rather an extension of normal male physiology that favours an R strategy. As we mentioned earlier, while a selective advantage is not enjoyed by those homosexuals who carry this gene, it is a benefit conferred on their straight kin.

Is homosexual promiscuity more a matter of an unfettered R strategy (Symons, 1979; Gallup and Suarez, 1983) than that of selective advantage? Perhaps a bit of both. An unfettered R strategy argues continual competition for fresh mates and this would favour (select) those heterosexuals with a measure of homosexuality. Male reproductive strategies favour low cost high reproductive rates when partners are readily available. Thus the homosexually-enabled heterosexual reproducer is likely to be gaining a double advantage. They are more attractive mates and more liable to reproduce. There is a distinct evolutionary gain to having offspring from as many women as possible, as diversifying natural selection and the balance population theory argue that a diverse gene pool provides a hedge against uncertain fitness requirements for future generations. In any case, a man risks little as his genetic contribution varies only marginally irrespective of how many female sex partners he takes, and in any case, he has limited insight into the genetic load his partner is contributing. For these reasons studies show that men are much less discriminating in choosing sexual partners than are women (Kenrick and Trost, 1989).

An example is probably in order. The Coolidge Effect is a famous example of undiscriminating male sexuality. US President Calvin Coolidge was in trouble with his wife. When visiting a model poultry farm it was observed that a rooster was able to have sex repeatedly. Mrs Coolidge asked that this be drawn to the President's attention (President Coolidge was 23 years older than his wife). 'Always with the same hen?', he enquired. When assured it was with different hens he asked that this be drawn to his wife's attention. The Coolidge Effect has been widely demonstrated in man and infra-human species. Novelty has several effects, including shorter refractory periods between sexual encounters (Bermant, 1976; Buss, 1994). This effect has several evolutionary advantages but clearly favours an R reproductive strategy. Men thus gain a wider genetic representation and insurance for their posterity against an uncertain future. Those men with a stronger drive will have the greater reproductive success. Those men who carry a heterotype for sex drive may derive an even greater benefit.

The foregoing discussion suggests that heterosexual men with one gay gene should have more offspring than their homozygous straight peers. At this point our discussion has gone far in advance of any empirical test of this theory. While it is the case that heterosexual men have more children than exclusively homosexual men, we have no way of separating heterosexual men who carry a homosexual gene from those who do not. If and when a gene conveying a balanced superior heterozygotic fitness effect is found, birth ratios will be test enough. However, it is possible to model the minimum differential needed to keep this advantage in the gene pool against a range of presumed selective values for the heterozygotic advantage. A surprisingly small differential is necessary to keep the homosexuality gene balanced in the population, albeit at low rates and invading very slowly towards a stable polymorphism. MacIntyre and Estep (1993) have modelled this differential, adjusted for differences in live birth rates between the sexes. They were surprised 'by the small differential heterozygote viability needed to maintain the disadvantaged homozygote in the population, 2% suffices'. Although this is a very small differential, other models report similar quanta. As an example, as long ago as 1959 Penrose noted that a differential of only a 1 percent increase in the fertility of carriers of phenylketonuria would balance the gene's disadvantage in homozygotes.

This differential is quite small and, as MacIntyre and Estep observe: 'the differential viability required to support the reproductively disadvantaged homosexual homozygote is smaller than the uncertainty limits of most mammalian and sociological studies' and 'a difference usually buried in noise'. Playing with their assumptions using the program *MathCad Plus*, we obtained similar results – at even this small differential it would take a little over sixty, 20-year generations for an invading homosexual gene to reach an equilibrium at 10 percent homosexuals, 46 percent heterosexuals and 44 percent straight heterotypes. Note that these proportions are speculative (a function of the assigned fitness quotient) and apply only to the one gene, two allele case. Note also that we have specified minimum levels here. As Jacques Gomila (1975) observed: 'the measure of fertility is always a measure of the lower limit of reproduction'. By increasing the differential, we lower the percentages of exclusively heterosexual genotypes needed to demonstrate a balanced superior heterozygotic fitness effect.

This is a simple model and reality is far more complex; so just how heritable may a homosexuality gene be? What are its natural limits in human populations? The era of research into fertility differentials was in the 1940s and 1950s and more recent findings are complicated by the advent of the contraceptive pill. Notwithstanding reliable contraception,

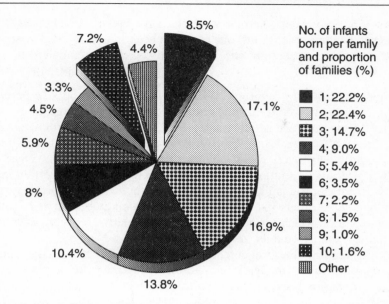

Figure 3.2 Proportion of population of 1881 generation in subsequent generation
Source: after Vincent, 1946: 150–153

and for a moment not worrying if a homosexuality gene is passed maternally or paternally, we have some evidence of the real limits of human
fertility and the impact of reproductive differentials. Vincent in 1946
reported a study of 500,000 women born in 1881. His results are displayed
in Figure 3.2. Families of 0–2 children were 61.1 percent of the total but
only contributed 25.6 percent of the next generation's children. However,
families of seven or more children who represented 6.3 percent of the
total furnished 20.9 percent of the descendants (Gomila, 1975). Extrapolating these frequencies, the latter women's descendants, if they carried the
same fertility rate in the year 2000, would account for over 90 percent of
the population. This argues that even a small differential advantage may
have a large impact over time. Yet many other factors offset the simple
mathematics of selection and it is worth quoting Gomila at length at this
point.

Penrose ... provided very convincing figures on the fertility of persons
living in such highly developed countries as the U.S.A. and the U.K.
Out of 100 pregnancies, only 85 come to term. Of these 85 percent, 3
percent are still births (2.55 percent of the total conceptions), 2 percent
are neo-natal deaths (1.70 percent of the total) and 3 percent die before
reaching maturity (2.55 percent of the total). Only 78.20 percent of the
initial conceptions furnish a sexually mature subject. Of this 78.20
percent, 20 percent do not marry (15.64 percent of the total). There

remain 62.56 percent who marry, of which 10 percent are childless (6.26 percent of the total). In all, out of 100 conceptions, only 56.30 percent lead to a new conception, and here again the cycle recommences.

(Gomila, 1975: 162)

Similar figures were reported in Vincent's sample with only 54 percent of his 1881 birth cohort having married by 1931. Marriage rates and fertility differentials are additive and may further reduce any one conception's future offspring. While improvements in health care and economics have slightly improved these figures, the moral is evident. Physical, psychological, social, cultural and economic factors disqualify certain individuals from reproduction, irrespective of their genetic propensities, advantageous or otherwise. All of these offsets would need to be factored into an equation which set out to calculate the relative fertility advantage of a homosexuality enabled man.

Notwithstanding the foregoing, it seems likely that a balanced superior heterozygotic fitness model is a plausible contender for a place as a selective scenario. Yet it has its problems.

Autosomal, X-linked, or even heterotic?

In this discussion so far we have assumed for the sake of simplicity a genetic propensity for homosexuality that is diallelic (has just two different alleles). While this is possible it is unlikely. However, to the problem first. The balanced superior heterozygotic fitness model advanced by Hutchinson (1959) and Wilson (1975) has assumed, in all the discussion since their work, that the genetic advantage lies on the male Y chromosome. That is, *men* pass on the gay gene and the superiority of the male heterozygote leads to a reproductive advantage. The reason it is male-linked in the popular imagination is simply that male sexuality intuitively suggests a certain Y-ness. A balanced advantage is unlikely to be so, as a Y chromosome normally occurs only once in each person. Any gene on the Y chromosome does not have an allele as there is no corresponding homologous Y chromosome from the mother, rather an X, and unless a Y gene is modified by an autosomal gene, cannot lead to a heterotic advantage. Nevertheless, a gene for homosexuality may be X-linked and generate a species of balanced superior heterozygotic effect but not for any mother's son (we will soon come to an X-linked 'overloving effect' which is a female version of the superior balance heterotic advantage). It may also be the case that the X chromosome passed on by some mothers influences (modifies) the fertility of their sons but this is not strictly a heterozygous effect.

Given these difficulties, it is hard to demonstrate a balanced superior fitness effect in men on anything other than autosomes (recall that autosomes are chromosome pairs other than our sex chromosomes). This is also unlikely. Current thinking about sexuality favours the notion that a complex number of genes on our sex chromosomes control sexual orientation with modifiers and triggers, some dominant and some recessive – the 'parliament of genes' (Ridley, 1994). It may be that the gene is not allelic at all but simply the result of a range of closely linked genes on only one sex chromosome of the pair. This is unlikely for reasons of molecular biology well beyond the scope of this book (fixity of inversions). Sexual orientation is almost certainly on the sex-determining chromosomes rather than on the autosomal.

If we assume that this is the case, it may also be that the gene has an X- or female-linked heterotic advantage. If so, this advantage does not accrue to the son and any man carrying a copy will not have a superior advantage. Any such offspring are automatically an evolutionary byproduct.

Too many gay men? Not enough gay men?

There is another difficulty with the balanced superior heterozygotic fitness thesis. Psychologist colleagues reading drafts of this section all asked why a straight man's libido was weaker than that of a homosexual man? Shouldn't this be the other way around? If heterosexuality is the optimum sexual orientation, as it must be by any reasonable definition of Darwinian fitness, then shouldn't the optimum type be a homozygous straight? As counterintuitive as this seems, population geneticists report many instances of seemingly inverted selection, and a scenario which equips homosexual men with superior sex drives while disqualifying them from reproduction is theoretically quite possible. Here we encounter directional versus disruptive selection again. Directive selection favours one optimum type, that is, it pushes a population towards one extreme, while disruptive selection favours two or more extremes. In this scenario the homozygous straight *is* an optimum type, an optimum type that is advantaged in certain men by a gene which may be only incidental to homosexuality. Remember that a homosexual variant which is moving to fixity (becoming a homozygous allele for that locus) is an impossibility. It would lead to the extinction of heterosexuals!

My colleagues' question leads to another more fundamental question. Why doesn't the heterotype take over and become the optimum type in a balance scenario? Given the strength of the procreative urge, is it not likely that most of us are heterozygous for the homosexuality gene? That is, why isn't homosexuality more a matter of stabilising selection selecting an optimum heterotype than of diversifying selection pushing for extremes? Do we all carry at least one gay allele? As we have no hard evidence either way, the only real guide to the penetrance of a gay gene is the percentage of exclusively gay men we observe in society. From this measure we may assume some rough frequencies for the variability of the homosexuality gene. Assuming the simplest case, a diallelic gene with complete dominance, the frequency for exclusively homosexual men should be around 25 percent of the male population, not the 3 percent Hamer et al. (1993) and others estimate are biologically gay. Then by the same mathematics, 50 percent of us would carry one gay gene. Why is homosexuality then such a much smaller part of the population? There is a discrepancy somewhere.

There are several answers to this and the obvious ones are incomplete dominance, and/or polygenics contributing to a smaller average penetrance of the homosexuality gene. Yet, if this were so we should expect a profile quite different from that found in the original Kinsey studies. Given the power of the proposed reproductive advantage (heightened sex drive) and that a large reproductive effect is most likely for balanced superior heterozygotic fitness to work, even if for a relatively low genetic penetrance, the homosexual gene should slowly colonise the gene pool and lift the percentage of gay men. This is demonstrated by the mathematics of mutation. As long ago as 1930 Fisher showed that the probability of any one advantageous but extremely rare mutant gene surviving is vanishingly small if the differential advantage it provides the heterozygote is also small (about a 2 percent probability for a 1 percent reproductive advantage). Thus if we use MacIntyre and Estep's (1993) 2 percent differential, it is almost certain that a beneficial mutant will be lost to random effects within the first few generations (Parkin, 1979). The corollary is evident. While it may be that the homosexuality gene was just lucky, it is more likely to provide a much higher fertility differential than MacIntyre and Estep's 2 percent, or is a hypervariable mutation. In either case, this should lead to a higher proportion of exclusively homosexual men than we see.

One way around the problem is to argue that homosexuality is a relatively recent mutation in our evolutionary history and that the frequencies we are now seeing are not a stable polymorphism but rather a mutant gene that is gradually invading the genome and moving towards a balance. While this would explain why there are lower numbers of gay men than might be expected, as an explanation it does not answer why we will not be overwhelmed with gay men at some later stage of our evolution.

But what about dual attractions?

By now there are probably loud mental protests from those who know the literature and are dubious of biology's mandate. Do not studies show that a majority of homosexual men have had heterosexual sex? What about bisexuality; the high rates of formerly married gay men; gay men who are parents; and those who donate to sperm banks; or have heterosexual fantasies? Are not all these factors weighing against this scenario? Yes and no. As we concluded in the last chapter, there are many types of homosexuality and each has its behavioural patterns and aetiology. These 'problems' may be illusory if we are speaking of differing types. However, this is an intellectual cop-out. To tackle the problem directly, dual attraction at whatever level may well be indicative of heterotic selection rather than evidence to dispute it. As it is beyond our scope to examine all these putative problems, we will just take bisexuality as a representative case of the dual attraction problem, comparing the two Weinberg studies (Bell and Weinberg, 1978; Weinberg et al., 1994b). This will base our discussion on some evidence rather than pure speculation. Several trends emerge from such a comparison but these are only indicative and should be treated cautiously, given changes in San Francisco's gay culture between the two studies, large differences in sample sizes and other procedural dissimilarities.

What may we expect to find if a balanced superior heterozygotic fitness effect is working in bisexual men? A heterosexual man with a homosexuality gene may have a broader range of sexual preferences. An increased sex drive may lead to sex with men because they are more readily available sexual partners than are women, or bisexuals may simply be an intermediate sex, both fish and fowl. This is not to suggest that all bisexual men are homosexually-enabled, or that all homosexually-enabled men are bisexual. Both are possibilities, but are a continuum of sexual orientations; we might expect a dose-dependent relationship with bisexual men having a larger dose or greater penetrance of homosexual genes than those whose heterosexuality is more pronounced. That is, the degree of penetrance of the polygene may have a rough equivalence to one's Kinsey ratings, with homosexually-enabled straight men closer to Kinsey 0s, than bisexuals, and so on (this is worth remembering when we come to the frequency-dependent sexual selection scenario). Then again, as Wilson (1975) noted from observations of sexual preference, a putative homosexual gene must have low penetrance and variable expressivity. It may be that bisexual men, whatever their Kinsey score, are heterozygotes in which an enhanced sexuality has 'leakages' towards indiscriminate promiscuity and variable sexual orientation. In either case, a heterosexual orientation should be dominant in bisexual men if the observed frequencies of sexual orientation are meaningful. Testing this raises interesting possibilities.

Natural selection usually selects against intermediate phenotypes. This leads to the prediction that whatever the reasons for their orientation, male bisexuals should be strongly selected to be more like heterosexuals than homosexuals. That is, heterotypes should favour dominance of the heterosexual allele, a necessary condition of heterotic advantage. As a heterosexual identity is the optimum type for paternity success (irrespective of a genetic component) bisexual men should trend more towards heterosexual attachments and behaviours than homosexual ones. Do they? In Table 4.2 of Weinberg et al.'s (1994b) study the ratio of sexual feelings (71.4/50.9); sexual behaviour (66.8/48.0); and romantic feelings (77.1/47.9) were typically straighter (Kinsey 0–3) in bisexual men than in gay men (Kinsey 3–6). Note, too, that while you would not expect bisexuals' sexual feelings to be exclusively heterosexual, their attachments and behaviour are another matter. Of the sample, 6.3 percent were exclusively behaviourally heterosexual and 14.6 percent had exclusively heterosexual romantic attachments. None of the respondents were exclusively homosexual for the three Kinsey dimensions. Analysis of these and other subtrends found that bisexual men 'were three times more likely to be heterosexual-leaning types than homosexual-leaning types' (Weinberg et al., 1994b).

Notwithstanding the first point, reproductive success is still a powerful urge in all men, irrespective of their sexual orientation. This leads to the prediction that both homosexual and bisexual men should display high levels of heterosexual behaviour while few heterosexual men will incline towards homosexuality. This prediction demonstrates that homosexuality is acknowledged as not leading to paternity success. This may be shown by a heightened desire to change orientation, or to have children, by higher numbers of partners in bisexual and homosexual men (more sex offsets reduced fertility) and higher actual paternity. Table 13.5 of the 1994b study of Weinberg et al. reports attempts to change sexual preference for self-identified men (their orientation may have changed to that currently reported). Rates of desire for change for heterosexual men were 7.4 percent, while those for bisexuals were 27.8 percent and for homosexuals 32.8 percent. The direction of change is even more revealing. Of the small numbers of heterosexual men who had wished to change orientation, 83 percent wanted to become bisexual; only one (16.7 percent) wished to be gay. Of the much higher numbers of bisexual men wanting to change, 58.1 percent wished to become heterosexual; 38.7 percent had become bisexual (not altogether an unexpected finding given that the sample was bisexual); and only 3.2 percent wished to become gay. Of the homosexual sample 75 percent wished to become straight, 13.1 percent bisexual and 11.5 percent had changed to become homosexual. Even more revealing is success at changing orientation. While no straight men were successful in changing identity, 46.7 percent of bisexuals and 18 percent of homosexuals were successful.

While this may be interpreted as the hegemony of heterosexuality and the desire to conform and be accepted, levels of sexual activity also support heterotic advantage. In the 1978 study Table 7 reports the total number of homosexual partners ever. Sixty-seven percent of homosexuals had over 100 homosexual partners. By way of contrast, Table 7.1 of the 1994 study reports only 28.6 percent of bisexual men had over 100 same-sexed partners. This is not a strictly fair comparison as we do not have data on the total number of heterosexual contacts for bisexual and homosexual men in these two studies. It may be that the bisexual men are simply having more heterosexual encounters than gay men and so achieving similar rates of sexual interaction but with different sexes, but on the whole the comparison is indicative. On the question of paternity rates, the two studies do not report rates but gave percentages of men who are parents. Extrapolating as best we can from these reports, it appears that bisexuals have a higher paternity than gay men.

We will spare you further figures; the point is made that bisexual men should favour heterosexual rather than homosexual behaviour, and preferences. All these trends are indicative of a heterotic advantage hypothesis. One would expect a polarisation towards the extremes of Kinsey identity with a smaller intermediate bisexual group. However, the thrust of evolution is towards heterosexuality and bisexuals should trend towards that direction. Those with a larger dose of homosexuality, who would be selected against, should show markedly reduced paternity and trend towards homosexuality. As the heterotype becomes more heterosexual in orientation it should be less obvious and more fit. That is, while not all bisexuals are homosexually-enabled, those that are should lie more to the Kinsey 1 end of the continuum and their behaviour should approximate heterosexual norms.

Box 3.1 **Testing the hypothesis**

1 Assuming the gene that influences sexual orientation also influences sexual drive they should vary in the same proportion.

2 Straight men demonstrating a balanced superior heterotic fitness effect should have more children than those men with two straight genes (homozygous straight men).

3 Homosexual men with two gay genes should have fewer children than both straight and homosexually-enabled straight men. That is, we are most likely to find the gene in exclusive homosexuals.

4 Point 3 should be dose-dependent. The greater the gene's penetrance the greater its reproductive liability.

5 The advantage conferred by the gay gene in straight men should be greater than the reproductive liability it causes in homosexual men.

6 Point 5 should balance at an advantage about 3–5 percent of the male population.

MODELS OF BALANCE POLYMORPHISM: SPERM COMPETITION

An interesting but implausible variant of the balanced superior heterozy-gotic effect is the sperm competition theory of MacIntyre and Estep (1993). In many species, particularly those who regularly have multiple births, females aid and abet an R strategy by a process of sperm competi-tion in which successive copulations during an ovulation fertilise their ova, thus gaining a range of fathers for a clutch or litter, ensuring several genotypes in their offspring. The advantage gained is both selective and adaptive. The most vigorous sperm will fertilise the most ova, ensuring a selective advantage of fertilisation by the most fit. However, the possibility of a fertilisation by a range of suitors also confers a possible adaptive advantage by having several different offspring, any one of which may react better to a suddenly changing environment. This type of sperm competition is possible but less likely in humans (Smith, 1984), where rates of discordant twinning and multiple copulations during a single fertile period (double-mating) are lower. In species such as our own which favour single births, the general idea of sperm competition is that the sperm of one male will out-compete those of another male inseminated within a short time of each other. This double-mating is then a straight race for the ovum. A variant proposed by Baker and Bellis (1995) is that kamikaze sperm directly attack and destroy rival sperm allowing the 'egg-getters' to race on unhindered.

The application of this theory to homosexuality is simple enough. Mac-Intyre and Estep (1993) note that sperm competition might account for a selective advantage for heterozygotes carrying homosexual genes, the genes providing a heterosexual sperm competitive advantage. What this advantage might be is unclear but would include fresher sperm, more motility, greater resistance to phagocytosis, and/or increased longevity. However, the homosexuality gene may be just a neutral passenger carried forward by virtue of a behavioural rather than a genetic advantage, and MacIntyre and Estep quote Margulis and Sagan (1991) on possible mechanisms.

Favoring the sperm of one male over that of competitors are such things as position during sexual intercourse, force and timing of pelvic thrusting, number and speed of ejaculated sperm, and proximity of the spermatic means of delivery – the penis – to the egg at the time of ejaculation. The charm and proficiency of a male – his ability to seduce a female and to continue to please after seducing her – of course also crucially determine his chances of entering and therefore winning the competition.

(Margulis and Sagan, 1991: 37)

While MacIntyre and Estep favour behavioural advantages rather than biological mechanisms, this is an open question. Does the advantage of having a homosexual gene lead to fresher sperm, more charming and seductive manners, or is it purely behavioural? Whatever the reason, the genetic mechanisms we explore in this chapter would work as effectively, and are of little immediate concern, as the main point of MacIntyre and Estep's paper is to model the differential required to maintain the homosexuality gene in the population under such circumstances. Their modelling suggests that as little as a 2 percent increment is necessary to gain a balance effect and this assumes the simplest case – one gene with two different alleles. Whatever the reason – sperm motility or charm, or the superior edge of the homosexually-enabled heterosexual, ensures a reproductive differential of at least the magic 2 percent over those without the gene.

This theory rests on assumptions of facultative polyandry, that women have more than one sexual partner in their lives. Facultative polyandry may occur in many forms. In some few cultures women may legally have more than one husband. In most societies, facultative polyandry occurs either serially through death and divorce and remarriage, or through pre- and post-marital affairs. Women may have extra-pair couplings (EPCs) through adulterous relationships or by consent, as in group sex, spousal swapping or prostitution. Then again, EPCs may result from non-consensual sex through involuntary sex, or rape, particularly multiple rapes which Baker (1996) suggests constitute about 70 percent of all forced sex and a major form of double-mating.

In its simplest form, sperm competition argues that men who enjoy monogamous relationships have what Buss has called 'paternity certainty' (Buss, 1996) and that this ensures their sperm do the job. Clearly, having only one source of sperm (however inadequate) ensures that a father's ongoing parental investment coincides with his genetic investment. Thus, the most fundamental form of sperm competition is excluding other sperm. Equally clearly, sperm competition theory assumes women are ready, willing and able to allow other sperm a chance and we will examine reasons for this in our section on frequency-dependent sexual selection. Here we have the whole basis of patriarchy – sexual jealousy, sequestering of mates, male promiscuity, the double standard and the like. However, one of the ironies of feminist challenges to such patriarchy is that women must have colluded in most forms of the double standard for it to exist. Robert Smith puts this most elegantly:

The biological irony of the double standard is that males could not have been selected for promiscuity if historically females had always denied them opportunity for the expression of the trait. If strict monogamy were the singular human female mating strategy, then only rape would place ejaculates in a position to compete and the potential role of sperm competition as a force in human evolution would be substantially diminished.

(Smith, 1984: 602)

While this theory is elegant in its simplicity, it is based on species favouring multiple births unlike our own (recall that the rate of multiple births in our species is about 1:80 for twins; 1:6,400 for triplets; and 1:512,000 for quadruplets). While MacIntyre and Estep are correct in assuming that sperm competition could still account for a reproductive differential in humans where single births are the rule, they do not take into account the *timing* of multiple copulations in their calculations. While it may be that the rate of cheating in our species is high and that women may have several sex partners, it is unlikely that they have sufficiently many successively at peak fertility to achieve the 2 percent differential – reproductive physiology is against it.

Man, like most mammals, faces time constraints in getting the job done. Peak fertility in women occurs for about two days after ovulation and then falls off rapidly. Average ovum fertility is probably only about 12 hours (Roldan et al., 1992). Thus, a successful fertilisation will only occur if mating is synchronised with ovulation. Baker and Bellis (1995) suggest that the short fertility of the ovum is a selective consequence in and of itself. They argue that nature has selected for a cryptic ovulation and short fertile life to promote sperm competition. Women may copulate with different men and introduce a whole range of selective vectors to determine male fitness, including differential vaginal phagocytosis, sperm storage and sperm warfare. That sperm are fertile for up to fourteen times as long as the egg suggests to them ovum evolution selected for efficient sperm competition. As they put it, 'Such short-lived eggs are, in effect, contraceptive adaptations that allow the female to minimize the risk of being fertilized by less competitive sperm and/or sperm from males who are assessed to be suboptimal in other respects' (Baker and Bellis, 1995).

However, this is only part of the story. We are all the successful products of a long period of sperm competition and any one orgasm contains millions of sperm of variable ability. Then again, the female reproductive tract is a formidable obstacle course for sperm. Out of the millions of sperm released in any one ejaculation, only thousands reach the cervical isthmus and less than twenty reach the ampulla, the fertilisation site (Suarez et al., 1990). 'This drastic reduction in sperm numbers implies a very strong selection indeed within the female tract' (Roldan et al., 1992). As we are all survivors of this direct selective pressure it is unlikely that our sperm will differ markedly in their ability to reach the ampulla. So primacy effects are less important than judging ovulation well. The journey to the ampulla takes about two days, so the likelihood is that the male who judges his mate's cycle well enough to inseminate her two days before ovulation will have the greatest number of fresh sperm at the site. Unfortunately, human females are continually sexually receptive and show few signs of ovulation and this may be a deliberate evolutionary tactic to bond mates – the so-called oestrus concealment or cryptic ovulation theory (Parker, 1987). For all the interest of sperm competitive accounts, a successful insemination is more likely a matter of timing than of multiple partners or of sperm competition.

A consequence of this selection of judgement and concealment may be the sequestering of women to ensure paternity certainty, but also that partners would have a clearer idea of their wife's fertile period than would outsiders. Baker and Bellis are dismissive of our ability in days gone by to pick fertile periods and they quote anthropological evidence of tribal societies in which even the connection between intercourse and conception is unknown. However, this flies in the face of their own discussion of increased human mate-guarding at peak fertility times and a fairly accurate folk literature on calculating effective abstinence which dates to the 17th Dynasty Egyptians. In China for at least the last thousand years, circular wheels were available for women to 'pick the coming of their moons, times for pleasure and times for getting sons' (Sun-Sung, 1996). Given that women would have an idea of their fertile periods argues that they would be well placed to organise copulations to achieve pregnancy. Double-mating could be organised to ensure that the desired extra-pair coupling was closer to the time of ovulation than the obligatory in-pair coupling necessary to ensure that the husband remains unaware and successfully cuckolded. We will return to the implications of this deliberate cuckoldry in our discussion of frequency-dependent sexual selection, but the point to be made here is that if women are aware of their fertile phase they do not have to rely on sperm competitive lotteries to ensure fertilisation by the most fit, but can deliberately select their pregnancies.

An even more telling difficulty exists with this theory. MacIntyre and Estep assume that the rate of sperm competitive advantage will generate a balanced superior heterozygotic effect sufficient to offset the reduced reproduction of homosexual men. Modelling their scenario in the light of Baker and Bellis's 1995 statistics suggests the effect would be too weak to provide a sufficient advantage to explain the penetrance of exclusively gay men at about 1–3 percent of the population. Several steps have to occur for this scenario to work: double-mating must occur sufficiently frequently for a sizeable percentage of the population to be conceived from EPCs. Baker and Bellis (1995) assume that 4–12 percent of British children are conceived 'to a sperm that has prevailed in the competition with sperm from another male'. However, the rate of EPCs should coincide with the rate of paternity discrepancy, averaging about 6 percent in the largest Western study to date (Edwards, 1957). Note that this is for all EPCs and that double-matings will be less than half of this 6 percent. As the in-pair copulator is as likely to be the successful inseminator as the extra-pair partner and either could carry a homosexual gene, we should use this revised double-mating rate as a rough approximation of the numbers of children born from sperm competition. Now this is precisely the rate of the most widely held estimate of exclusively gay men in the population (3 percent). But to achieve this figure MacIntyre and Estep need, first: for *all* double-mating successes to be the result of a homosexual or allied gene; second, that all such matings pass the gene to all offspring irrespective of gender; and third, that the offspring repeat the process indefinitely.

Box 3.2 **Testing the hypothesis**

1 Homosexually-enabled straight men should enjoy a sperm competitive fertility advantage, compared to homozygous straight men, based on one or more of the following:
  • longer penises
  • more vigorous (motile) sperm
  • greater concentrations of sperm per ejaculation
  • fresher sperm
  • engage in more vigorous pelvic thrusting
  • prefer rear-entry sex over other positions
2 Homosexually-enabled straight men enjoying a sperm competitive advantage should be better at assessing peak ovulation in their partners than homozygous straight men.
3 Homosexually heterozygous straight men enjoying a sperm competitive advantage should engage in higher rates of sexual intercourse, with more partners, than homozygous straight men.
4 There should be high rates of facultative polyandry in all human populations.
5 Homosexually-enabled straight men enjoying a sperm competitive advantage should be better at gaining and retaining exclusive sexual partners compared to homozygous straight men.

MacIntyre and Estep's sperm competitive theory collapses if we just note the impossibility of the first assumption, let alone the rest. Not only is MacIntyre and Estep's theory statistically improbable but it is also theoretically cumbersome. A much simpler explanation might assume that women are choosing their partners to select more robust men; or equally that they are more likely to be seduced by a homosexually enhanced heterosexual suitor. This is more probable than assuming a homosexual balance effect predicated on vaginas full of competing sperm!

An intriguing possibility flows from this theory which is amenable to being tested. One major cause of differential fertility is age. Older men have fewer conceptions (Buss, 1994). Therefore, one of the ways a sperm competitive advantage might demonstrate itself is in the ages of homosexual men's parents, which should be younger than population averages. There is a considerable debate on this question, although for other reasons. One of the naive theories of homosexuality is that it is a consequence of 'stale sperm'. As older men have both reduced sperm counts and more damaged sperm, parental age should correlate with incidence of homosexuality and, by implication, with that of homosexually-enabled straight men if a sperm competitive advantage is age-dependent.

For all these reasons sperm competition as a balance effect is best suited to species with multiple copulations and births where advantages of one genotype may out-compete others. The indiscriminate and repeated copulation required is not characteristic of our species.

MODELS OF BALANCE POLYMORPHISM: DENSITY AND FREQUENCY-DEPENDENT SELECTION

Now we briefly consider an insight provided by Wayne Getz (1993) of the Department of Entomology at the University of California, Berkeley, who was the first to link homosexuality to frequency and density-dependent relationships. Getz developed a series of mathematical models of the rate of homosexuality as a function of the frequency of its gene(s) and the density (size) of the population(s) which contain it. His model is general and could apply to any combination of alleles. Unlike the heterotic advantage and sperm competition theories, we are not considering a selective scenario here, as no causal mechanisms are suggested beyond reproductive success. The value of such formulae is that they allow us to model the likelihood of homosexuality expressing itself in a stable, unstable, or balanced way within a community. Although Getz's paper does not suggest mechanisms by which homosexual genes invade a population and become selected beyond a reduced desire to mate or compete, his model provides a basis on which other scenarios may be tested. Getz, as with other population geneticists, is less interested in the actual mechanics of selection than in its outcomes. His paper in the *Journal of Theoretical Biology* is a mathematical overview of the possible scenarios by which polymorphism may arise. Such models are non-empirical and say nothing about actually occurring frequencies or densities. However, Getz's paper is an important contribution linking homosexuality to density and frequency-dependent relationships for the first time and is the point of departure for my own selective scenario. We will consider the nature of frequency and density-dependent relationships before turning to a scenario which depends on it.

Sir Ronald Fisher (1930) first pointed out that: 'if the selective value of a genotype is negatively related to its frequency, a balanced polymorphism might ensue' (cited in Clarke, 1975a). Fisher was interested in Batesian mimicry among butterflies. Batesian mimicry is a selective system where, for example, certain types of edible butterfly come to resemble ones that are unpalatable. This only works if the mimicking species is far less common than the ones they are mimicking. Fisher noted that the gene frequency of this relationship readily led to balance polymorphisms.

Certain palatable types of butterfly such as the swallowtail are polymorphic in both shape and colouration. Although the genes controlling morphology (appearance) are complex and are thought to be controlled by a single locus with many modifier alleles (Hodson, 1992), they express themselves in a wide variety of forms with some variants mimicking unpalatable species. As Clarke (1975b) notes: 'In situations of this sort, the selective value of a morph inevitably depends upon its density ... When the mimetic form is relatively rare, predators encountering its particular visual pattern will more often meet distasteful models than palatable mimics. Their avoidance of the pattern will therefore be strengthened'. However, the reverse is also true and when there are many examples of the mimetic form, predators are more likely to encounter palatable types and so come to associate its appearance with palatability.

As you can see, this will result in a balancing situation. The numbers of any particular form of the swallowtail relative to the butterfly it is modelling will depend on the overall genotype frequencies within the species, the total numbers of the mimetic species and the total numbers of the modelled species (Clarke, 1975b). So Batesian selection is both frequency- and density-dependent. In the frequency case, the relative proportions of mimicry genes in the population will affect the selective balancing, with those most closely resembling the unpalatable species being the most likely to survive. However, this is also density-dependent and there is considerable evidence that the overall success of Batesian mimicry is due to the total numbers of prey population (Plomin et al., 1980). As Wright (1969), in his review of gene frequency theory notes, mimicry is an expensive selective system and in each generation of predators, many of the models and mimetic species are lost, as each generation builds up 'templates' of palatability and unpalatability. The more there are of a particular type, the more there are to be eaten. So 'search images' of prey are density-dependent, as well as selecting against common types and sparing the rare (Clarke, 1975b).

The pattern of selection in these two systems often leads to a balance at a low level of gene frequency for the mimic. Rarity has its value. If there were too many of the palatable mimics relative to the unpalatable, the search templates would overlap and birds and other predators would wake up to the mimicry. So if a particular gene for mimicry becomes common, then a strong selective pressure arises to balance (eat) the

Table 3.2 Approach to equilibrium in a simulated selection experiment due to the rare-male advantage in Drosophila pseudoobscura

| Generation | Eye colour of parental pairs | | | |
| | Experiment 1 | | Experiment 2 | |
	Orange	Purple	Orange	Purple
1	80	20	20	80
2	60	40	29	71
3	68	32	38	62
4	56	44	35	65
5	31	69	41	59
6	63	37	50	50
7	62	38	52	48
8	60	40	50	50
9	50	50	44	56
10	46	54	47	53

Source: after Ehrman, 1970: 193

mimics. As predation thins out the numbers of palatable mimics relative to the original unpalatable models, a balancing selective pressure arises with a new generation of predators learning that this type tastes terrible (the more there are the more likely each predator will eat a bitter-tasting moth). The selective force becomes in turn selected against. In this scenario intermediate types are fair game and have a selective value approaching zero. There is a large body of literature which has shown how frequency and density can lead to balance polymorphisms at quite low levels.

Of particular interest to our discussion is the combination of frequency-dependent and sexual selection vectors. Work by Claudine Petit in 1951 and Lee Ehrman in 1965 (Petit and Ehrman, 1969) on the workhorse of population genetics, the fruit fly Drosophila, independently showed that rarer forms of the male fruit fly are more likely to reproduce. As their numbers increase, their reproductive advantage vanishes and selective forces reduce their reproductive differential. However, as they become rarer it then picks up again. Petit first discovered this phenomenon when working with two strains of Drosophila, the wildtype and bar-eyed mutant, sex-linked condition that changes eye shape (Plomin et al., 1980). In Petit's experiment the coefficient of mating success is the ratio of the number of females mated per mutant male to that of females mated by wildtype males. Measuring mating success of randomly mating females, she found that the frequency of bar-eyed males fell from 93 percent of the total male population early in the experiment to 6 percent, but their mating success ratio increased as they became rarer (Table 3.2). Ehrman (1970) and others have shown similar results. The question is: what advantages do these males enjoy as they become rarer? In fruit flies this is still uncertain. What is clear is that this advantage is a consequence of sexual selection on the part of the females; they are actively discriminating with which males they will mate and seem to be using olfactory cues when they do so. Rare females do not seem to have such an advantage. Males mate indiscriminately with: 'anything resembling another *Drosophila* – including other males, females of other *Drosophila* species, dead or etherised flies, and even inanimate objects' (Plomin et al., 1980). How such a rare male mating advantage evolved is still a mystery, given the vulnerability of intermediate forms.

So much for fruit flies. However, the parallells to homosexuality are readily apparent. As we noted in our discussion of heterotic advantage, one of the problems of balance accounts of polymorphism is to explain why there are not greater numbers of homosexual men than there are. The models we have just described would account for both the relatively small numbers of exclusively gay men and for the continuance of the heterotic advantage (whatever it is) of the homosexually-enabled straight heterotype. Frequency-dependent counter-selection (reproductive inefficiency) would keep homozygous homosexuals at a very small percentage of the population, intermediate types would be strongly selected against, and an overdominant heterotype would be constrained by density-dependent selection (we will discuss probable causal mechanisms in the next scenario). One intriguing possibility of this general model is that frequency-dependent selection may be more important than heterozygous advantage in maintaining polymorphism. As Clarke (1975b) noted, we are then 'faced with the intriguing possibility that heterozygous advantage may be as much a byproduct as a cause of polymorphism'.

How might this work? Clarke and Petit's formulae are single vector and can lead to fairly straightforward modelling of homosexual outcomes using speculative frequencies or densities. Getz's model is more complicated, using as it does two parameters of mating and parental success and so his formulae are more specific and complex. From these models, it is clear that under some conditions a wide range of polymorphisms may result. Some of these will lead to a heterotic advantage and they may be maintained either as stable or unstable balances. While in the frequency-dependent case at equilibrium the average selective value is not necessarily maximised, it may become a potent generator of diversity within populations (Clarke, 1975b). However, we come to an important point here and one that Getz assumes but does not explicitly mention. While the advantage derived by a polymorphism may result in a stable or fluctuating gene balance this is not necessarily a completely biological equation. It may well be that this balance is causally genetic but behavioural in consequence. This may lead to *behavioural* polymorphisms.

Let us consider as an example a gene that leads to reproductive vigour as a result of its frequency. Recall the problem we encountered in the first of our scenarios – why don't we have a much higher proportion of exclusively gay men than we do? Why is this a relatively rare gene? Imagine for example the heterotic advantage of a gene that increases a homosexually-enabled straight man's charm or aggressive drive (we will consider this in the following selective scenario). If the gene were rare in a population it would relatively advantage those who carried it. It would then equip these men to become more successful competitors and seducers than the average homozygous man and to enjoy a much higher reproductive success. However, this edge may be short-lived (recall that a successful mutant by definition reduces the fitness of the previously optimum type by becoming the new optimum type). The frequency of these genes would then increase in the population. Charm becomes devalued and the gene's fitness reduced as there would be so many powerful males vying for a mate 'that they would waste time and energy on strife among themselves' (Clarke, 1975b) and lose the mate. As Darwin observed of dominant rutting stags, they often fight to the point that both become exhausted, allowing the prize to be claimed by a far inferior male. Under these circumstances it is easy to see how a behavioural polymorphism may lead to the gene's frequencies becoming balanced, allowing for both homozygous straight men and gay men to coexist with what under other circumstances should become the dominant type. We turn now to consider what behavioural and physical benefits may support such a balancing act.

MODELS OF BALANCE POLYMORPHISM: FREQUENCY-DEPENDENT SEXUAL SELECTION

If the genesis of a book such as this arises from dissatisfaction, then my main concern is with social constructivists who blindly ignore the mounting evidence for a biology of homosexuality. This dissatisfaction is closely followed by a considerable despair at the constant confusion in the literature of sexual desire with mate choice. As Patrick Bateson (1983) notes: 'In a society in which spouses are freely chosen, it is easy to confuse the influences on sexual preference with those on marriage.' He goes on to remark that anthropologists are having to remind us 'again and again' that in a great many societies mates are arranged rather than chosen. Yet this does not rule out sexual desire in these societies and it would be naive to think that within arranged marriages one's object of desire is always one's mate – not if adultery and divorce statistics are any indication – and it goes without saying that the Western experience is not much different. The important point here is that, despite styles and practices in marriage in our species, women *choose* sexual partners, if not marriage partners.

My selective scenario has as its starting point that women control the gay gene's penetrance. While it seems reasonable to assume that the persistence of obviously deleterious genes must be linked to heterotic balancing effects, and as MacIntyre and Estep (1993) note: 'this is a principle which seems to cry out for application to human sexuality', none of these scenarios will work if women decide otherwise. Perhaps the reason balance polymorphism models seem counterintuitive and often somewhat fanciful is that they neglect female choice. Even so, these models have provided clues for a selective scenario of frequency-dependent sexual selection. Hutchinson's (1959) classic contribution first connected the idea of heterotic advantage to homosexuality; Getz's 1993 paper raised density and frequency-dependency; Hamer's (Hamer et al., 1993) that homosexuality's cause is most likely maternal; and MacIntyre and Estep (1993) that male competition is the limiting factor in the spread of the homosexual gene. These insights are incorporated into a selective scenario which I hope will place balanced heterotic models right in the mainstream of evolutionary theory.

Two ideas are basic to my scenario. Women are attracted to men who carry gay genes because they admire the benefits these men gain from carrying them. Even so, they are suspicious of, and will reject, any man who has homosexual tendencies as this may reduce the reproductive fitness of their potential offspring. As Gallup and Suarez (1993) put it: 'females should be selected for being careful comparison shoppers when it comes to mate selection'. From these two ideas the corollary flows: men who have a measure of gayness in their makeup will be desirable mates and enjoy a reproductive advantage relative to their homozygous peers. Those with a larger 'dose' of gayness will be relatively more disqualified from reproduction than those with a smaller dose. A frequency-dependent balance is thereby struck, with sexual selection being the determining factor. This scenario makes several advances on the other heterotic models: it acknowledges the central role of female choice in the biology of homosexuality; it firmly marries a heterotic advantage with social selective factors, bridging the gap between physical and social evolution; it provides for a continuum of sexual orientation from heterosexuality to homosexuality, acknowledging a polygenic pattern of inheritance; and readily allows for the limiting effects of balancing selection.

As we observed in our discussion of a balanced superior heterozygotic advantage the problem is not so much to discover causal mechanisms for the homosexuality gene's survival but to explain why it has not become more evident. We need to derive a model which will allow a relatively steady but small proportion of exclusively gay men in a population, near a level where the gene is about to, but does not quite, extinguish itself. In this selective scenario this balance is struck by accepting that all but the most concealed of homosexually-enabled straight men will be strongly selected against. As these 'concealed' men gain a greater breeding advantage their numbers will increase and the homosexuality gene (and homosexual behaviours) become more frequent. This in turn will lead to strong counter-selective pressures as women become more discriminating, reducing the gene's frequency to the observed rates. A frequency-dependent sexual selection scenario permits this balance to be struck assuming several conditions:

- That sexual selection or female mate choice is the proximate behavioural cause sustaining a gay gene.
- That women will desire the best possible genes for their offspring and so choose better mates than themselves. That is, they are not assortatively mating for the selective characteristics.
- That men will be relatively non-discriminating with whom they have sex, even if they desire high status marriage partners.
- That there is a high proportion of ex-nuptial children conceived before, during and after marriage.
- That women will not mate as often with those they suspect might be gay.
- That the greater attractiveness of homosexually-enabled heterosexual men will give them a reproductive advantage, but
- That an enhanced ability to charm (seduce) women will be balanced by an increasing counter-selective pressure as the proportion of gay genes in the population increases.

How probable is this selective scenario? Let's start with sexual selection.

Sexual selection or female choice

Sexual selection is the choosing of sexual partners or indeed one's mate on the basis of behavioural or other characteristics that are not immediately obvious enhancements of one's reproductive fitness. Darwin was quite baffled by females choosing mates on characteristics which did not seem useful to the species. For example, many birds, such as the peacock, develop enormous tails which, although colourful displays and attractive to peahens, are otherwise a nuisance, interfering with finding food and avoiding predators (Hodson, 1992). Darwin in *The Descent of Man* (1871) devoted over half of his book to sexual selection, subtitling it *and Selection in Relation to Sex*. Darwin was puzzled by two forms of sexual selection. The first, intrasexual selection, seemed to rely on the ability of males to out-compete each other for females. This led to sexual dimorphism. Males are heavier and stronger and have evolved specialist equipment such as antlers to aid in the fight for mates. Darwin was not so worried by this male-to-male competition as it could be accommodated within a theory of individual natural selection, but observed that it often led to the death of the most fit and to a lot of selective energy being expended in rather useless defensive equipment and behaviour.

Yet it was the second form of sexual selection, mate choice or epigamic selection, which gave Darwin and his successors such a hard time. The necessity of males having to charm their prospective mates led in his view to counterproductive secondary sex characteristics such as the peacock's tail. Females seemed to be choosing mates on traits other than those which had a direct reproductive advantage. If they chose mates on the basis of their penis length, for example, this would be directly selective but choices made on tail size, or the shape of a nose, or beard density had little obvious reproductive benefit. Yet males of many species were being selected for these characteristics. The task of evolutionary theorists since Darwin has been to discover selective values for these characteristics, usually by arguing they are clues to reproductive health, the so-called good genes theory (Ridley, 1994). It uses up a lot of resources to be bigger, heavier and continually grow nice beards, so an animal that puts on a fascinating display must be exceptionally healthy or vigorous. Females then look for these indirect clues for reproductive vigour in choosing a mate.

Still, this doesn't explain the existence of the peacock's tail whose genes require a reproductive differential to become fixed in a population, and it skates over the enormous problem of how bad genes survive in the gene pool in the face of selective pressure which should favour a close competition for favoured genes on any selective trait (Prout and Eaton, 1995). Darwin at first thought that 'sexual selection would have been a simple affair if males were considerably more numerous than females' (Darwin, 1871). Then presumably the fittest would win the day and reproduce. However, in most higher species, sex ratios are basically similar and this led Darwin to think that it was just a matter of relative fitness. The matching principle would favour matings between the more vigorous and healthy animals and this would lead to a reproductive differential. Pairings between unhealthy couples would produce less offspring than the more fit. Characteristics such as beautiful tails or dense beards are then important signals of health and, by implication, of reproductive vigour. However, these secondary sex characteristics do come at a cost and women, in preferring peacock tails or hairy men, are selecting traits that, while, acknowledging health and reproductive vigour in their suitors, are also transferring costs as well as benefits to their sons. The way around this difficulty is to realise that fathers pass their robustness to their daughters as well as to their sons but without the costs. In this way the mother derives a genetic benefit above and beyond that conferred to her sexy sons. For this reason it is likely that the greater part of the benefit derived from sexual selection is provided by female offspring. So, while matching for reproductive fitness is a major plank of epigamic selection producing larger litters and more clutches per season (Wilson, 1975), many other mechanisms sustain it (Trivers, 1985).

Sexual selection has a lot in common with artificial selection, the careful moulding of characteristics in a thoughtful way by selective breeding. One of the less palatable aspects which kept sexual selection so controversial in Darwin's day was a Victorian disquiet with the idea that women were breeding their menfolk, however unconsciously. By consistently preferring certain male traits, women were shaping the species as deliberately as any farmer (Ruffie, 1986). Darwin's work showed that this was so for other species, and research since then suggests similarities in women's aspirations. What are these traits?

Sexual selection has proven one of the most controversial aspects of evolutionary theory and theoretically productive, with an enormous quantum of research output. Women clearly select for men across a spectrum of characteristics and some of these are reasonably good indicators of reproductive vigour. What makes men attractive to women is, on the whole, more to do with social dominance (Barber, 1995), and with skill and prowess (Ford and Beach, 1951), than with physical appearance (Buss, 1994). When physical appearance is a factor, women select more for aspects which are 'indicative of his physical strength such as stature, masculinity, maturity, dominance etc.' (Singh, 1995), rather than for male beauty. When male beauty is a factor, the delta shape of broad shoulders and narrow waist (Lavrakis, 1975); wide face and square jaws (Cunningham et al., 1990); bilateral symmetry (Johnstone, 1994; Thornhill and Gangestad, 1994); weight (Manning, 1995); and waist-to-hip ratios (Singh, 1995) are more to do with sending 'honest signals of male quality' (Moller, 1990) than with beauty per se. What is important in these studies is the order of the effects. Women choose bread-winning resources first, then dominance characteristics, and then looks. Note that these findings are for long-term mates, not necessarily for casual sex partners. How important a role does charm play in what seems a very pragmatic business?

On the nature of charm

Now we come to the crux of this scenario. Women choose mates who will be good providers and who will invest resources in their offspring, and look for a mate similar to themselves to minimise conflict in their relationship – the matching principle – or positive assortative mating at work. At the same time they are trying to beat the status quo and hope for a mate with a better pedigree than their own. It is likely that women have an evolved preference for certain types of men and have developed a keen ability to distinguish between offers. Men traditionally offer health, intellect, virility and resources and use aggression and charm to push their case. Homosexually-enabled straight men with access to both masculine and feminine traits will be able to offer sensitivity, creativity and better communication skills in addition to the traditional male offerings. Given that women have a range of possible mates with equivalent prospects, the homosexually-enabled straight man with a greater measure of feminine appeal will succeed at the margin. At the same time, women's discriminant ability will be finely attuned to hints of unmanliness and too large a dose of homosexuality will rapidly disqualify a potential suitor, given that one of the most consistent findings of sexuality research is strong disapproval of effeminate men (McCreary, 1994).

Social psychology tells us that two main factors are working in women's mate choice – one is a strong preference for men who will be good breadwinners and the other is for similarity to themselves (McKnight and Sutton, 1994). There is a certain tension between these two objectives. Women are looking for a minimum safety of someone quite like themselves but hoping for someone better. Women select by similar ethnicity, religious and political beliefs, social status, geographic propinquity, shared interests and common goals. The conventional wisdom is that with strong sociocultural assortative mating, sources of marital conflict are minimised and parental investment is maximised. Women also match by physical characteristics. What is important varies from culture to culture, although there are certain similarities: women are unlikely to marry men shorter than themselves; beautiful women seek handsome mates; and so on. Up to this point, similarity provides baseline expectations but unless the woman sees herself as having little to offer, she will try to maximise her offspring's fitness by seeking men with a superior genetic endowment. Given that all these characteristics are obvious and well distributed throughout the population, it is unlikely that she will marry far from her own potential; she has far too many competitors for that to happen. For this reason, male characteristics such as greater height, strength and endurance, which signal virility, may be less important at the margin than other more subtle signals of male superiority.

Similarity can also work in other ways. Women have expectations of men which are not part of male socialisation. They admire men who are warm and caring, who are nurturant, good communicators who share feelings, who are creative and have flair, who possess wit, charm and sensitivity (Hudson and Henze, 1969; Buss and Barnes, 1986; Howard et al., 1987; Buss 1989; Sprecher et al., 1994). There is also considerable evidence that gay men are brighter (Weinrich, 1978); more creative (Weinrich, 1977; Ruse, 1981; Cooper, 1994; Hewitt, 1995); better communicators and more socially adept than the average male (Wilson, 1978); and less disturbed (Strickland, 1995). While it is impossible to unscramble the relative social and genetic contributions to these traits, or to see them as exclusively feminine, they are characteristic of and much admired by women.

Homosexual charm is legendary and the diminished (but still evident) antipathy felt by heterosexual women towards gay men (Kite and Whitley, 1996) may in part reflect a certain similarity of outlook. As we explored in the last chapter, there are different masculine and feminine pathways in the fetal brain and early hormonal influences affect their development (Breedlove, 1994). It is important to realise that these are separate pathways and more androgynous individuals may result from the development of both rather than from one suppressing the other (Byne and Parsons, 1993). One of the advantages the homosexually-enabled heterotype may enjoy, in addition to increased virility, is traits traditionally thought of as feminine, which women recognise and with which they feel comfortable and, in recognising a certain familiarity, positively select for them. Thus, the reproductive differential which keeps the homosexuality gene in the population may be a marginal superiority of the homosexually-enabled straight heterotype, which reflects charm and a certain similarity of traits.

What is the nature of this charm and how does it work? Twin purposes are served in selecting mates who are both charming and sincere. Sources of possible marital conflict are minimised by selecting for nurturant traits and mates who have the self-confidence to try to charm are also likely to be successful in their careers, at least to the extent that self-confidence equals access to resources. Consistently, in answering questionnaires on what they want in a mate, 'women have expressed a greater preference than men for such personality characteristics as expressiveness, kindness and considerateness' (Sprecher et al., 1994). Charm is an indicator of emotional compatibility and these nurturant traits promote a sense of security in women that their chosen mate is following similar agendas as themselves, a favourite rule of social psychology – that similarity breeds safety. Charm is also indicative of poise. Under-confidence in a male suitor is a distinct liability. Poise equals self-confidence and signals that the suitor is comfortable in his suit and that the 'courtship gifts' he displays for his intended anticipate real resources he will provide for their children – a major concern for women in mate selection (Bailey et al., 1994). So traits such as intelligence, creativity and flair are perhaps subtle signposts for self-confidence and a success potential beyond sheer virility.

It is unlikely that these traits are more important than signs of obvious virility and perhaps the major advantage the homosexually-enabled straight man enjoys is as uncomplicated as an enhanced sexuality. However, the ability to seduce and satisfy a partner is as much a behavioural trait as it is a physical one and, in competition for mates, charm may have a synergistic relationship with virility. What is clear is that charm has its boundaries. At one limit 'too charming' is seen as deception and insincerity and at the other limit as possible effeminacy.

Women who have a finely attuned discriminative sense would select for this characteristic within a discrete behavioural range and secondarily to obvious bread-winning and virility potentials. Then again, as Barkow (1989) observed, women who select charming men ensure that their male offspring are also charming, thus maximising the numbers of their grand-children.

A reproductive differential?

By now you are probably wondering why heterozygous males enjoy a reproductive advantage in this selective scenario? Given that there are roughly equal numbers of men and women why doesn't a simple matching principle apply, with each pairing with someone similar to themselves (positive assortative mating) and then each couple having as many children as they desire? What would make the heterotype have more children than anyone else? Several interrelated factors may be at work here.

In *The Descent*, Darwin distinguished two factors which lead to repro-ductive success in a sexually selective system: the male's ability to charm (seduce) the female and the male's ability to out-compete other males in finding a range of mates. Perceptive readers will notice that R strategy underlies these abilities and perhaps the primary reason for heterozygotic success is simply a male promiscuity reproductive strategy. Yet from our earlier discussions, you will recall that women's strategy is aimed at the opposite – binding a mate close to the nest and being choosy with whom they marry, given a lesser reproductive capacity. As women are the limi-ting variable in the system, we would expect that a K-stable strategy would prevail and for this reason would nullify the heterotic advantage of a straight man with a gay gene. Fortunately, this difficulty is overcome by female infidelity. As regrettable as it may be, there is ample evidence (Bellis and Baker, 1990; Buss, 1994; Einon, 1994; Baker and Bellis, 1995) that women are promiscuous, if not as flagrantly as men, at least as calculatedly. As Symons (1979) and Barkow (1989) note, at least part of the difficulty is in our curiously conservative view of women as being wholly monogamous and mating for life, pair bonding with a single partner in the manner of ducks or gibbons. This is not so for our species and evidence from paternity testing research indicates that up to 30 percent of married women have children who cannot be products of the marriage, even if their spouses think they are (Baker and Bellis, 1995; Buss, 1996).

Monogamy is rare among mammals and Baker and Bellis (1995) review several studies of human infidelity in defence of their sperm competitive theory. To show that infidelity is not entirely pointless they quote the traditional medical view that between 10 and 15 percent of children are genetically unrelated to their fathers. They support this with a range of studies which show rates of paternity discrepancy from 2 to 30 percent (Schacht and Gershowitz, 1963; Harpending in Trivers, 1972; Philipp, 1973; Neel and Weiss, 1975; McLaren in Cohen, 1977; Salmon et al., 1980; Smith, 1984; Macintyre and Sooman, 1992). In two of the larger studies to date, Ashton (1980) in Hawaii, with a sample of 2,839, gave a more conservative paternal discrepancy rate of 2.3 percent; and Edwards (1957), in a large Metropolitan London sample (2,596), found a rate of 5.9 percent. Perhaps the best estimate of parental discrepancy is around 10 percent (Macintyre and Sooman, 1992). It should be remembered that this is a measure of successful inseminations, not of the myriad infidelities necessary to produce them. On the other hand these figures often include situations where the male partner is aware of and may even consent to an ex-nuptial child, or where the mother is unaware or uncertain of their child's ex-nuptial paternity, so this figure may be an overestimate of infidelities that produce a child. For these reasons, researchers tend to speak of extra-pair copulations (EPCs) rather than infidelities, as you will recall in our discussion of EPCs in the sperm competition section of this chapter. There are a multitude of studies which point to high EPC rates in both sexes and to the theoretical complications this brings (Kinsey et al., 1948, 1953; Broude and Greene, 1976; Smith, 1984; Macintyre and Sooman, 1992; Einon, 1994; Johnson et al., 1994). Baker and Bellis (1995), for example, found in their sample of 4,000 British women that the more sexually experienced a woman, the more probable she would have at least one EPC: '17% double-mate within their first 50 copulations, 50% within their first 500, and over 80% after 3,000 copulations.' Clearly, infidelity is a characteristic human behaviour in both sexes.

Nevertheless, it is with successful pregnancies that we are concerned here. While many pregnancies may be unplanned, many are deliberate, particularly in an age of reliable contraception. Why might a woman choose deliberately to cuckold her partner? It is clear that consciously or unconsciously, women are following their own R strategy, albeit in more limited and selective a fashion than their menfolk. A variety of casual fathers makes for a more varied genetic succession and for offspring from superior males who are otherwise inaccessible as mates. A certain measure of understated polyandry has characterised most cultures and in an era of sexual permissiveness and ex-nuptial children, the 3 percent differential needed to ensure a frequency-dependent sexual-selection for a homosexual heterotype is assured. Indeed it might even become a positive selective strategy pursued by women who are dissatisfied with their mates. As Kenrick et al. (1993) have shown (Figure 3.3), men are more than willing to have sex with women whom they would not consider as marriage partners. Perhaps women at a disadvantage, with a disability, or just dissatisfied with their spouse, may have extramarital affairs with

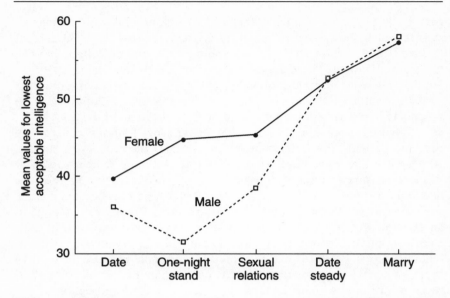

Figure 3.3 Relationship between mean values for lowest acceptable intelligence
and involvement level

Source: after Kenrick et al., 1993: 956–961

higher status males to deliberately cuckold their husbands and ensure a
range of genotypes in their children, which is selective both in terms of
genetic variability, as well as gaining the superior traits of the extramarital
lover. While this is speculation, it is a rich field for future research and
if the numbers of married women with fertile partners seeking donations
from sperm banks is any indication, is more than likely to be a significant
finding.

A related factor is competition between women for high status mates.
This would also favour the homosexually-enabled straight man. While it
seems paradoxical to the whole tenor of our discussions here, women
may well compete for a scarce resource in choosing such a partner. As
we have seen, there may be a correlation between homosexuality and
factors such as virility, intelligence, attractiveness and sensitivity. Given
that there are relatively few men who possess feminine-type traits while
displaying conspicuous masculinity, women may compete among themselves to attract and hold such a mate and sexual favours may be an
important part of this strategy. Returning to Kenrick's study you will see
from Figure 3.3 that females were willing to have sex before steady dating.
If several women are using this strategy to bind a homosexually-enabled
male then the reproductive differential is easily met. Evidence is circum-
stantial at best and some theorists even doubt that sex-for-bonding is a
demonstrable human strategy (see Smith (1984) for a review). However,

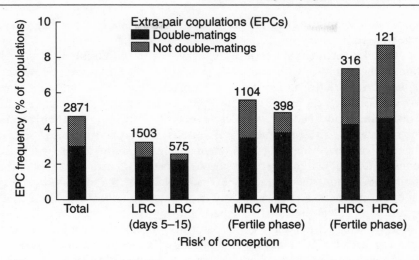

Figure 3.4 Association between double-matings, contraceptive use, and fertility
(UK)

Notes: LRC: low risk of conception (oral contraceptive; sterilisation; menopause).
MRC: medium risk of conception (barrier methods; intrauterine devices).
HRC: high risk of conception (no 'modern' contraceptive).

Source: Baker and Bellis, 1995: 197

there is comparative evidence and Hrdy (1981) notes such female competition in primates.

But are women cuckoos? The problem of parental investment

What if women are cuckoos, persuading others to help raise their offspring? As the cuckoo lays her eggs in other species' nests and hopes the
parents will raise her offspring for her, so too rates of double-mating
(Figure 3.4) suggest that this is a tactic deliberately employed by many
women, if the rise in EPCs towards the woman's fertile period is any
indication. Within several primate species, paternity uncertainty is swiftly
resolved by the newly dominant male aborting the offspring of his van-
quished rivals (Hrdy, 1981). In human affairs, infanticide is not a favoured
tactic and many men choose to ignore possible breaches of marital fidelity,
wisely turning a blind eye and raising extraneous offspring as their own.
We have little data on the extent of deliberate, conscious, double-mating
and the figures quoted above may be skewed to madly passionate
(uncontrollable?) affairs, extramarital rape and simple confusion on the
part of the pregnant bride as to who was really the father. While human
sexual intercourse is a conscious act, parenthood may not always be a
controllable one, as failures of contraception attest. Many extramarital
conceptions may be simply accidents. Notwithstanding these caveats,

deliberate extramarital sex aimed at reproduction is a tactic which makes eminent evolutionary sense.

Parental investment is a term which is widely used to imply that women choose their mates with ongoing spousal support in mind. However, *mating* in its strictest usage is sex for reproduction rather than marriage. Women may well choose fathers for their children where ongoing parental investment is not an issue. Conscious decisions to improve their reproductive success in subsequent generations by maximising the genetic diversity of their offspring is a great selective tactic as the woman's genetic investment remains the same irrespective of who contributes the other half. After selecting the best possible man to pair-bond, taking on other partners is the only way a woman can improve her genes' posterity short of reproductive incest. Putting this another way, women should be selected to cheat on the paternity of their offspring if they can get away with it. There has been a curious blindness in the literature on forces selecting women to cheat. Given that women have so few chances at their posterity, it would be unusual if it were not so. While it may have been that in times of scarce resources (the usual state of our species for most of its existence) women would have tightly bonded to resourceful husbands, times have changed. The pioneering work of human sperm competition theorists such as Robert Smith, Robin Baker and Mark Bellis, which highlights actual rates of ex-nuptial infidelity, may be pointing to the evolving direction of a sexual selection less tied to parental investment considerations. If this were so, then our scenario would result in a greater selection for charm, than bread-winning capacity in casual mates.

Today this may be a possibility, but women's tactics have been shaped by millions of years of depending on males for resources, through repeated pregnancies, childbirth and childrearing. These realities would ensure strong parental investment and a husband. In Robin Fox's words women look for men who are 'controlled, cunning, cooperative, attractive to the ladies, good with the children, relaxed, tough, eloquent, skillful, knowledgeable, and proficient in self-defence and hunting' (quoted in Wilson, 1978). Yet nothing stops these women having reproductive affairs other than the cost of being caught by one's spouse (Broude and Greene, 1976). The double standard that has disadvantaged unmarried women for so long paradoxically advantages married women. Men are less worried about the consequences of sex than women and, as we noted, will have sex with partners they would not consider marrying. It is a safe bet that women who follow this path would have a ready supply of casual mates whose superior characteristics they could never hope to marry.

Our focus here has been on women cheating in marriage, as marriage is an inevitable state for most of us, be it legal or otherwise. Even so, it is not necessary to marry to advance a homosexual gene for charm or virility and so gain a heterotic advantage. Nothing in the foregoing implies that women have to marry but parental investment needs probably make it more likely. With increasing sexual liberation, women have many more opportunities for pre-marital sex and a significant percentage ranging from 10 to 40 percent of women enter marriage, or remarry with children not of their new spouse. This raises the intriguing possibility that in an era of considerable resource security, illegitimacy, extra-nuptial pregnancies, marital discord, divorce and remarriage are all nature's way of advantaging women's reproductive interest.

Anyway, not to lose sight of the point here, while competition between women for men is as obvious as the nearest teenage social, this competition results in a reproductive differential for the homosexually-enabled straight man. This may be tested. If we identify those characteristics which typify these men we should be able to see how women respond to such profiles in their dating and reproductive choices. Wiegmann et al. (1996), in their illuminating paper in the *American Naturalist*, provide an analytical model that with minor modification would readily model the penetrance of such profiles.

Deception

Many species gain a direct benefit by deceiving potential mates about their abilities (Trivers, 1971). Homosexually-enabled men might not be the best stock available but may pretend to be. For example, it has long been established that the Arts attract proportionally higher numbers of gay men. Weinrich (1977), commenting on this, observed that effeminate boys, who as a group become proportionately more gay men, are also 'unusually adept at stage-acting and role-taking – at an age long before they could know that the acting profession has an unusually high incidence of homosexuality', a finding confirmed by Hewitt (1995). It may well be that gay men have a heightened ability to portray an appropriate image and personality that would attract a mate and this may well be unconscious. So the aspects of charm we have explored may not directly translate to a genetic superiority but are designed to signal that they do. Is this a problem? Here we go round in circles. Is a secondary sex characteristic, such as a large tail or wonderful beard, of direct reproductive benefit? Yes, if it leads to a mate in the face of stiff competition – but then again a longer penis will probably be more useful if your mate has been sleeping around and you want your sperm to get there faster (and one wonders why bulging cod-pieces are no longer a part of male display). The whole issue of secondary sex characteristics' selective value is vexed and difficult to demonstrate and overshadowed by primary ones. The point is moot. Why then do a greater sensitivity, better communication skills and other so-called feminine characteristics signal genetic superiority? We have partly answered this in our discussion of charm but it is not really necessary that such features signal genetic superiority, rather that they seem to. For our 'how-possibly' scenario, gay virtues may only need to be apparent, if not real. That the homosexually-enabled straight man can gain a mate is all that is asked and, as we have noted, this is a wonderful ability to have passed on to your male descendants, even if it is just simply charm.

I came to this insight reading Robert Trivers' *Social Evolution* (1985). Our species, as with many others, is selected for controlling the information we give about ourselves. As Trivers notes:

> One of the most important things to realise about systems of animal communication is that they are not systems for the dissemination of the truth. An animal selected to signal to another animal may be selected to convey correct information, misinformation or both.
>
> (Trivers, 1985: 395)

Trivers recounts how the female scorpionfly has evolved a display which signals to males bearing food that she is female and receptive. She ducks her wings and hopefully the male responds by offering her a 'nuptial gift'. But scorpionfly males have also evolved the ability to display as if they were females – a common trait called behavioural mimicry – and in 22 percent of cases this persuades the male bearing prey to relinquish his gift. The moral is obvious: deceit works. Now it is not necessary that this be a deliberate deceit. One can hardly think of scorpionflies having the neurons to think through the consequences of their actions, but it works and in our scenario it is unlikely that homosexually-enabled straight men would be conscious of their actions, seeing them as normal male behaviour. From an evolutionary psychologist's perspective such behaviour is entirely usual. Ours is a female display species and women often go to unusual lengths to attract males. The woman using lipstick for red lips, blusher for skin tone, and padded bras to accentuate her curves is using deceitful practices to emphasise her health and fecundity but is not consciously lying about her virtues. And so it is with our homosexually-enabled men: the roots of their behaviour may be entirely unconscious.

Nevertheless, the point has to be made that whether gay virtues are of superior genetic potential, or only seeming to be, the scenario works either way.

What is more interesting is not that we are selected for deceit, but that we would also be strongly selected to detect deception. Returning to Trivers' example, the prey-bearing scorpionfly has gone to some trouble in catching his morsel and wants to be sure that the recipient responds appropriately. This leads to a complex system of deceit, deception detection and reciprocity which is dynamic and in which the drift to a stable equilibrium is more a function of the discriminative ability of the one choosing, than of dissembling skill. This assertion flows directly from the different investment the sexes have in any one mating: the man risks little, the woman risks a great deal. For the frequency-dependent sexual selective hypothesis, the ability to detect homosexual traits will be a very strong selective pressure. Women will disqualify men at a hint of gayness as, presumably, gay genes directly reduce their reproductive fitness. Unlike other forms of deception, in which a complex system of paybacks allows for second chances, in this system gayness is the kiss of death.

Implications for a frequency-dependency relationship follow from the strength of this selective vector. As the frequency of the homosexual gene increases in the population, so too increase the chances of its detection and, given these selective pressures, the woman's choice would be conservative – when in doubt, don't. Remember that this model relies on our sexual orientation being controlled by a complex of genes rather than there being different genes for heterosexuality and homosexuality. For this reason, there will be a continuum of behaviours which correlate with the degree of sexual orientation. The relative frequencies of intermediate sexualities will be directly controlled by this selective deception detection. For this reason it is likely that homosexual and heterosexual phenotypes will aggregate. This is in accordance with the various Kinsey and other studies which show low rates for intermediate sexualities.

Box 3.3   Testing the hypothesis

1 Homosexuality should be distributed in the community with a range of behavioural phenotypes.
2 Many of these subtypes should be behaviourally indistinguishable from heterosexual males.
3 Masculine and feminine pathways should exist in foetal brains.
4 Women should be much better at subtle interpersonal signal recognition than men.
5 The probability of a woman rejecting a man's first sexual overtures should decline as male quality increases.

HOMOSEXUALITY AS AN EVOLUTIONARY BYPRODUCT

In all probability, homosexuality is adaptive in its own right but there is also the possibility that it is merely a vestige of evolution. Intuitively, the reduced reproductive success of homosexuals argues that this is so. Given the sexual inversion viewpoint so popular in the earlier part of the century, homosexuality was neatly slotted into an 'also rans' category. Those whom nature deems less equipped to reproduce are shunted into 'futile sex'. Despite a clear lack of evidence supporting this view, it is pervasive in both popular accounts of homosexuality and in the scientific literature.

Even kin selection theory, which argues that homosexuality is adaptive, has as an unstated subtext that homosexuals are less interested in *directly* perpetuating their own genes. Of course the problem with this view is that it anthropomorphises the blind and impersonal forces of evolution. To speak of 'selecting' and such other terms suggests that nature actively intervenes to select out the unfit, in this case, homosexuals. Such a reading is incorrect. Evolution is essentially a reactive process. The less fit are selected out by natural attrition and this is a consequence of relatively random forces of natural selection, catastrophe, climatic change, mutation and the like. From this perspective homosexuality is probably just a consequence of other processes, in essence a byproduct.

Perhaps homosexuals have little choice in their homosexuality: they carry a mutation, having a defective sexual orientation which leaves them chasing inappropriate sexual partners and so are disqualified from reproduction. We will explore this, but a more intriguing possibility exists – that homosexuality is really a question of differential fertility rates between mothers and sons, an evolutionary balancing act but a relatively benign one, at least for mothers.

MODELS OF EVOLUTIONARY FUTILITY: AN OVERLOVING EFFECT

We turn now to Hamer and colleagues' overloving effect, a rather brief afterthought to their search for the gay gene. In the media circus that arose following their first paper in 1993, one of the more informed questions that kept arising was 'how might this putative gene be selected?' and Hamer and his colleagues were challenged to explain its existence. Unlike the models we have already examined, Hamer's 1994 book proposed a heterotic effect which operated not on the offspring but on the parent. In all the speculation that followed no one seemed to notice that this firmly assigned any gene leading to male homosexuality to the evolutionary dust bin. Rather than the gene conveying some relative advantage to offspring, the children of Hamer's 'fertile females' are byproducts of evolution.

The ultimate purpose of all sexual behaviour is sexual reproduction and human society is constructed to reflect the sexual nature of our species. This unoriginal assertion is neither trite nor are its ramifications all that obvious, despite constant analysis in fine-grained detail. Sexual politics and overlays of 'correct intersex behaviour' notwithstanding, man desires woman and woman needs a mate. Whatever aids in perpetuating ourselves is good, whatever hinders is bad, at least to the extent that evolution has a morality. So assume for a moment that we are designed to target those whose gender marks them as appropriate sexual partners. Given the central importance of reproduction, it is not hard to accept the further assumption that this desire is coded in our genes; that our genes target the opposite sex as appropriate opportunities for reproduction and that the strength of this desire is proportionate to the genetic dose we receive. That is, we have both a genetic direction and impetus. Such assumptions are implicit in both modern biology and synthetic evolutionary theory (Pollard, 1996; Reik, 1996).

When Dean Hamer was challenged to explain why a gene for homosexuality might exist on the X chromosome, he drew on these assumptions in proposing an overloving effect. Because homosexual men and heterosexual women share an attraction to men, several investigators have asked themselves over the years whether gay men might not then share similar brain structures with straight women (Breedlove, 1994). Hamer took this one step further in asking why this might happen. Imagine that a gene encodes for women a desire to have sex and imprints men as appropriate sexual targets. Women who have a stronger dose of this gene would have greater sexual drive and all things being equal would have more children than those women with a smaller dose. Two ideas are central here. The first is that this gene causes a differential reproductive rate which carries the gene forward to future generations and the second is that it is passed on to sons and affects their sexual orientation and preference.

Here we have another instance of balance polymorphism but unlike those we considered previously as an evolutionary advantage, here an uneasy balance is struck from a selective viewpoint. According to Hamer's scenario, men who receive a copy of this gene are disabled from reproducing as they adopt the sexual orientation of their mothers, having a desire to have sex with men. This reduces their reproductive success. However, their mothers are having more children (and more sons than other women) and this ensures their genetic message passes to subsequent generations despite the reduced reproductive fitness of their sons. That is, the mother's greater reproductive success balances their son's reduced sexual fitness. Here the genetic advantage lies with the mother. She has a greater sexual drive, more children than other women and as she will produce as many daughters as sons, presumably her daughters will enjoy this reproductive advantage too and pass forward her genes in greater numbers. As such, the mother has an evolutionary advantage while her homosexual sons are byproducts of this advantage. Put another way, male homosexuality is an accident of another process and not genetically selected.

Hamer's overloving gene seems at first glance counterintuitive. Why is it a benefit to a mother if she has a gene disqualifying her children from reproducing? The answer is that sex itself is a polymorphism, not just a means for arriving at polymorphisms (Ruffie, 1986). It is a question of complete dominance and altered sex ratios: 'In men with sex chromosomes XY, any allele on the X chromosome behaves as a dominant, because there is no corresponding allele to mask it on the other chromosome' (Hodson, 1992). So a mother passes a dominant trait to her sons if it is X-linked, but may not do so to her daughters who get two copies of the X chromosome from each parent. Most X-linked traits are recessive in women, who act as carriers in passing these genes to half their offspring. Colour blindness, Duchenne muscular dystrophy, haemophilia type A, fragile X syndrome, and nephrogenic diabetes are examples of such recessive traits. While most such X-linked traits are recessive and quite rare, there are examples of dominant traits in which women receive an X-linked gene from both parents. This is what Hamer proposes for homosexuality. Indeed, this is an interesting case of overdominance because Hamer suggests that a normal tendency to desire men is carried heterotically with what must be a normal wildtype gene given extra emphasis by an overloving effect on one or both chromosomes.

How does this lead to a balance which maintains the homosexuality gene in the population? William Rice (1984) provided the general insight in his modelling of sex chromosomes and the evolution of sexual dimorphism. He observed: 'The major prediction from this analysis is that genes coding for sexually dimorphic traits should be located disproportionately on the X-chromosome.' Hamer applied Rice's general observation to homosexuality:

> this type of model is especially attractive for a gene on the X chromosome because an X-linked gene will be found twice as frequently in women, who have two X chromosomes, as in men, who have one X chromosome. As a result, the gene would have to increase childbearing in women only half as much as it reduced reproduction in men. Genes that hurt the reproduction of one sex while helping the other are not just a theoretical construct; they have been experimentally demonstrated in many different organisms and seem to play a key role in the evolutionary process of sexual selection.
>
> (Hamer and Copeland, 1994: 183)

Modelling this balance polymorphism, as little as a 2 percent reproductive advantage enjoyed by the mother over her sisters would keep the homosexuality gene in the population at the conservative 3 percent of population level used by Hamer.

At present, evidence for an overloving gene is relatively slender and relies on statistically demonstrating a maternal-line effect. This rests on three legs: that mothers of homosexual men have more children; that they have more homosexual children than mothers of straight men; and that their sisters and maternal aunts and cousins and nieces do likewise. In the absence of a definite marker (and as we saw in Chapter 2 the existence of such markers is hotly contested) the overloving effect has had a mixed press. Hamer's initial study (Hamer et al., 1993) found clear evidence of a maternal-line effect. With reference to Table 2.1 (see p. 55) not only was the incidence of maternal-line gay relatives higher but it conformed to an X-linked pattern that supports the overloving effect. Compare the rates of maternal uncles and maternal cousins through aunts. This shows an almost identical percentage and this is unlikely if the homosexuality gene were carried autosomally. In that case you would expect the rate of maternal gay uncles to be twice that of gay maternal cousins. If it were a single dominant diallelic gene the rate would be 25 percent as against 12.5 percent. Nearly identical rates suggest it is X-linked because, as Hamer notes:

> I realised that the explanation lay in the special rules that govern the inheritance of the X chromosome. Unlike on the other chromosomes, where uncles and nephews share twice as much genetic information as cousins, in the case of the X chromosome, maternally related cousins actually share more genes, an average of 37.5 percent. The explanation for this is that sisters share an average of 75 percent, rather than the usual 50 percent, of their X chromosome DNA.
>
> (Hamer and Copeland, 1994: 97)

Of course, another explanation for these numbers is that the gene is in fact autosomal and the variation is caused by simple mechanisms of differential fertility. As Hamer himself observed, given that gay men have markedly reduced reproductive rates, fewer children may be inheriting the gene from their fathers than from their mothers: 'This would automatically result in more gay relatives on the maternal than on the paternal side, even if the gene was not on a sex chromosome' (Hamer and Copeland, 1994). For this reason, the near identical rates of gay maternal uncles and cousins is a critical issue in supporting an X-linked overloving effect.

Box 3.4 **Testing the hypothesis**

1 Men and women should both have sexual orientation pathways which allow early developmental imprinting on either sex.
2 Children should be aware of sex differences from an early age and imprint on appropriate sex targets prior to puberty.
3 Women who have a stronger dose of this gene would have more children than those women with a smaller dose.
4 Women with a stronger dose of this gene would have more homosexual sons than women with a smaller dose.
5 Women who have a stronger dose of this gene would have maternal relatives who demonstrate points 3 and 4 also.
6 The incidence of gay maternal uncles should approximate that of gay maternal cousins.

MODELS OF EVOLUTIONARY FUTILITY: HOMOSEXUALITY – A CONTINUOUSLY OCCURRING MUTATION?

All the theories we have considered in this chapter assume that a gene for homosexuality exists and that it is balanced in the population, carried forward from generation to generation by virtue of some selective advantage it confers or receives. What if the gene were simply a continuously occurring mutation without selective value? We have seen that homosexuality is ultimately a byproduct of evolution, however much it advantages the heterozygote. What if homosexuality were nothing more than a fragile point at which genetic inversions resulted during meiosis. Is this simple explanation a sufficient selective scenario for the survival of homosexuality?

A classical mutation?

There are three main types of mutation: substitution at a single base pair; the loss or addition of base pair/s; or the large-scale rearrangement of chromosomal material (Hodson, 1992). Spontaneous mutation is the ultimate source of species variability and is the engine of evolution. The rate of mutation at any one locus in a species has been variously estimated since the work of Fisher (1930) to occur at any mammalian locus from 1:100,000 to 1:1,000,000 times (Hodson, 1992). Goodenough (1984) estimates higher animals such as man have about 50,000 functional genes. At these mutational frequencies, she estimates that about half of an adult's gametes will carry at least one new mutant allele and notes that 'mutation provides the population with an abundant supply of new alleles at each generation'.

However, virtually all these new mutations are deleterious and estimates of the mutational load (reduced viability) carried by a species approach 50 percent. Goodenough (1984) quotes J.F. Crow on this point: 'The species pays a high price for mutation and the evolutionary possibilities that derive from it.' Figures on the viability of any particular mutant locus differ significantly depending on its degree of penetrance, growth rates of the population, etc. Mutant genes may be lethal, deleterious or neutral but are rarely beneficial, either immediately, or eventually, as with the balanced superior heterozygotic fitness effect which for homosexuality would start from puberty onwards. What about the idea that a repeated mutation at a point would alter frequencies to bring about evolutionary change eventually? While mutational pressure alone may lead a new gene to fixity or to a stable polymorphism, given an average mutation rate per locus of 1:100,000 it would take about 20 million years to even start getting an appreciable change in the frequency of a new allele within a population. This calculation led Goodenough (1984) to conclude that 'mutation, while critically important to evolution in providing genetic variability, does not in and of itself bring about significant changes in allelic frequencies'. Selective pressure can drive a mutation to quickly become the optimum type but this is usually the result of environmental and other factors, not mutation alone. For this reason it is unlikely that homosexuality is a repeatedly occurring spontaneous mutation, at least in the classical sense.

A hypervariable mutation?

Dean Hamer, in his book *The Science of Desire: The Search for the Gay Gene and the Biology of Behavior* (Hamer and Copeland, 1994), notes recent advances in molecular genetics which have identified hypervariable DNA sequences which 'change their structure at rates hundreds or thousands of times higher than the normal rate of spontaneous mutation'. Hamer cites the example of the fragile-X gene, the result of increased copies of trinucleotide repeat sequences:

> In most people these sequences are present in 6 to 50 copies, but occasionally they elongate to 200 to more than 1,000 copies – an expansion that causes severe mental retardation and other abnormalities. The 'full mutation' has survived and is present in about 0.1 percent of all X chromosomes, even though these people almost never have children, and several percent of all X chromosomes have a slightly elongated form of the repeats.
>
> (Hamer and Copeland, 1994: 185)

Reasons for this level of variability are unknown, although Hamer suggests there may be some advantage in having a flexible genome which 'at the bottom line' permits DNA variations that severely limit reproductive potential to occur at relatively high frequencies. Support for Hamer comes from William Turner (1995), who proposes a theory of maternal male foetal wastage linked to homosexuality. He suggests this is due to fragility in the Xq28 region, and noted a marked association of X-linked male semi-lethal conditions with male homosexuality.

Turner calculated the sex ratios of mother's and father's siblings and that of their children for ninety male homosexuals drawn from his own sample and a larger if somewhat more speculative sample of pedigrees of famous homosexuals drawn from the literature and a re-analysis of Henry's (1941) data. Turner found markedly imbalanced ratios of maternal uncles to aunts in all categories of his study. For his ninety homosexual men the ratio of maternal uncles to aunts was 132/209. On the maternal side for his combined studies the ratio was 241/367 and the overall male/female ratio of maternal relatives was 310/628. Turner took these figures as a measure of male foetal wastage in the maternal line and this contrasted markedly with ratios of the paternal line which were much less significant (205/177). Turner also calculated a ratio for lesbian women's maternal aunts and uncles of 92/92 which again reinforces his, and our, hesitancy to equate lesbianism with male homosexuality.

Of marked interest in his study was that 28 percent of homosexuals' (including lesbians') mothers had no live-born brothers and 'a further 37% had but one apiece' (Turner, 1995). Turner contrasts this with large scale demographic data which show population rates of women having no brothers at 3.97 percent and only one brother of 7.49 percent. This difference leaps into significance when Turner compares his own figures to the ratio of male/female offspring of fathers and mothers carrying Xq28 male semi-lethal disorders. His comparison data drawn from the literature showed a ratio of 255/508 sons-to-daughters for presumptive male carriers of these conditions yet only 1232/1057 sons-to-daughters for presumptive female carriers. The similarity with his maternal ratio and those for the semi-lethal condition, a much higher rate of suicides, male stillbirths and never married among his homosexual sample, all suggest that whatever is causing these problems at the Xq locus is also implicated in male homosexuality:

> Fetal wastage is universal and frequent. Most occurs in the first few weeks after conception, and affects males more than females . . . The X chromosome is involved in this more than any other . . . This distorted sex ratio (302/610, M/F ratio = 0.495), which involves a high rate of male fetal wastage, corresponds very closely to that of the offspring of fathers in families having male semilethal Xq28 . . . Further, the ratio of all children born to the mothers of these Xq28 corresponds almost exactly with the ratio of those children born to mothers of homosexuals.
>
> (Turner, 1995: 126)

Turner's study is not without its problems. A significant proportion of his sample came from public record sources such as the 'biographies of famous homosexuals', permitting little independent verification of the pedigrees he relies on. Using the pedigree data of Henry (1941) although a little more empirical was again beyond direct verification. Then again many of his summary conclusions conflated gay and lesbian totals despite his acknowledging that they were of apparently differing cause. Of course this study is only suggestive, being comparative in nature, and should be seen as no more than indicative. However, it *is* interesting and Turner makes a number of points that merit further study. Not only does his study suggest the cause of homosexuality lies in the relatively fragile Xq region but it suggests a particular vulnerability on the part of males to disturbances in this region. Turner interprets his findings in molecular terms, suggesting that a molecular imprinting effect accounts for the gradual strengthening of deleterious effects in one's heredity. His data suggests that mothers of homosexuals were themselves born to fathers who carried semi-lethal Xq28 linked genes. The relevant genes coming from unaffected grandfathers are modified by mothers, who are also unaffected by its consequences only becoming manifested in the grand-children. The causes of molecular imprinting are still unclear but seem to involve a process of anticipation where a trait becomes more pronounced through successive generations because alterations to the gene are cumu-lative (Hamer and Copeland, 1994; Reik, 1996). That such a process can directly influence behaviour has been recently found in schizophrenia (Thibaut et al., 1995). For reviews of this fascinating process see Erickson and Lewis (1995) and Haas (1996).

In summary, both Turner and Hamer raise the possibility that instead of homosexuality being a balanced polymorphism it may well be a hyper-variable mutation which in Turner's words 'would require an appreciable and not inconsiderable mutation rate'. Both rely on analogies with the fragile X syndrome to make their point although Turner goes further in suggesting that as with fragile X the process by which the homosexuality gene is activated is in the gradual methylisation of specific trinucleotide repeat sequences or cytosine–guanine pairs. The methylisation process of genes which is more active when passing through mothers gives rise to genetic disorders in their sons at a rate parallel to the degree of methylis-ation. Turner concludes: the fact that females carry two X chromosomes 'may only be one of the reasons why homosexuality occurs in females at a rate half that of homosexuality in males; another reason might be that females carry a shorter, or unmethylated, permutation'. The way ahead to test this possibility is to correlate the incidence of semi-lethal male disorders in families with homosexual sibs directly. We turn now to a consideration of homosexuality as social evolution.

Chapter 4

Homosexuality as social evolution

There is, I wish to suggest, a strong possibility that homosexuality is normal in the biological sense, that it is a distinctive beneficent behavior that evolved as an important element of early human social organisation. Homosexuals may be the genetic carriers of some of mankind's rare altruistic impulses.

(Wilson, 1978: 143)

If we cannot find a gene for homosexuality does this rule out biosocial explanations entirely? While social constructivist critiques would like to think that homosexuality needs a gene to be positively selected from generation to generation there are other ways of achieving the same end. What has to be remembered is that the ultimate purpose of biosocial theorising is to explain how we increase our overall genetic representation in subsequent generations. The analysis of individual traits such as homosexuality is to see how they contribute to this end. If the goal is to pass on as much of our genetic message as we can then a whole variety of cultural prescriptions and individual choices will effect this goal. The survival of our genotype is as much a matter of individual action as it is of physical (biological) evolution. If we act wisely then we increase the chances of our genes surviving. When our individual efforts are aggregated across a population, the same selective pressures which apply to our physical evolution decide the relative merits of any one individual action. This coevolution then selects for behaviours which work and discards those which don't, so social evolution is as much about differential survival as physical evolution. What has to be remembered is that we as individuals are not selecting for any one trait but for the continuity of our entire genetic message. Evolution on the other hand retains individual traits that favour current circumstances. In practice, social and physical evolution work together to decide one's genetic future. Even when one's genetic endowment hinders one's reproductive chances, social evolution selects for traits and behaviour which advance survivability. That is, social and physical evolution are additive, and deficits in one area may be overcome by advantages in the other. It is on this basis that homosexuality as a behaviour which reduces one's reproductive chances may nevertheless advantage one's genetic destiny.

What is important in this equation is that this process has been going on for a long time. As a consequence we all share common genes and our nature reflects our social evolution. *Homo sapiens* is a social species and the basis of our social organisation is cooperation among those with whom we share a reproductive interest. As in all social species this bond is strongest with relatives whose genes are closest to our own. Theories of homosexuality which rely on social evolution posit an advantage to homosexual behaviour which aids relatives' reproduction, ensuring that close copies of their own genes are carried forward. What these mechanisms are, and more importantly why homosexuals decide to disqualify themselves, are interesting questions we will address. However, social evolution in this scenario ultimately favours genotypes rather than behaviours. How likely is a social evolution of homosexuality?

On the nature of natural selection and human evolution

Andrew Huxley (1983) noted: 'It is often forgotten that Darwin himself made no claim that natural selection is the only mechanism in evolution.' It may be that homosexuality is not a matter of physical but of social evolution. We may have unconsciously fallen into characteristic patterns of behaviour which are not programmed by our genes but whose similarity, ubiquity and perseverance in our species argue a certain utility. Are there positive evolutionary strategies which some of us follow at the expense of direct reproduction? It is entirely possible that homosexual behaviour is so inherently beneficial that it arises again and again as circumstances dictate its necessity. Yet does social evolution follow the same logic as physical laws of mutation, natural selection and inheritance? It seems so. Good ideas reward those who use them. Whether homosexuality provides immediate reproductive benefits is an open question but superior sexual strategies, and that is what we are ultimately talking about, will aid our survivability and this is the first step towards a 2 percent advantage.

If social evolution has a mechanism analogous to inheritance as its driving force, it is imitation. The rapid evolution of our species may be entirely due to our capacity to imitate each other – a more literal case of 'monkey see, monkey do' than we might imagine. There are immediate analogies between natural selection and imitation. This is best seen in technological advances. Chance events, or a craftsman puzzling over ways to better his craft, gave rise to new technologies and these to a direct reproductive differential. The artisan who first filled an animal skin or hollow gourd with water to cross a desert enjoyed a direct reproductive success over those who stayed and died of thirst. In a less obvious way, social innovation may provide similar advantages. The first ape-man who accidentally associated a sound with food and gave it a recognisable meaning for his clan set our species on the road to the glories of language. Technological and social innovation translates to direct benefits for the individual and to imitation by those with whom they associate. The point is that we spend most of our time with near relatives, and the benefits of social evolution may be more a matter of kin favouritism than of individuals surviving to reproduce.

As an evolutionary process, imitation is as direct a mechanism as selection but infinitely faster than differential survivability:

> [Social innovation] is analogous to transmutation of species by mutation, selection and inheritance, but in the latter case the effect is picked out by differential survival, a process immensely slower than imitation by a human successor, and correspondingly evolution is an immensely slower process than even traditional development of human skills.
>
> (Huxley, 1983: 12)

Now for theorists since the seminal papers of Alexander, Durham and Irons (Chagnon and Irons, 1979) the key question has been: does social evolution obey the same laws as physical evolution? Are characteristic human action patterns rigorously selected for and against on the basis of their utility? If so, what mechanism translates social or technological success into evolutionary imperatives? Is it reproductive success, behavioural flexibility or the sheer inescapable logic of 'this works, that doesn't, go ye therefore and do likewise'. This is a large question and an interested reader should start with William Durham's *Coevolution: Genes, Culture and Human Diversity* (1991) and Charles Lumsden and Edward Wilson's *Genes, Mind, and Culture: The Coevolutionary Process* (1981).

For our purposes, it is sufficient that these action patterns exist. The rapid evolution of social arrangements, skills and organisation, led to a circular process in which social change necessitated further social action, leading to rapid evolution. The paradox of rapid social evolution by trial and error, is that it led to a fixity of behaviour as our species fell into effective ways of responding to certain common dilemmas. This in turn led to typical response patterns, or behavioural scripts which were easily learned and reinforced by custom. The commonality of human laws and customs reflects the utility of these behavioural scripts. While our species is a very new player on the evolutionary block, we have rapidly acquired fixed social responses because they work and in working pay fitness-enhancing dividends. Still, while rational purpose is an immensely faster process than natural selection, it is ultimately constrained by our fitness, and as Gallup and Suarez (1983) note: 'Evolution is not represented by the survival of the fittest but by the perpetuation of the most reproductively viable configuration of genes.' We all die, so whatever advantages we accrue in life, or the social and technological advances we may model, are meaningless unless these enhance our reproduction or that of our relatives. Unless we do so, our contribution to evolution is zero. So social evolution must eventually pay a dividend in enhanced reproduction. How then does homosexuality pay us a coevolutionary dividend?

KIN SELECTION

It is not immediately obvious why we humans invest as heavily in our kin as we do. Parental investment starts at conception and ends with the courts ensuring that our last bequests conform to customary rules for benefiting our descendants and kin. In the following discussion, which has as its premise that we seek to maximise our genetic representation in subsequent generations, it is well-worth remembering that we humans already share most of our genes in common with our primate cousins and with each other. It is estimated that we share about 98.8 percent of our genes with chimpanzees of the species *Pan paniscus* (Gribbin and Gribbin, 1993) and the extent of genetic variation within humanity is less than 0.1 percent (Lewontin, 1993; Hamer and Copeland, 1994). These figures suggest that human variability rests on relatively few genes and that most of these are deleterious mutations which are succumbing to normalising selection. However, the variability we see is sufficient to identify kin and we have a great interest in the welfare of our descendants. Why this is so is one of the great understated problems of human evolutionary theory. Darwin's theory of natural selection argues that parents, usually mothers, care for their offspring because it is a duty of nature. That we might desire offspring may be explained by a reproductive urge but this does not explain why we favour our descendants over others of our species. Many, if not most species, put little effort into offspring and even in those which do, ours does to an unusual degree. In our species, the long delay before children are capable of helping themselves is usually given as the reason for favouring kin but this parental investment does not explain why we have not organised childrearing communally as have many social species.

This difficulty increases as we move from Darwinian to genetic explanations. The genetic basis of behaviour is, as we saw in the last chapter, an open question. While it is relatively straightforward to argue that reproductive urges are encoded in our genes, it is more difficult to argue that complex social behaviours such as childrearing or kin favouritism are also genetically encoded. We will come to consider why genes may

nish in this respect but the difficulty remains. Parental investment
d bonding therefore suffice as reasons for the preference relatives
clearly show each other, however slender an explanation this may be.
How does this preference for our kin select for homosexuality?

There are several kin selection accounts of homosexuality which date
to Robert Trivers who, in a one-liner in 1974, suggested it as a possible
mechanism for homosexuality. Kin selection refers to practices which
favour kin over unrelated members of one's social group. Such favouritism
increases kin's chances of reproductive success and as they carry common
genes to our own they increase the likelihood of replicates, close copies
of our genes, being passed to future generations. Any action which
increases the prevalence of our genes in the next generation, including
the indirect reproductive benefits of kin selection, is called inclusive fitness
(Hamilton, 1964). As we are all fairly closely related genetically, in practice, kin selection tends to operate on familial rather than consanguineous
lines and includes adoptees and stepchildren and in-laws and spouses who
are genetically unrelated (Futuyma and Risch, 1984; Sherman and
Holmes, 1985; Barkow, 1989). Wilson (1975, 1978), picking up on Trivers'
idea, popularised the notion that perhaps homosexuality's prevalence
might be explained by the benefits exclusive homosexuals derive from
helping kin.

The literature on kin selective accounts of homosexuality is fairly
muddled and one of its difficulties, detracting from its plausibility, is a
confusion of kin selections. Kin selection scenarios take three main forms.
First, it may be that a gene for homosexuality is maintained in a population by kin selection. This type of kin selection preserves a homosexual
gene because we select for replicates and homosexuality is transmitted
as part of this package. In this scenario, the deleterious effects of the
homosexuality gene are balanced by kin selective advantage. Second,
there may be a gene for some other behaviour whose action is enhanced
by kin selective means. Thus Wilson (1975, 1978) suggests that a gene for
altruism may promote homosexuality, which is then a social consequence
of its action. In this scenario, homosexuality is just a social behaviour
without a genetic basis but arises as a consequence of a gene for some
other trait. The third form of kin selection for homosexuality is purely
social with no genetic component. Homosexuality is chosen because the
homosexual opts for a non-reproductive lifestyle and relies on relatives
to ensure his genetic destiny. In practice, these three scenarios shade into
one another and most kin selective theorists use them interchangeably
without realising the confusion this creates. As we will see, kin selection
has had a bad press and perhaps the reasons reflect this conceptual
confusion.

KIN SELECTION FOR A HOMOSEXUALITY GENE

Perhaps the most straightforward account of kin selection is that there is a gene for homosexuality and that a social behaviour, altruism towards kin, selects for it. It is worth starting with Wilson.

> The homosexual members of primitive societies may have functioned as helpers, either while hunting in company with other men or in domestic occupations at the dwelling sites. Freed from the special obligations of parental duties, they could have operated with special efficiency in assisting close relatives. Genes favoring homosexuality could then be sustained at a high equilibrium by kin selection alone. It remains to be said that if such genes really exist they are almost certainly incomplete in penetrance and variable in expressivity, meaning that which bearers of the genes develop the behavioral trait and to what degree depends on the presence of modifier genes and the influence of the environment.
>
> (Wilson, 1975: 555)

Wilson suggests that men who feel at a reproductive disadvantage for some reason may instinctively subordinate their sexuality into non-reproductive lines such as homosexuality, which frees up time and resources to support close kin. These kin would then have a better chance of reproducing and of carrying forward genes common to both the homosexual and his kin. If this differential were sufficiently large, then the greater survival of common genes would balance the loss of specific qualities that could only be passed on by direct reproduction. Wilson's theory assumes homosexual men have a reduced reproductive potential, that they deliberately compensate for this and that their immediate relatives are markedly more fecund than the population average. How likely is this scenario?

There is virtually no evidence for or against the kin selective hypothesis (Buss, 1994; Dickemann, 1995). What slender research there is tries to demonstrate that gay men have greater resources than heterosexual men (Hewitt, 1995), the implication being that they will use their wealth to benefit kin (Salais and Fischer, 1995). However, there are no studies which demonstrate that homosexual men's near relatives have larger families and few studies which show that gay men favour their kin more than heterosexual men. While James Weinrich (1977) spent a goodly proportion of his doctoral thesis arguing that tribal shamanists were often ritually homosexual and that this necessarily benefited their kin, part of the difficulty in evaluating the merits of this scenario is that the increasing pace of social evolution over the last three millennia has taken us far from the tight tribal group in which the effect has presumably arisen (Dickemann, 1993). The utility of the kin selective hypothesis as an explanation of homosexuality depends on the assumptions one cares to make about its genesis, yet gazing into the twilight of human antiquity is always a chancy business. Comparative anthropological studies of present day tribal cultures fail to demonstrate a shamanist-homosexuality effect at anything like the universality necessary to support a kin selection hypothesis (Futuyma and Risch, 1984). Perhaps the implication is that homosexuality is a behavioural script which has reached its use-by date. What once was a sensible strategy in the small close-knit tribal groups which typified most of human evolution is no longer suited to a mass society. Here we face the difficulties of extrapolating from cultures which are no longer representative of the overwhelming mass of humanity (Weinrich, 1995).

For these reasons, the kin selective hypothesis of homosexuality has not commanded a huge following even though kin selection is one of the great successes of biosocial theorising, explaining many other puzzling aspects of natural selection. Still, the scenario has even more fundamental problems. As we noted in Chapter 1, mathematics is against kin selection for homosexuality. The kin selective account assumes that those of us who choose lifelong celibacy can still enhance our genetic interests for, in Trivers' words, 'One need merely assume that the nonreproducer thereby increases the reproductive success of relatives by an amount, which when devalued by the degrees of relatedness, is greater than the nonreproducer would have achieved on his own' (Trivers, 1974). However, what is ignored in this succinct equation is that genes limit rather than enhance our genetic representation *in subsequent generations* via replicates. Our genetic interest in this instance is not served by passing on as complete a copy of our genes as we may, because this would include detrimental genes which will decrease and further devalue our overall inclusive fitness. That is, passing on a detrimental gene may limit the spread of all of our genes. What flows from this is that simply having more replicates in the next generation is an inadequate explanation of homosexuality. What matters is the relative advantage of these replicates.

A goodly proportion of the conceptual confusion inherent in kin selective scenarios of homosexuality flows from not distinguishing between two vital but separate questions: *what causes homosexuality to spread* and *what helps it survive.* Even if we assume a gene for homosexuality (or rare altruistic impulses) as Wilson does, kin selection is still an inadequate explanation in and of itself for homosexuality's survival, for at least two accounts of kin selection see homosexuality as a deleterious behaviour. While there is no genetic link between a gene for homosexuality and kin selection (it is not necessary here to assume a gene for kin selection), inclusive fitness mechanisms underlie most genetic scenarios of homosexuality, making kin selection a likely vehicle for homosexual transmission but not for its long-term survival. There is a fair bit of fuzzy thinking here. Kin selection *is* an efficient strategy for maximising one's inclusive fitness; the game plan is to pass *all* of one's genes forward, but this is *not* an explanation for any particular gene's survival.

For conceptual clarity, separating these two questions let us more clearly assess the kin selective scenario's merits. Increasing one's overall genetic representation in the next generation is only part of the story and selection still operates on the genes we promulgate, good and bad. For this reason, a gene for homosexuality is less likely to survive if homosexuals are simply assisting kin to have more children. Logically, increasing the numbers of reproductively disabled relatives in subsequent generations will decrease rather than increase one's overall genetic representation, irrespective of how many close relatives one has in the next generation. Even if homosexuals recognised their reproductive disability early on and put a large measure of resources into their kin, they would simply be aiding the diminution of their overall genetic contribution by having more homosexually disabled relatives, *unless of course the homosexual gene confers some other reproductive advantage to those kin*.

So, helping relatives to have more children will not retain the homosexuality gene long-term. A supposedly deleterious trait such as homosexuality, even if over-represented in the next generation by a kin selective advantage, will quickly become rarer unless it is replenished in future generations, or your relatives are fiercely inbreeding, or it provides a markedly increased fecundity. Homosexuality does run in families and may be expressed in subsequent generations but even if these extreme forms of kin selection increase the occurrence of homosexual genes passed forward, this still does not answer why the gene(s) persist. If they do, kin selection theory merely returns us to the problem we started with in the first paragraph of Chapter 1; that increases in inclusive fitness flow from a continuing reproductive advantage, not simply from having more nieces and nephews.

Let us now support these assertions. What is crucial to the above argument is not the raw numbers of offspring produced but the degree of advantage conferred by kin selection. For example, if our relatives' reproductive advantage is *smaller* than the ultimate liability of having homosexual offspring, then although passing on the homosexuality gene may provide a substantial head-start advantage for a few generations this will inevitably be extinguished. Assume that a homosexual celibate has five brothers (5.6 offspring is the average in current populations not practising reliable contraception) and that via kin selection he helps each of his siblings have an extra child. In the first generation there will be thirty offspring and this generational scenario then repeats itself. Let us also assume that the approximate incidence of male homosexuality in subsequent generations is 25 percent (about the incidence for fraternal gay twins) and for the sake of simplicity we will assume that all offspring

Table 4.1 Differential reproductive success and descendants via kin selection
and direct reproduction

No. of direct descendants by generations	Kin selective	Direct
1	6.00	5.00
2	30.00	25.00
3	135.00	125.00
4	607.50	625.00
5	2,733.75	3,125.00
6	12,301.88	15,625.00
7	55,358.44	78,125.00
8	249,112.97	390,625.00
9	1,121,008.36	1,953,125.00
10	5,044,537.62	9,765,625.00

Note: Assumes a kin selective advantage of 17 percent and an exclusive homosexual
penetrance of 25 percent per generation

are male. Now if these homosexual offspring are celibate, what happens
to an initial kin selective advantage over subsequent generations even if
each heterosexual brother has an extra child? We will compare this to a
straight man with four brothers only, each producing five children. From
Table 4.1 you will see that the initial reproductive advantage lasts for
only three generations and despite an ongoing kin selective advantage,
after ten generations produces less than half as many offspring as the
heterosexual man, so the advantage is quickly extinguished. Assuming a
range of reduced, rather than non-existent reproductive capacities, leads
to the same result only more slowly. Modelling reproductive success
against an inherent reproductive liability shows a kin selection disadvantage rather than a gain.

However, this is only half the story. What we are interested in is
the coefficient of relatedness of descendants expressed as number of
descendants times degree of relatedness. Will a head-start advantage
manifest itself in a greater degree of cumulative inclusive fitness overall?
From Figure 4.1 you will see the above scenario represented in inclusive
fitness terms using a simple weighted sum method. Although there are
substantial theoretical difficulties with this method (Grafen, 1982; Gayley,
1993) it is robust enough for our illustrative purposes. The cumulative
percentage of both men's reproductive strategies is evident and is the
same as before.

To take the converse case, what if the initial reproductive advantage is
larger than the reproductive liability of producing homosexual offspring
– wouldn't this rescue kin selection as a selective mechanism? Yes and
no. What must be remembered from Chapter 3 is that we are not talking
about the survival of individuals but rather the frequencies of particular
genes in a population. Individual survival is only a proximate means for

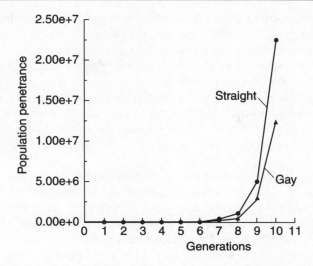

Figure 4.1 The difference in population penetrance of direct versus indirect
inclusive fitness

Note: Calculation uses simple weighted sum method to calculate total population
penetrance of two genotypes selecting by direct and indirect (kin-selective) reproduction

homosexuality's survival. The net effect of having a positive selective
pressure from kin selection is to ensure that the overall proportion of
homosexual genes increases in the population. This in turn gradually
alters the balance of kin selective reproductive gain versus homosexual
liability from a positive to negative ratio by increasing the percentages
of nonreproducers. We have here what population biologists call a predation cycle. Kin selective breeding success ensures more relatives but
more reproductively disabled ones in your direct line. So as the advantage
turns to a disadvantage, producing more homosexual kin reduces one's
genetic representation in subsequent generations. Of course these gay
relatives are all assisting their kin to gain a kin selective advantage also,
but because they are all related the scenario becomes one of diminishing
returns, which ultimately limits even this saving grace.

Somewhat paradoxically, this liability is self-correcting and lets us avoid
too intricate mathematics. As you accumulate a higher incidence of homosexual descendants, your relatives' very breeding success will sow the
seeds of its own destruction. More gay descendants means a declining
reproduction to the point that, having almost flushed themselves from
the gene pool, the game resets itself and continuing kin selective altruism
once more becomes an advantageous strategy to follow. In an ideal
world, this kin selective edge should eventually balance itself against a
reproductive liability at whatever level of advantage you care to specify,
gradually oscillating until a stable balance is reached. However, in the

real world, varying rates of kin selection among kin ensures that we have a dynamic solution in which the kin selective advantage never reaches zero, the point at which the homosexual gene should extinguish itself, but often comes close. The mathematics of this scenario are tricky (Grafen, 1982; Kitcher, 1985) but at least some advantage may be achieved by inclusive fitness means. This dynamic scenario is a common one when modelling predator–prey relationships and could easily theoretically account for the rapid spread and subsequent survival of a supposedly deleterious homosexual gene in the human population by essentially social means.

So far so good, but we must now specify a realistic level of advantage and this is where the ultimate difficulty lies with this version of the kin selective scenario. What must be remembered is that each of us are not just aiming at replicating our genes but at maximising them in subsequent generations. Realistically we have most direct control of our own reproduction and to a lesser extent that of our children. Beyond this point our genetic posterity is out of our hands. So rather than a dynamic model of reproductive success being appropriate, we must use a linear approach for at least these two generations (this assumes kin selective altruism is a conscious process). Kin selection will work only to the extent that each person can gain an advantage greater than that of his own direct reproduction and greater than that of his peers. So the homosexual man following a kin selective strategy is in competition with the rest of his species. As each of us automatically enjoys a replicate advantage by virtue of his siblings also feeling a compulsion to have children, a person following a kin selective scenario is gambling that he can exceed the number of children he would otherwise have himself by increasing his relatives' reproductive rates. When looked at this way, kin selection only works where reproductive advantage is markedly above any realistic level of enhanced reproduction.

To put this in perspective let us look at a simple break-even scenario. Ruse (1981) noted that in forgoing having his own children a man would have to increase a sibling's level of reproduction by 100 percent just to break even in selecting for replicant genes. Another way to achieve this is to increase several siblings' reproduction by a margin which would provide at least twice as many children as he could have himself. Returning to our example, this requires the gay man's five brothers to have an extra child each. As Baker and Bellis (1995) noted, given the constraints imposed by infant mortality and limitations on fertility, average family rates of offspring historically were quite low (about three children surviving to reproduction). So it is highly unlikely that there have has been sufficiently large enough reproductive differentials between gay and straight lines to support such a high level of kin selective advantage across the millennia. Kin selection as presented by Wilson and others seems an improbable gamble statistically.

Putting this another way, kin selection may spread the homosexuality gene but does not aid its ultimate survival. So an initial positive reproductive advantage to heterosexual relatives will ultimately decline as a function of its success. What this suggests is that homosexuality is maintained in the population by other than kin selective means even if kin selection may have first spread the genes throughout the population. It may be that the gay gene provides an advantage by balanced superior heterozygotic fitness or other heterotic means, which is aided and reinforced by kin selection. This is probably implicitly assumed in Wilson's (1975) mention of 'sustained at a high equilibrium'. However, this is best explained as heterotic advantage, and gene transmission by kin selection without this advantage is going nowhere. Reproduction by proxy obeys the same laws as direct reproduction but at a diminished advantage for homosexuals.

As a consequence, having even limited numbers of offspring outweighs the advantages gained from kin selection. If it were otherwise, straight men would limit their own offspring to maximise their inclusive fitness via their siblings' children. Clearly this is a nonsense and so the largest component of genetic success is derived from direct rather than indirect reproduction. In the battle of the genes, heterosexuals also automatically enjoy inclusive fitness advantages from their kin having children. So it is the impact of homosexual genes rather than the reproductive differential provided by homosexual men helping their relatives which must be the ultimate advantage derived from kin selection. The mathematics of this scenario is far more complex than our simple analysis and in the real world, as we have seen, homosexual men do have children, although at lower rates than do exclusive heterosexuals. Perhaps this partial reproduction offsets the difficulties of reaching a sufficient advantage via kin selection. However, this is unlikely over the long term, as partial reproduction also presumably proportionately reduces resources and opportunities available for kin selective altruism (for a contrary view see Weinrich, 1987b).

KIN SELECTION FOR GENES OTHER THAN HOMOSEXUALITY

As discussed in Chapter 3, homosexuality may be caused by genes which are only incidentally linked to homosexuality. That is, a gene for increased sex drive may carry a homosexual gene forward in subsequent generations simply because it is commonly linked at genetic recombination. The reproductive advantage of an enhanced sex drive, or a greater seductive potential, or whatever, ensures that the homosexuality gene is balanced in the gene pool, despite its deleterious impact on reproduction. In an analogous way, perhaps homosexuality is a consequence of some other genetic process which is selected for by kin selection. Wilson, in promoting kin selection as a vehicle for homosexual transmission, is unclear on the precise mechanism. In his earlier discussion (Wilson, 1975) he appears to favour homosexuality as a gene selected in its own right. However, in his more extended treatment Wilson implied that it is a consequence of some other genetic process: 'homosexuals may be the genetic carriers of some of mankind's rare altruistic impulses' (Wilson, 1978). The implication is that the genes being selected for are those of altruism rather than of homosexuality. Presumably then, homosexuality is a choice consequent on a recognition of some disability likely to reduce the person's reproductive potential. Unlike the first form of kin selection discussed above, the genesis of this process is genetic, with the kin selective trait being under the control of a gene for altruism or whatever. This meets the statistical difficulties we noted above because the gene itself confers some advantage which increases relatives' fecundity.

Perhaps the major difficulty of this variant of kin selection theory is in establishing a necessary connection between poor reproduction and choosing a homosexual lifestyle. We will return to this matter in our discussions of homosexuality as a lifestyle choice. We now need to consider what advantage is being selected for by kin selection. Although there are many accounts of kin selection almost all assume that homosexual men are more altruistic than heterosexual men (Trivers, 1974; Wilson, 1975, 1978; Weinrich, 1977, 1987a, 1995; Irons, 1979; Ruse, 1981, 1988; Hughes, 1988). Irrespective of whatever other benefits homosexuality may bestow, if homosexual men reproduce less than their sibs, they impair their own and their sibs' inclusive fitness. Only by a system of payback which enhances kin's reproductive fecundity may this breach of inclusive fitness be repaired. This assumes that homosexual men are conscious of this necessity and that they feel an empathetic obligation to reward their kin with resources to enhance their fecundity. Although generally left as an unstated corollary, they must do so at a rate much greater than that of their kin to them. This seems to be one of the sticking points of the shamanist theory in which the flow of resources to the tribal shaman seems as much from kin as towards them (Churchill, 1967).

Debra Salais reviewed this point, finding there were no empirical tests of the altruistic assumption and proceeded to assess the proposition that gay men are more empathetic and by implication more altruistic than their heterosexual peers (Salais and Fischer, 1995). Her sample was seventy-six homosexuals and fifty-one heterosexual men drawn from a matched population from Dignity, a gay group loosely attached to the Catholic Church, and a sample of undergraduate and postgraduate psychology students. After all demographic, age and locality variables were matched, the gay men were significantly higher on a 64-item empathy scale than her heterosexual sample. Salais and Fischer note a consistent relationship between empathetic responses and altruism in the literature, while acknowledging that altruistic tendencies may not readily translate to altruistic actions. This small study, the only empirical test of the altruistic hypothesis to date, should be treated cautiously as the authors note that this finding does not suggest that this inferred altruism would necessarily advantage kin. Gay men may prefer to place their resources with other gay men, a finding of more than one study (Hewitt, 1995).

Beyond this study, there is little empirical support for altruistic genes as a vehicle for kin selection. However, we may model aspects of a kin selection hypothesis. The essence of all forms of inclusive fitness is genetic selfishness, that is, the individual is selected to look after his or her genetic interests first because they are the unique possessor of their complement of genes. Only identical twins share the same unique message, which perhaps goes part of the way towards explaining the special relationship they enjoy – a special case of genetic selfishness. This selfishness is at once the major hurdle that kin selection theory has to surmount: selfishness should first be applied to oneself, then to kin. This could be tested. Given that 20–40 percent of identical twins are discordant for their sexuality, it should be possible to assess the direction of helping provided by the gay twin to his straight brother. This genetic selfishness would be reflected in a rate of helping that should be double that given to other siblings who only share half their genes.

However, assuming that we favour kin because we have a genetic propensity towards kin altruism, or, in Barkow's (1989) words, 'a gene that will promote the development of a psychological mechanism likely to increase the probability of altruistic behaviour', then we must have a valuing system. Kin selective altruism is not altruism in the usual sense, that is, behaviour which is selfless, rather it is prosocial behaviour which returns a benefit to both the homosexual and his kin. The homosexual celibate will evaluate the costs of helping to ensure that he receives due benefit from such help. Barkow (1989) identifies four calculations underlying this process:

> These calculations include assessing (1) the value of any aid to its potential recipient (that is, the extent to which the aid proffered would increase the inclusive fitness of the recipient); (2) the probability of risk to the donor of the aid (the probability that supplying the aid would reduce its fitness); (3) the probability that the recipient of the aid does indeed bear a copy of the gene for altruism.
>
> (Barkow, 1989: 48)

To these three, Barkow adds a fourth, that of the 'fitness-investment-potential of the recipient', that is, the degree of reproductive fitness both realised and potential. Now if these sorts of calculations underlie the homosexual's decision to forgo direct reproduction by aiding kin, then Wilson's hypothesis is directly amenable to test. The homosexual's patterns of aid should benefit kin rather than non-kin; should then aid kin in proportion to the degree of relatedness; and then aid kin commensurate with their assessed degree of future reproductive fitness investment potential. Rather than these genes being Wilson's 'rare altruistic impulses' we should all have genes for altruism, as presumably we all share in the benefits of inclusive fitness and should be selected to give what help we can to kin, irrespective of our sexual orientation.

So a further test would be that homosexual men are helping relatives at levels far above a heterosexual baseline. This is a necessary condition to ensure the reproductive differential required by Wilson's scenario. This level of helping should be dramatically and immediately obvious, as a homosexual man in forgoing having his own children would have to increase a sibling's level of reproduction by 100 percent just to break even in selecting for replicant genes (Ruse, 1981). Note however that this assumes that homosexuals are *forgoing* reproduction. What is important is the assumed reproductive potential of these men. If the potential homosexual is irrevocably disabled from reproduction by his condition, then the above necessity at least to double a relative's offspring is spurious, as any increase gained by kin selection, however modest, would be a net gain. Clearly, homosexual men do have children but not as many as heterosexuals. Are there types of homosexual men who would have no children irrespective of the powerful evolutionary urge to paternity?

As we are all the winners of a long evolutionary struggle and each of us has an unbroken lineage back to the earliest humans, and through them to our hominid and primate ancestors, and on in succession to the earliest single cell organism that reproduced, this is a powerful urge to gainsay. If reproduction is deliberately forgone, then ensuring succession by replication would need to be supported by powerful altruism; anything less would see the gradual extinction of these genes.

Given that we are a social species we habitually engage in prosocial behaviour, most obviously to our mates, who are usually genetically unrelated. Genes for cooperation, or prosocial behaviour, or even altruism, would have a strong selective advantage and would encourage behaviour which builds the social bond. For Wilson's kin selective hypothesis to work, homosexual men would need to show marked patterns of helping near relatives and these patterns would show a finely developed fitness-investment-potential. As Barkow observed in his general discussion of this point, we would select for relatives who are liable to return our investment by breeding prolifically. Age and gender and other variables would be key determinants for helping. For example, a greater return on helping would be gained from younger siblings, who presumably have a greater breeding potential and return us an extra head-start dividend. In a sexually liberated society (unrestrained breeding scenario) perhaps gay men should favour heterosexual brothers pursuing R breeding strategies rather than sisters so as to maximise their potential reproductive return. Obviously, this helping calculus is not entirely based on biological variables. Sexual preference and other social variables would mediate altruistic behaviour, with gay men less likely to aid determinedly bachelor sibs, or for that matter gay ones.

This scenario also assumes that we have a highly discriminating sense of relatedness and that we are able efficiently to assess coefficients of consanguinity. Here at least is a theory that readily permits possibilities of empirically testing the kin selection hypothesis, by assessing the direction and quantum of help given by homosexual men to their siblings. Given our discussions in Chapter 3 on the degrees of paternity uncertainty approaching 30 percent in some cultures, we could assess the amount of help given by homosexual men to their siblings and then by DNA fingerprinting assess their degree of relatedness. Full siblings, those sharing both parents, have a coefficient of 50 percent, half siblings only 25 percent. If the kin selective hypothesis is working, homosexual men should invariably help the closer sibling. How we assess relatedness in these circumstances would depend on our knowledge of paternity (or maternity) and this would need to be controlled for. Given the findings of Baker and Bellis (1995), there should be sufficient numbers of gay men who have siblings they think are full relatives but are not, for this to be a viable test of the hypothesis. Beyond that it is an open question how humans recognise their kin. While animals depend on olfactory and other clues, the matter is undecided for humans (Porter, 1987). As our species views relatedness on familial rather than consanguineous lines this should provide an ideal test of the altruism hypothesis, made all the more rigorous when you consider that we all share the vast majority of our genes in common.

So where are we? This variant of the kin selection hypothesis is more theoretically robust than the first because it does not rely on a gene for homosexuality which should always trend towards extinction. A gene for altruism (or whatever) would be a positive gene and counterbalance a reduced reproductive potential. The homosexuality gene may then be either close linked to the altruism gene or to a purely personal or social choice; the genetic effect in either case is the same – helping kin. The only difficulty with this view is the perennial question of why the altruism gene does not spread throughout the community and reach a point of fixity in which all possessing it share its benefits equally? The simple answer is that it has and that kin selection is more a matter of resources and opportunity than special genetic advantages. When viewed this way Wilson's kin selective scenario for homosexuals seems less a matter of 'rare altruistic impulses' than of simple necessity faced by a potentially disabled reproducer.

KIN SELECTION AND A SOCIAL PREFERENCE FOR HOMOSEXUALITY

What if homosexuality is not inherent? Although there are links between homosexuality and shamanism in some contemporary tribal cultures, what if there were no necessary connections between kin selection and homosexuality? Some men may choose to be gay and some gay men may choose to favour kin. If sufficient benefits accrue to those men who adopt a gay lifestyle, they may provide sufficiently attractive models to encourage those around them to aspire to homosexuality. As we are more likely to imitate those with whom we have the greatest degree of contact and these are likely to have been kin in our antiquity, perhaps imitation is driving kin selection for homosexuality. Under these circumstances homosexuality may become a hereditary occupation reserved for younger kinfolk, a feature of several contemporary shamanist systems. In these circumstances, kin selection may only have an incidental relationship with homosexuality. Michael Ruse first pointed this out when he noted that the kin selective hypothesis does not necessarily require 'special genes separating homosexuals from heterosexuals' (Ruse, 1988). Ruse was making this point in considering whether we might all have a genetic capacity for homosexuality but the point applies equally if we do not. Kin selection might work just as well if homosexuality was not inherited but simply a matter of choice. In assessing this proposition we face another instance of the preference versus orientation problem we explored in Chapter 1 – which came first: a recognition of reproductive disability, or the homosexuality?

The literature abounds in studies showing that some gay men have much higher than expected incidence of effeminate characteristics in childhood and adolescence, the so-called sissy-boy syndrome (Whitam, 1977; Grellert et al., 1982; Green, 1987; Zuger, 1988, 1989; Bailey et al., 1991; Pillard, 1991; Bailey et al., 1993), leading Weinrich (1995) to observe that 'an association between gender nonconformity *in childhood* and homosexuality *in adulthood* is so well supported it is undeniable'. Still there are methodological problems in just accepting gay men's recollections that they were nonconformist children (Ross, 1980). Looked at from the other end, effeminate children would need to become gay adults in sufficient numbers to show that early gender nonconformity leads to homosexuality and this is less overwhelmingly demonstrated in the literature. That many gay men were not sissy-boys and many sissy-boys do not become homosexuals must make us cautious of this linkage. In any case, for this kin selective scenario to work it is not necessary that early effeminacy reliably signal a poor potential reproducer; it is sufficient that either the person or their kin decide that it might be so. Even this assumption is unnecessary. Simply deciding that a gay lifestyle is attractive and lucrative enough is sufficient if it allows resources to flow to kin to offset loss of one's own genetic contribution. Notwithstanding, the implication drawn from most of kin selective accounts is that early effeminacy signals an impaired reproductive capacity and a choice of a gay lifestyle.

Despite the apparent simplicity of this version of the kin selective scenario it is not without its difficulties and is bedevilled by the problem – is a homosexual lifestyle a choice made by heterosexuals with poor prospects, or is homosexuality a recognition of the inevitable and kin selection a reaction, or tactic to offset reduced reproduction? As we have seen it may well be both and there are many homosexualities, but Wilson argues it is genetic and that homosexuality is inherent and that kin selection selects for replicates. However, as we have seen, kin selection in these circumstances is an inadequate explanation of a homosexual gene's survival. The difficulty is that unless kin selective accounts argue for a gene for homosexuality, then helping behaviour may select for one's genetic posterity but not necessarily for one's homosexuality. Put another way, if there is no gene for homosexuality why would helping kin necessarily transmit homosexuality from generation to generation ahead of any other behaviour? If, on the other hand, homosexuality arose before its recognition (that there is a gene or some other cause for homosexuality), then kin selection may be a consequence of the cause rather than social evolution and a discussion of its relevance to the homosexuality debate belongs in the set of selective scenarios covered in Chapter 3, not here in a discussion on social and cultural evolution. If, however, homosexuality is a matter of choice or imitation then a more immediate difficulty presents itself. Ruse (1988), in his commentary on kin selection poses two questions that need to be answered if we will accept homosexuality as a lifestyle choice:

> First one looks for reasons why the homosexual (or rather person-who-is-to-develop-into-a-homosexual) would be a less than efficient personal reproducer. One expects the future homosexual to have been, potentially, a rather poor quality heterosexual. Second, one looks for reasons why the homosexual would be good at aiding close relatives. One looks for abilities in the homosexual that suggest he/she could turn society towards the reproductive ends of his/her family.
>
> (Ruse, 1988: 135)

To these questions I would add a third, even more fundamental to my mind – why should a man who disqualifies himself from direct reproduction *necessarily* choose homosexuality as a compensation? In 1987 James Weinrich asked rhetorically 'why wouldn't the reproductive altruist be asexual rather than homosexual?' (Weinrich, 1987b), a question he had answered at length in his doctoral thesis (Weinrich, 1977). The answer to this question is implied in Wilson's assertion that such men are not neuters: they do have a sex drive but one that is unlikely to favour successful reproduction. More immediately, we might ask: why they do not turn to other forms of heterosexual expression ahead of homosexuality. To demonstrate a kin selective effect one has to show a causal link between Ruse's two questions. Why should poor reproducers choose homosexuality rather than asexual bachelorhood, or if their sexual drive is strong, why don't they patronise prostitutes and still be good providers to their relatives and offspring?

For homosexuality to have arisen in anticipation of reduced reproduction is a scenario less suited to kin selective explanations than if homosexuality were an inherited trait. We will turn to this choice versus orientation problem in a moment, but for now let us consider how homosexuality may have arisen if it were a choice rather than a necessity. The potentially deficient heterosexual faces choices predicated by a sex drive he has to meet. The easiest and least expensive way is to favour prostitutes. Prostitution has not been called the world's oldest profession without good reason. Prostitution exists precisely because men need and will pay for sexual outlets beyond marriage. As discussed in Chapter 3, a male R strategy demands such opportunities. Men report, on average, twice as many sexual partners than women and higher rates of intercourse (Baker, 1996) and this poses a slippage problem. Given equal numbers of men and women, who is servicing these men? As Dorothy Einon has found, there is little evidence for a few hypersexual women meeting this demand and a whole lot of prostitution and not a little male bragging is needed to make the numbers balance (Einon, 1994). Prostitution has always served as a direct outlet for men who disqualify themselves from reproduction and meets the need, if not nature's reproductive intention. Can such men afford prostitution? No more or less than the kin selective hypothesis would argue – superior resources are reputedly available to these men.

By now you are probably unhappy with this line of argument and saying to yourself 'But surely some men choose prostitution and others homosexuality?' Clearly homosexuality has a powerful penetrance and many men feel compelled to express themselves this way but this is an argument for an inherent capacity, not a lifestyle choice. The point is that kin selection by and of itself is an inadequate explanation for homosexual choice, if choice it is. The implicit assumption in Wilson's theory is that men who are both sexually deficient and sexually repressed choose homosexuality as a sexual outlet. Yet apart from anthropological studies which link *some* homosexuals to shamanism or other positions of power and respect (Weinrich, 1977; Symons, 1979; Adam, 1985), few studies convincingly show that homosexuals are aware they will become poor reproducers, or what benefits they will derive from their homosexuality to offset their supposed pathology (Buss, 1994). In the absence of a convincing connection, the kin selective account is questionable. That is, it may well be that men who doubt their capacity to be fathers may use kin selection to increase their inclusive fitness but why they also become homosexual is another matter.

A poor quality heterosexual?

Are homosexuals aware that they will be 'potentially, rather poor quality heterosexuals'? As Michael Ruse (1988) noted in his extended review of this question there are variants of the kin selection hypothesis, all of which view homosexuality as a disease but none argues this perspective convincingly. The assumption of kin selective accounts is that the homosexual-to-be is aware of their dubious capacity as a potential heterosexual parent and chooses homosexuality as an adaptive response to this diminished capacity. Not only does this theory assume that homosexuality is a sickness or at the best bad (non-reproductive) sexuality, but it relies on notions of sexual inversion unsupported by the evidence. We have reviewed the inversional hypothesis at length in Chapter 2 and will not return to it here. What is rarely stated but implicit in inversional accounts is that homosexuality leads to illness and is dysfunctional for that reason. Michael Ruse (1988), in his chapters 'Is homosexuality bad sexuality?' and 'Homosexuality as sickness: The arguments', makes several points worth noting. Conditions have changed enormously since the days of our tribal forebears and there is no evidence that homosexuals are potentially psychologically unhealthier than their heterosexual peers (Pillard, 1988); indeed they may demonstrate much lower than expected levels of psychopathology (Bell and Weinberg, 1978). On questions of physical disability, Ruse argues that homosexual men are not born innately (potentially) unhealthy, irrespective of the health of gay culture today. Gay cultures do have much higher rates of sexually transmitted diseases (Garrett, 1994) but this is a consequence of sexual activity levels, not of orientation. In any case, public health care and increasing affluence ensure that homosexuals can be as healthy as the rest of the community, even in an era of HIV/AIDS.

We must also philosophically challenge the idea that homosexuality is bad sex, which implicitly supports inversional theories. The syllogism used to support the bad sex notion goes something like this: sex is designed for having children; homosexual sex does not produce children; therefore homosexual sex is bad sex. While this is logical it is not factual, a weakness of syllogistic reasoning pointed out as far back as Aristotle. Any number of points may be challenged in this syllogism but it is sufficient to challenge the central premise, that sex is designed for having children. While this is true it neglects that sex has many other purposes and that labelling any one usage 'bad' leads us to question all other usages. For example, is contraceptive sex bad, or masturbation, or for that matter practising celibacy? Clearly, the notion that homosexuality is bad sex is a dubious proposition. I will leave you to read Ruse's treatment of the illness and bad sex arguments, but in brief there is no real evidence to support a bad sex notion.

Suffice it to say that kin selective accounts rely on notions of maladaption, Wilson's 'rare altruistic impulses' notwithstanding, and are contrary to the weight of evidence which suggests that homosexuality provides an adaptive advantage ensuring its survival. James Weinrich in his reply to critics of biosocial views of homosexuality best met this challenge by noting that 'The reason why sociobiologists first explained homosexuality adaptively is because they first try to explain everything adaptively. (And please note that I wrote "first" not "always")' (Weinrich, 1995). Weinrich goes on to note that persistent human behaviours well above the mutational equilibrium are 'probably in some way the result of adaptive evolution of behavior and not a pathological mutation or aberration' even if the behaviour no longer services the purposes for which it evolved. We depart from Weinrich at this point because much of his work assumes a kin selective effect. Weinrich assumes that homosexuality is advantageous, although it is explicit in his theorising that homosexuality does lead to reduced reproduction. So if some men sense their reproductive potential will be diminished why then do they choose homosexuality as a compensatory sexuality? As there has been no compelling reason advanced for choosing homosexuality ahead of other alternative sexual expressions, kin selection theory at present does not really address same-sex attractions.

PARENTAL MANIPULATION

To this point we have viewed the advantages and disadvantages of homosexuality from the perspective of the homosexual gene carrier rather than of their parents or close relatives. To the extent we considered the offsprings' interests it was to assume that they would benefit from whatever advantage was passed to them from the parental generation. For example, in our discussion of sexual selection in Chapter 3, we assumed that a mother's preferences served her children's reproductive interests as much as they served her own and this assumption certainly underlay our consideration of kin selection. However, this is unlikely, and in reality the interests of parents and children differ for the good reason that a child is totally related to himself but only half related to either of his parents. So a certain degree of parent–offspring conflict is inevitable, as each maximises their fitness. As just one example, parents may wish to maximise their investment by supporting as many offspring as possible, a strategy which argues a relatively equal allocation of resources to all their children. However, from the offspring's perspective he or she is the centre of their genetic universe and their own genes are more important than those of their parents or siblings. For this reason any one offspring would wish to enhance their fitness by increasing their share of parental resources. This argues either an unequal allocation of resources to all offspring and/or a conflict of goals between the child and its parents.

Robert Trivers (1974) first articulated the consequences of this parent–offspring conflict in his seminal paper in the *American Zoologist*. A number of points flow from his analysis but perhaps the most important is that parents have the whip hand in this conflict of interests; children are dependent on their parents. Trivers notes that if any 'gene in the offspring exacts too great a cost from the parent, that gene will be selected against even though it confers some benefit to the offspring'. This acknowledges the relative power differential between parent and child and points to one solution of this inevitable conflict: that parents will deliberately manipulate their children and their reproductive potential to minimise conflict and to ensure the greatest reproductive benefit (inclusive fitness) for themselves. In an ideal scenario, all offspring would compete equally and this would equalise parental allocation of resources. However, this ideal is complicated by any number of factors which argue that children do not compete on a level playing field. Older children will have a head-start advantage and so on. So, as conflict is inevitable, parents may favour strategies enhancing the reproductive potential of some children over others. Traditionally, this has favoured male first-born offspring in Western culture (Dickemann, 1993).

There are many reasons parents may decide to manipulate their children. However, a consequence of an unequal allocation of resources is that some children may be sidelined in the reproductive stakes in order to advance the fitness interests of their parents. How might this favour homosexuality? The parental manipulation scenario is a species of kin selection/inclusive fitness strategy in which the parents' rather than the child's interests are served. The parents decide which offspring are the best potential reproducers and invest resources in them at the expense of their other children. Often this choice is driven by customs such as primogeniture, or by gender, or a purely arbitrary choice (Dickemann, 1995). The point is that often this choice has little to do with the reproductive competence of the child and is between children with equal potential. The parents are following a K strategy with a vengeance, maximising resources for just a few of their many offspring. What of the other children disadvantaged by this process? They choose homosexuality as a default sexual outlet, responding to their parent's desire for them to suppress their sexuality to better support their favoured kin. To the extent the child has a reduced reproductive potential as a result of parental manipulation, they have to choose kin selective altruism as a way of ensuring their genes are replicated.

How likely is this strategy? If kin selection has little going for it, parental manipulation has not a lot more. The scenario is essentially the same as the kin selective one with an additional level of explanation superimposed. The theory has stirred little interest since it was first advanced by Trivers and mostly attracted critical comment or brief reviews for the sake of completeness (Ruse, 1981, 1988; Futuyma and Risch, 1984; Dickemann, 1993, 1995). Does changing the focus from the child's interest to that of the parent rescue kin selection as an explanation of homosexuality? Probably not. The parental manipulation scenario still has all the difficulties of the kin selective account – does the mathematics of kin selection support the survival of a homosexuality gene and so forth. Its sole advantage is that it posits a link between a reduced reproductive potential and homosexuality. The parents decide on the relative fitness of their children, presumably from a more informed perspective than that of the child, and in so doing encourage some to become homosexual. Becoming homosexual provides the child with a sexual outlet which then does not compete with the favoured offsprings' reproduction.

Yet the difficulty is still in seeing a necessary connection between say, being a second son and becoming homosexual. The same mathematics that makes genetic accounts of kin selection unlikely also work against parental manipulation. The best way for a parent to get the maximum return on their genetic investment is to encourage all their offspring to reproduce furiously. If parents decide that a child should be assigned a subordinate lifescript, thus reducing their chances of reproducing, this is counterproductive. They would derive more inclusive fitness from a diminished but still active reproducer than from scripting their child to be gay. The advantage they receive from this child's altruistic kin selection is unlikely to offset the losses the child and the parent face in the child withdrawing from reproduction. Parental manipulation only makes sense if the parents detect early signs of genes for homosexuality or any other deleterious trait, and decide to cut their losses in encouraging their offspring to become nest helpers (Trivers, 1985). If so, we return to our starting problem: how does the gene survive reduced reproduction? If being steered towards a life as a celibate member of the clergy is simply a matter of choice on the parents' part, it still does not necessarily equal the child becoming gay, irrespective of what current Western stereotypes of the Catholic Church might suggest (Dickemann, 1995). In tribal cultures this might be ritualised and mandated but this is still quite speculative (Lang, 1990; Dickemann, 1993).

Perhaps the weakness of this theory is that it sees homosexuality as more a matter of choice than of genetics. Parents may decide their sons are poorer potential reproducers but in the absence of any study which demonstrates the basis on which parents decide to manipulate their children, it is difficult to see any advantage to disabling the reproductive potential of their heterosexual offspring whatever their disabilities. If, on the other hand, homosexuality is an innate predisposition that more than likely will out, then parents encouraging kin selective altruism in their offspring is not a matter of choice but a counsel of despair in the face of the inevitable, and can hardly be labelled 'manipulation'.

Selective benefit

So what is interesting in the parental manipulation scenario is not so much the mechanism but the direction of selective benefit. As Trivers (1974) notes, inclusive fitness can produce two types of celibate: those whose interests coincide with those of their parents and those whose interests differ. Coincidence of interests should then also lead to coincidence of inclusive fitness between the parent and the child. For example, if the parents were astute and observed early effeminacy or whatever signs of a poor reproducer, and could counsel their child towards an appropriate nonreproductive outcome, presumably the inclusive fitness benefits of both would be similar, if reduced. However, this is a less likely outcome than children having their inclusive fitness lowered while increasing their parents'. Trivers acknowledges this:

> What is clear from the present argument, however, is that it is even more likely that the nonreproducer will thereby increase his *parents'* inclusive fitness than that he will increase his own. This follows because his parents are expected to value the increased reproductive success of kin relatively more than he is.
>
> (Trivers, 1974: 261)

A consequence of this line of argument is that it should lead to ambivalent and unhappy pseudo-gays unless they are convinced their parents accurately diagnosed an inevitable homosexuality. At this point it is tempting to wander off into the happy valley of Freudianism and to speculate on the role of cloying overprotective mothers and of hostile fathers psychologically castrating offspring, all in the name of kin selective altruism! However, restraining ourselves, it seems that unless the parents are accurately diagnosing their children's impairment (in which case the parental manipulation theory makes some sense as the best palliative available to offset inevitable losses of inclusive fitness) they must be producing offspring who will be 'ripped off' by their parents' actions.

Parents have several choices in how they might manipulate their offspring to their best selective benefit.

They may simply choose to invest differentially, as in primogeniture, where the bulk of resources are reserved for the first-born, a tactic which becomes a self-fulfilling prophecy and the remaining children are forced to compete from a disadvantage. For example, European colonial expansion was the province of second sons who were encouraged by their parents to seek new lands to found cadet branches of the family (Boone, 1986). This tactic, which at first seems to be putting all your reproductive eggs in one basket, does make sense when levels of parental investment risk/return ratios are examined. As Dickemann (1993) notes:

> For his parents, the senior son is a high-investment, lower-risk tactic, the cadet a lower-investment, higher-risk tactic providing insurance in case of failure of the senior line, and possible familial gain through dispersal and colonization.
>
> (Dickemann, 1993: 60)

Following this strategy, it is difficult to see how homosexuality would *necessarily* follow, even if actively encouraged by parents in subordinate offspring. Presumably the drive to reproduce is strong enough to reject parental injunctions in even celibate occupations (as has been amply demonstrated by the transgressions of the Church hierarchy). While homosexuality may be a compensation for sexual frustration, it is hardly a compensation for not having children. Put another way, this form of parental manipulation should select for aggressive ambisexuality rather than homosexuality.

Parents may also decide to invest in one or other sex and this choice may well be directed by the social and economic circumstances of the times rather than by genetics. Dickemann (1993) provides an extended review of the possibilities of allocation by sex but if we pursue the notion of parental manipulation as a socially selected path for homosexuality we can propose a few testable hypotheses. First, if inclusive fitness is at work it is more sensible for mothers to select for daughters than for sons, as they share more common genes (on their double X chromosomes) than fathers do with their sons (or daughters). Inclusive fitness/kin selective accounts of homosexuality should then favour reproductive daughters and homosexual brothers who support them. This is unlikely given men's vastly superior reproductive potential, but gay men do outnumber lesbians four-to-one. Second, given fathers' paternity uncertainty and mothers' closer genetic similarity, mothers should be more involved in parental manipulation than fathers. While fathers would be equally willing to manipulate daughters or sons to become homosexual, they will have less of an incentive than their wives to do so. Third, given these provisos, mothers should invest heavily in daughters to attract the best possible mates and exact a heavy bride price to reinvest in other female offspring. Fourth, mothers should produce more daughters than sons. As only a few males are needed to do the job they are a relatively plentiful sexual commodity. While this is the pattern in some societies it is not in others and is a somewhat farcical scenario, however logically it flows from the inclusive fitness hypothesis. In a species with a near 50:50 sex ratio such as our own, such a selective pressure towards daughters would immediately generate a counterbalancing selection for sons.

A by no means final, possibility is that parents might choose whom to favour on the basis of some perceived attribute of their offspring and that this is most likely to work in disadvantaging children perceived to be poor potential reproducers. We have already considered the selective benefits of this choice here and in our kin selection section. Despite an intuitive link between effeminacy and gender nonconformity and homosexuality; studies that do establish a link between early gender nonconformity and homosexuality (Weinrich, 1995); and that it may be possible that parents are accurately predicting their offsprings' reproductive success, this still does not resolve all the difficulties we noted with the kin selective accounts. It merely separates the questions 'What causes homosexuality?' from 'What allows it to survive?' Parental manipulation, or kin selection, or inclusive fitness may be vehicles for the spread of homosexuality but are inadequate accounts of homosexuality's survival and, as we have seen, this is by far the more fundamental question.

So it can be seen that there is a difficulty at the heart of the parental manipulation hypothesis. If homosexuality is innate, inevitable, or at least of high penetrance, then parental manipulation for homosexuality and kin selective altruism is a good compensatory tactic but not a likely explanation of the gene's survival. If this is not so, then it seems inevitable that parents' wishes to advantage one child relative to another would run counter to the child's best interests, conflict seems inevitable and remaining exclusively gay becomes uncertain.

A SOCIAL ADJUSTMENT

There remains the possibility that homosexuality is simply a convenient social behaviour which benefits society sufficiently to reserve a place for gay men. Such theories are independent of evolutionary theory to the extent that they are responses to other pressures rather than 'orthodox adaptionist accounts' (Weinrich, 1987b). Such explanations, which ignore ever-increasing evidence for homosexuality's biology, are, in Trivers' view, explanations of last resort, seeing homosexuality as maladaptive (Trivers, 1985). Nevertheless, it may be that homosexuality is more than a byproduct of evolution and that it may serve evolution's purposes while meeting entirely personal or social agendas. There are several such theories which range from the purely social constructivist (Gallup and Suarez, 1983) to those with a more developmental flavour (Pollard, 1996). Given our ta^r of explaining homosexuality from a biological perspective it is proba' more useful and certainly more comfortable to review one of the more developmental of these social theories.

Robin Baker and Mark Bellis (1995) have proposed an intriguing genetic theory which they say models 'a balanced polymorphism'. Their work was discussed when considering sperm competition and frequency-dependent sexual selection in Chapter 3. While they claim a genetic basis for their scenario, shorn of its sperm competitive elements, a close reading suggests that homosexuality may be entirely developmental or social in origin and they model a selective scenario that is less fanciful than many in this category. Baker and Bellis start with the entirely obvious point that we have the capacity for both heterosexual and homosexual sex – that is, in their view we are behaviourally polymorphic. They then note that most homosexual activity occurs in the adolescent period prior to heterosexual intercourse. Adolescent males, they say, are clumsy novices desperately in need of sexual practice before forming lasting reproductive liaisons. Homosexual sex provides a relatively anxiety-free opportunity for novices to practise with an equally inexperienced friend in a mutually reciprocal way. So far their scenario is a standard recapitulation of the developmental theory of homosexuality shorn of its identity formation aspects and well in accord with the evidence. On this superstructure, Baker and Bellis argue that if homosexual sex is effective practice for later heterosexuality, then those who experiment this way will become more competent heterosexual lovers than their peers, at least at an earlier age. This head-start may then equip them more effectively to seduce and reproduce earlier than the majority of their age mates.

Baker and Bellis then begin the evolutionary part of their scenario by noting that 'A lifetime of exclusive homosexuality is rare (1 percent or less), even in societies where nearly everybody is bisexual . . . In all probability, therefore, exclusive homosexuals are the small and reproductively maladaptive tip of the adaptive iceberg of bisexuality.' Accepting for the sake of argument that we are really talking about bisexuality rather than homosexuality, Baker and Bellis go on to state that 'We know of no data for male humans on the number of children born to bisexuals compared to heterosexuals.' They then introduce data from Essock-Vitale and McGuire (1985) and their own nationwide UK study of 4,000 women, to show that although heterosexual women from 39 years onwards have more children than bisexual women, at earlier ages up to 25 years 'bisexuals were four times more likely to have children than heterosexuals by age 20' (see Figure 4.2).

This reproductive head-start is, they suggest, the key to the survival of bisexuality. Baker and Bellis assume, 'in the absence of any evidence to the contrary', and freely acknowledging that this may be refuted, that the same early advantage pattern applies for bisexual males. If this were so, then the downside of bisexuality in adulthood, which on their figures

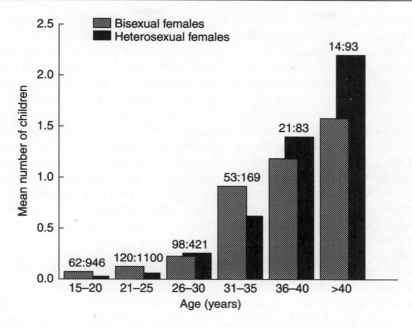

Figure 4.2 Reproductive success of bisexual and heterosexual women at different ages (UK)

Source: Baker and Bellis, 1995: 117

would be a mildly reduced overall reproductive rate vis-a-vis their straight peers, is compensated by a head-start advantage. You will recall that one of the vectors of reproductive success is a smaller intergenerational turnaround time: descendants who breed sooner increase their proportional genetic success in subsequent generations. This leads to:

> a pattern ... in which bisexuals reproduce earlier but may have fewer children over a lifetime could well indicate a balanced polymorphism, bisexuals and heterosexuals achieving equal reproductive success over time but through different strategies.

(Baker and Bellis, 1995: 118)

How plausible is Baker and Bellis's scenario? First we have to decide if what they are modelling is an innate or an acquired strategy. Clearly, they see bisexuality as an innate behaviour, inevitably so in a book on the evolution of sperm competition. However, in acknowledging its variability 'The level of polymorphism for bisexuality seems to vary ... from a few percent in Europe to nearly 100 percent bisexual in ... Melanesia' and its cultural basis in their scattered but extensive anthropological review, they provide a convincing picture of a highly variable, socially acquired and culturally determined behaviour. That is, there is little in their theory which could not be more simply explained as an acquired behaviour following a social evolutionary logic. If from adolescent anxiety you develop an inclination for homosexual sex and this continues through into later life then the slight reproductive disadvantage accruing to bisexuality – increased disease risk, marital discord and the like – may well be offset by early practice effects. Only if we require a gene for bisexuality for the behaviour to reinforce the effect in subsequent generations would an inherent explanation be necessary but even then this advantage is as likely to be imitative, as inherent. Baker and Bellis have fallen into the trap of equating a biological capability for an outcome of natural selection and there is no necessary connection between a capacity for bisexuality and expressing it. This is amply demonstrated by that old gay joke that 'if God had wanted us all to be gay, he would have given us all anuses'. It is the behaviour here which needs explaining, not the capacity.

On the flipside Baker and Bellis are acutely aware of the problem of bisexual behaviour and go on to pose the same questions we are pursuing here – what is the advantage that keeps the behaviour in the population and what stops the behaviour becoming universal? To this they add: 'Why is the level at which the polymorphism balances different for males and females and different in different populations?' The first two questions are neatly answered by their offsetting an early head-start advantage against slight reproductive disadvantage compared to heterosexuals. We will consider the adequacy of this balancing act shortly but let us first deal with this last question, which poses a more immediate difficulty. Baker and Bellis argue that inexperienced females are at a lesser disadvantage in the copulation stakes, quoting Ford and Beach (1951) as their authority. Indeed they suggest that a measure of female ineptness may be a positive selective advantage because 'only the more competent males may be able to copulate successfully with a relatively inexperienced female', and presumably this advantage includes the ability to charm and seduce a reluctant partner. That women are pursued as partners, and that they have less immediate pressures on them to perform sexually, suggests to Baker and Bellis that there is 'less selective pressure on females to gain their practice and experience when very young'. They go on to note that this may account for the 'much slower rate at which females come to experience homosexual interactions compared with males', only half of whom have done so by age 25.

That there is this variation between males and females is a major difficulty for their genetic scenario and may be interpreted not as a female evolutionary advantage 'probably more subtle than being concerned with basic reproduction', but rather that lesbianism is a separate preference. We are not dealing here with one type of homosexuality, but at least two. An obvious extension of their theory, which may be easily refuted on their own evidence, will make this point. Baker and Bellis make no mention of the point that young bisexual males should mate with young bisexual females for both to gain a head-start advantage. Yet they say that head-start advantages accrue to bisexuals of both sexes, so logically an early sexual achiever should gain the greatest advantage by picking a bisexual mate, reinforcing a positive genetic trait for shorter intergenerational turnaround times. This compounding advantage should then come to dominate the gene pool in a millennium or so as the optimum type and we should see younger and younger mothers pushing a secular trend hard up against the ultimate biological limits to motherhood. As reported in the *World Annual and Statistical Yearbook* (United Nations, 1995), in most countries there is a trend towards later marriage and reduced fertility, for social and economic but not genetic reasons. If Baker and Bellis are right, we should also find a direct selective advantage to both sexes that should iron out the different percentages of male and female bisexuals (about four-to-one) and the relative differences in the ages of onset of bisexual behaviour – after all, it takes two to tango.

So while Baker and Bellis show that some bisexual women have a head-start advantage, this must be for different reasons than for bisexual men who gain their advantage by becoming early sexual achievers. That women are homosexual (or bisexual) four times less often than men, come to their lesbianism later, and as a consequence have a markedly reduced head-start advantage, suggests that this is not the selective advantage enjoyed by some bisexual women, or at the very minimum is not genetically selected. A far simpler explanation for the few that do might be that men traditionally prefer younger women (enhanced fertility) and they are attracted to a more available (that is, bisexual) partner. It may be in all this that bisexual women enjoy a sperm competitive advantage in their mate selection strategies but not for head-start reasons.

In posing the question 'Why is bisexual behaviour a disadvantage if it is shown by too great a proportion of the population?' they also mention that bisexuality is a virtually all-encompassing normal and unproblematic behaviour in some cultures, so their question becomes unanswerable in these terms. Clearly, if in some cultures it is a normal and expected pattern of behaviour, the problem would be to explain the odd instances where it did not occur. Still Baker and Bellis are addressing a real problem because homosexuality is not the optimum phenotype and does have disadvantages in many cultures. Even if everyone is bisexual, then everyone shares the same relative advantage enjoyed by the bisexual man. The advantage becomes nullified by the inclusiveness of a behaviour shared by all. Why then is it advantageous in some cultures and not in others?

Returning to this broader issue, Baker and Bellis are aware of the weaknesses of their theory and their rejoinder might be to remind us of the limiting conditions which rein in homosexuality and place it at a relative disadvantage. While Baker and Bellis do not directly acknowledge these problems with their scenario they are well aware of them and try to meet them by proposing that the downside of bisexuality (or exclusive homosexuality for that matter) is an increased risk of sexually transmitted diseases and, as a consequence, reduced reproduction rates. They then try to quarantine those populations who have high or universal rates of bisexuality from these infective consequences with a wonderful argument which goes something like this: bisexuals have a much greater risk of nasty sexually transmitted diseases (STDs); therefore populations with high rates of bisexuality should have high rates of STDs. The high incidence of STDs will lead to a lower rate of bisexuality as a consequence of infection; yet there are some societies which have longstanding traditions of bisexuality involving all the men; so these societies must be geographically and sexually isolated otherwise they too would have high rates of STDs and low rates of bisexuality.

Despite the elegance of this aspect of their argument, it does not work and leaves not a few questions unanswered. Baker and Bellis (1995) note that 'In large, mobile human populations, such as Europe and the United States, bisexuals are relatively uncommon', the implication being that in these societies there is only a small advantage to being bisexual and/or the rates of STDs are high. Evidence suggests that this is unlikely. Baker and Bellis base their argument on the *proportion* of bisexuals in the community. That is, a society with a low rate of bisexuality/homosexuality must have a high rate of STDs (or other disadvantages). World Health Organisation and other data suggest that the incidence and spread of STDs throughout the world is quite the reverse, with some of the worst-hit areas being relatively isolated African and Asian communities (Garrett, 1994). A reply to this confounding datum would be to invoke the *novel environments defence* and suggest that these are atypical times and that in our evolutionary past, geographic and sexual isolation allowed the pursuit of this selective strategy. Baker and Bellis at least partially use this defence in acknowledging the virulence with which an STD can spread through a population. However, what is a more important is the *rate* of sexual contact. A society in which bisexuality is universally practised may have equivalent copulation rates to a society in which only a small percentage of bisexuals may have many partners. The incidence of exclusive homosexuality in the West is low, from 1–3 percent. We have already reviewed the incidence of promiscuity among gay American males in Chapter 3 and this may result in as many bisexual contacts as in an all-embracing but often highly ritualised bisexuality in another culture. If there were no differences in rate of bisexual contacts, what would drive Baker and Bellis's scenario?

A positive side?

Not wanting to throw cold water over Baker and Bellis's scenario entirely, it does have several quite significant aspects. If we accept that men and women are following different reproductive agendas then we can use such of their strategy as it applies to men. You will recall from Figure 3.4 in Chapter 3 (see p. 111) that the incidence of double-mating and extra-pair copulations in the West was highly significant, approaching 80 percent for more experienced women. If you do not have to worry about defending a sperm competitive scenario, or explaining lesbianism, then Baker and Bellis have modelled a quite interesting balance hypothesis for male homosexuality that need only depend on socially constrained behaviours. As a variant of the frequency-dependent sexual selection hypothesis of Chapter 3, it may provide an alternative, but social, mechanism for the maintenance of homosexual behaviour. If the incidence of STDs was a significant constraint on a homosexual lifestyle in the past, then the balance of an early advantage to a bisexual may be struck not by comparing his reproductive success to heterosexuals but to those men who choose an exclusively homosexual lifestyle. The advantages to the bisexual man then offset the reproductive losses from those who choose an exclusively homosexual lifestyle.

Why does bisexuality persist beyond the early reproductive phase? Another of Baker and Bellis's strengths is their definitional clarity. While their theory does not really answer why exclusive homosexuality remains a significant proportion of the population (on their figures a not insignificant 29,000,000 men worldwide are exclusively gay or will be when they grow up), it does suggest how they are maintained within that population. If we define exclusive homosexuality as not having had heterosexual sex in the last five years, a definition which allows for adolescent homosexuality and for married men coming out (Weinberg et al., 1994b), few, probably only about 3 percent, are exclusively homosexual, about as many as remain bisexual throughout their lives. Yet many men have had a homosexual phase early in their lives. The numbers of men who continue with homosexual contacts past early adulthood are small and their theory explains why this is so – a head-start advantage is by definition an early advantage achieved while young. One test of their theory would be to see if the entirety of a bisexual man's offspring are born earlier than population averages for first and subsequent children, as a head-start advantage presumably also applies to subsequent children. Perhaps they bunch more than the average family too? Maybe exclusive homosexuals are not 'the small and reproductively maladaptive tip of the adaptive iceberg of bisexuality' but rather bisexuality's other half.

THE CENTRAL THEORETICAL PROBLEM OF
SOCIOBIOLOGY

Perhaps the best way to conclude a four-chapter discussion of homosexuality's place in the sun is to throw a little doubt on everything we have discussed thus far. The central tenet of our discussion of homosexuality has been differential reproductive success, or having a greater representation of one's genes in subsequent generations than other members of one's species. To summarise, reproductive success may be demonstrated three ways – you have more children than the average; you bring more of them to their reproductive maturity than the average; or you have more robust offspring, who reproduce sooner than others, ensuring your generational turnover time is shortened. A related scenario supporting differential reproductive success is inclusive fitness strategies aimed at assisting kin also to pursue these ends – thus ensuring that replicates, close copies of our genes, are maximised. Differential reproductive success is the key to balanced superior heterozygotic fitness scenarios and to kin, sexual, and parental selective models. The problem with these selective scenarios is that in most countries fertility rates are declining. That people will consciously restrict the number of children they have becomes the central theoretical problem of sociobiology and of our remaining discussion.

Although Daniel Vining was not the first to observe the problem that declining fertility rates posed for theories based on differential reproductive success (Alexander, 1975; Daly and Wilson, 1978; Symons, 1979), his article in *The Behavioral and Brain Sciences* in 1986 drew a sharp reaction in the biosocial community. Vining started his analysis by noting that:

> Sociobiology predicts that individuals will behave so as to increase their genetic representation in the next generation. Individuals, then, should exploit positions of power to increase their number of descendants relative to those below them. Rarely, however, do we observe such behavior in modern human populations.

> (Vining, 1986: 167)

Vining goes on to note an inverse relationship between cultural and biological contributions of individuals possessing status and power and poses the question of how long 'modern culture' can sustain itself if 'a high relative frequency of certain traits is necessary to its survival; these same traits are heritable across generations; and those endowed with these traits are demonstrating lower than average reproductive fitness'. He uses data drawn from a number of sources to demonstrate that a profound demographic transition is underway in the Western world, which first began in France, the United States and Britain in the 18th and early

19th century, had spread through Europe by the end of the 19th century, and to all industrial economies by the end of the 20th century. Apart from a post World War Two fertility bump, most Western nations this century are approaching replacement population values or have declining populations. Vining demonstrates a relationship between national affluence, education, declining mortality, technological and industrial competence and declining birth rates which is readily apparent to anyone with the most recent *Encyclopaedia Britannica*, or United Nations' *World Annual and Statistical Yearbook*. He goes on to show an inverse relationship within countries between economic and social rank on the one hand and birth rates on the other. He caps his analysis by demonstrating a direct relationship between social success and reproduction in pre-industrial Europe and in the third world today.

Having made a convincing case for an inverse relationship between social and reproductive success, Vining then considers what violating this central dogma might mean for evolutionary theorising. He notes that virtually all sociobiologists have taken some note of this 'prevalence of non-fitness-maximizing behaviors in modern culture', but also points to a curious reluctance to grapple with what this means for modern evolutionary theorising. Vining reviews several attempted rescues of this theoretical difficulty by those who have squarely faced his problem and we will briefly examine their scenarios before considering what Vining's challenge might mean for homosexuality.

Perhaps the commonest rescue attempt is what Vining dubs the 'novel environments hypothesis'. The period of his analysis, barely 200 years, represents less than 1:500th of our species' immediate history and a vanishingly small part of hominid evolution. If there is one defining characteristic of our species' evolution it is the rapid growth of our reasoning powers and of a frontal cortex which has led to a marked behavioural plasticity, probably a response to the dramatic climatic changes of our recent history (Gribbin and Gribbin, 1993). Authors such as Daly and Wilson (1978) note that as a consequence of these rapid changes we have evolved many behaviours which, although once appropriate, are currently unhelpful. No doubt you will have noticed throughout this book that theorists constantly use this argument to resolve inconvenient facts troubling their view of homosexuality. However, declining birth rates *is* a current trend which needs explanation and to label it as an evolutionary holdover does little more than, in Vining's words, 'push the mystery of non-fitness maximizing behaviors around'. So we are left with a problem which even proponents of the novel environments proposal acknowledge (Wilson, 1978; Lumsden and Wilson, 1981; Dawkins, 1982).

A possible answer is provided by what Vining acknowledges as a plausible theory provided by Jerome Barkow and Nancy Burley (Burley,

1979; Barkow and Burley, 1980; Barkow, 1989). Barkow and Burley start with the rapid growth of human intelligence and speculate as to what this meant for women who faced strong pressures to maximise their childbearing. The rapid rise of intelligence gave women the foresight to anticipate the 'dangers, pains and inconveniences of childbirth and child-rearing' (Barkow and Burley, 1980) and the ability to control their fertility. Faced with these difficulties, women would seek to maximise their invest-ment in just a few children rather than spend a lifetime raising offspring. Thus intelligence provided enormous benefits to the female of the species but at the 'one great selective disadvantage' (1980) of threatening her fitness. To counter this disadvantage, a whole range of cultural traits evolved to promote childbearing, including strong pronatalist dogmas and rewards for having children. Barkow and Burley pose a rhetorical ques-tion asking why human society should so universally pressure and reward women, if they were not reluctant to have children? At the same time, innate traits developed to counter the rise of intellect such as concealed ovulation, continuous sexual receptivity and a strong sexual desire. Rather than limiting intelligence, evolution balanced its disadvantages.

> With the growth of intelligence, early hominid females eventually understood the relationship between ovulation, copulation, and fertil-ization. They used this new knowledge to control their fertility, reducing it to the point of eliminating their genes from the gene-pool. Since intelligence itself was of high adaptive value, selection reduced not female intelligence but [male] awareness of ovulation.
>
> (Barkow and Burley, 1980: 172)

Vining agrees with Barkow and Burley's model but notes that modern Western culture has now given women the tools to cope with concealed ovulation, continuous sexual receptivity and a strong sexual desire by using reliable contraception. Rising affluence has also profoundly changed cultural scripts, transferring wealth and information into women's hands, providing them with an autonomy from male dominance and access to an independent lifestyle. Contraception has provided a sexual freedom independent of reproduction with a consequent lessening of procreative pressure. Women once again are able to anticipate and control their fertility, leading to Vining's paradox. Barkow and Burley's model directly anticipates the situation that now prevails in developed nations and Vining notes that sexual freedom is most likely among more intelligent women whose education will facilitate them choosing non-normative life-styles, whose greater resources will permit them to follow new directions, and to have greater access and understanding of reproductive techno-logies. Thus, although Barkow and Burley's model explains why this problem arose, and how it was selected against in the past, it does nothing to anticipate a resolution of this current evolutionary conundrum.

Vining's fundamental postulate and homosexuality

Vining's conundrum poses a major challenge to our understanding of the possible roots of homosexuality's evolution. Throughout the entirety of our discussion the central premise of the scenarios reviewed was maximisation of reproductive fitness by increasing one's genetic representation in subsequent generations. If there is a gene for homosexuality it is balanced in the population by a reproductive advantage it holds over the heterosexual wild-type. Only in our examination of homosexuality as a byproduct of evolution do we have a model which is not affected by Vining's challenge. Addressing this problem is all the more urgent because we started with a challenge from the social constructivist camp to explain homosexuality in the light of evolutionary change. How then do we meet Vining's challenge?

Perhaps the simplest answer to this conundrum is to argue that homosexuality genes are being spread among the less well-endowed sectors of the community. This is unlikely. Although it is an unpopular truth, intelligence, defined as the ability to handle a complex technological world, has a large hereditable component (Plomin et al., 1980; Henderson, 1982; Sternberg and Grigorenko, 1997). We have already noted Weinrich's (1977) review of the link between homosexuality and higher intelligence. While there is some dispute about this, if it were so, given that gay men inherit their intelligence in considerable degree from their parents, it would follow that these parents are precisely those who are most likely to reduce their fertility. This argues that proportionately, homosexuality must be in as rapid a decline as Western fertility. It may well be. We have no figures and no real facts on which to base an argument. At present though, the gay community is articulate and intelligent (Weinrich, 1978), educated and socially competent (Bell and Weinberg, 1978; Strickland, 1995) and affluent (Hewitt, 1995), a mix unlikely to come from the poorer sectors of our community.

There is a certain theoretical comfort in the novel environments hypothesis but at best it is a weak defence. Perhaps homosexuality spread as a consequence of processes which no longer have much utility? As Huxley (1983) observed, cultural evolution proceeds at an infinitely more rapid pace than physical evolution and perhaps homosexuality is a phenotypic adaptation that now owes little to genotypic selection. Unfortunately for this view, the constantly unfolding evidence for a biological basis argues that physical evolution is not yet finished with homosexuality. What is uncertain is the pace of human physical evolution. Our bodies are poorly adapted to the environments which we have fashioned and have a physiology more suited to loping through the savanna than sitting in front of a computer. Moreover, changing physiology may provide only indirect clues to the pace at which behavioural traits encoded in our genes are selected and evolve. We have precious little insight into this area, although one of the central thrusts of evolutionary psychology is to demonstrate how much our evolutionary past still influences our social practices. In this respect at least we would agree with Wilson that 'our cultures are jerry-built on the Pleistocene' (cited in Ruse, 1979).

William Irons (1983), in grappling with Vining's conundrum, proposed a theory which argues that in rich times or rich environments the elite members of a group limit their fertility to enable better use of resources to maximise the reproductive success of their offspring. With adequate resources infant mortality is reduced and this permits a quality not quantity approach to reproductive success. Irons gives few examples to support his point, so I would like to trespass into his area of ethnography and by example make two points supporting his theory and provide a rebuttal of Vining's apparent misreading and critique of Irons' work. Let us start with a tribal wisdom which limits population because the custodians of the land are conscious that climatic variations are cyclical and that the ultimate carrying capacity of the land is set by the worst point of the cycle. To breed to capacity in times of plenty is to hasten the bottom of the cycle and tribal cultures have developed elaborate rituals to prevent this. In Arnhem Land (just below the Tiwi on Melville Island, which Irons uses as an example), Aboriginal custodians enforce elaborate greeting ceremonies and other rituals which limit casual access to marginal areas and so restrict population pressure on resources (Peterson, 1975). In similar ways Irons argues that our tribal ancestors limited their offspring in rich times, while in poor times this was an automatic consequence of resource scarcity (in our example, carrying capacity). This represents a selection pressure for quality offspring rather than quantity. Irons argues that in modern societies this logic fails because the mortality differentials are the same in both rich and poor environments, so pursuing a limiting strategy is maladaptive.

Vining challenges Irons' argument by questioning 'why survival rates should not be higher in richer environments, at all parities' and why 'quantity should ever have to be sacrificed for quality in such environments'. He also decries Irons' theory as one without psychological or physiological mechanisms, which 'remains largely obscure'. This is not only a misreading of Irons' work but is also inaccurate.

In defence of Irons' brief theorising, his argument seems quite plausible on at least two grounds. First, our forebears, by following an attenuated K strategy, while limiting quantitative reproductive success, may well have achieved the same goals by parental investment and kin selection. Second, selecting for quality offspring would ensure higher survival rates and presumably shorter intergenerational times. If this were so, reproductive success is then more a matter of inclusive fitness than direct reproduction gains, with offspring quality a matter of tribal survival. In Aboriginal

Australian life, infanticide and other eugenic measures were once routine, obeying this harsh selective logic (Peterson, 1975), particularly when faced with multiple births. The mathematics of these forms of reproductive success would be so multivariate as to defeat quantitative modelling but in simple case scenarios, would predict a reproductive success equivalent to direct reproduction at high rates of infant mortality.

One of the key issues poorly canvassed in Vining's paper is that evolutionary processes do not stop with the invention of reliable contraception; indeed they may be given a sharpened impact. The core of Vining's argument is a challenge to explain how reduced reproduction of the brightest and best does not result in being overwhelmed by a tide of averageness when the mortality differentials are negligible. Irons' argument may well provide an explanation and incidentally explain homosexuality's penetrance. What is often forgotten in contemporary evolutionary theorising is the ecological dimension to natural selection. While natural selection works on individuals, the sum of its effects works on groups. The end of individuals' maximising reproductive success is often not the survival of the fittest but species extinction as when an aggressive new mutation overwhelms the gene pool. What is ignored in simple linear models of maximising reproductive fitness is that lag times often obscure the ultimate adaptiveness of a trait, a point Irons makes himself in discussing the nexus between population growth and resources in the Tonga of Malawi and the !Kung Bushmen (Irons, 1983). Tribal cultures which routinely practised war games, banishment, infanticide, abortion, senilicide and abstinence as population control measures were well aware of the cost of exceeding the real carrying capacity of an ecological niche, and that rich times and places became poor times and places if population was not routinely limited. Given the extreme climatic variations and relatively short interglacial periods our species has endured in its brief evolution (Gribbin and Gribbin, 1993), it is not surprising that we might be selecting for maximum quality rather than maximum numbers as a way of meeting this most pressing of selective parameters. It goes without saying that the brightest and the best would be the most aware of the perils of lag time before overbreeding effects became apparent and not coincidentally usually are in positions of responsibility to do something about them on everybody's behalf. The evident worth of Irons' answer is readily apparent when we consider the human population explosion this century and looming environment degradation. When viewed this way the parity issue is resolved, and is positively selected for when the ultimate consequences of overbreeding become evident.

Not wanting to neglect the purposes of this book, it has been suggested by some theorists to whom I will pay the courtesy of anonymity that homosexuality is a response to population pressures and that homosexuals decide on homosexual lifestyle as an ecological response. Notwithstanding

Irons' argument, this is a nonsense as nonreproduction would equal the extinction of their genetic contribution, homosexual or otherwise. The point of Irons' argument, as I interpret it, is that there are other ways than having a multitude of offspring to ensure one's genetic success. In Chapter 3 we explored several models of heterotic fitness which achieved their ends not by direct reproduction but by relative advantage. The model of frequency-dependent sexual selection accommodates itself to Irons' theory and explains how, within a declining population, homosexuality would be both positively selected and at the same time limited. With the addition of an ecological dimension to the homosexuality debate we can see that a homosexual reproductive advantage conferred on heterosexuals would be positively selected as long as it were relatively rare. When its incidence became more evident it would be counterselected. The net effect of these two forces would be continually to improve the characteristics being selected for and this rests comfortably within the thrust of Iron's argument.

Perhaps the most important point in support of this position is that women exercise the constraining selective variable, choosing mates for the best possible genes. One of the strongest findings from studies of sexual selection is that women are preoccupied with the genetic potential of their prospective suitors, where men are far less choosy. That women follow a strategy of maximising genes rather than maximising offspring is as much a matter of selective pressure as of the biological limits of childbearing. The advantages a homosexually-enabled man has in attracting a mate also help retain the homosexuality gene without long-term deleterious effects to the species. This might well be the ultimate solution to our problem. No matter how many people there are, homosexuality will help us select for quality genotypes, or at least what women perceive as quality.

Chapter 5

The seven deadly sins of sociobiology

No matter how much today's scientists assure us they are being com-
pletely objective, they don't think there is anything wrong with
homosexuality, even if they themselves are gay, as some of the recent
ones have been – the Normality of heterosexuality is always assumed,
always left unexamined. And Normal heterosexuality requires Normal
males and females. Normal requires Abnormal and so the circle goes
on . . .

(Ardill, 1996: 12)

This last chapter serves two purposes. First, it provides an opportunity to
present a differing view of the morality of evolutionary research from
that generally available in the literature. Second, it briefly attempts the
more traditional task of summarising research. The first objective in my
view is probably far more important than the second. At the risk of
interpolating personal experience into a theoretical review I would defend
this view. When my colleagues and I started researching this area after
relatively placid careers in less controversial fields we were ill-prepared
for the storm of abuse that broke over our heads. The gay media particularly had a free kick at our expense despite the basic and quite
conservative research we were undertaking (counting heads). Once we
had recovered, the experience was instructive and brought home just how
emotionally charged questions of sexual orientation are. That this spills
over into rarefied levels of academic argument is evident from the
increasing numbers of homosexuals doing doctorates to push their career
barrows (entirely laudable) and to help resolve their own sexuality (less
so). Perhaps being straight allows a certain distance from the angst but
the level of bickering, misinformation and just sloppy reasoning from
both gay and straight commentators was annoying and ultimately dis-
heartening.

While the genesis of this book was an approach from a publisher, the
spur to doing it was trying to solve the wonderful intellectual puzzle that
homosexuality presents, militated by the strongest expressions of concern

from colleagues and friends. Partly this was a purely professional worry about the consequences for our careers but also their more deeply felt concern that homosexuality was an area best left fallow. Musing over this view in the years of writing and researching this book I came away with an entirely personal conviction that much of the advice to leave homosexuality alone was little more than internalised homophobia and that gay men suffered this as much as their detractors. In chewing over my data with perceptive gay colleagues, several agreed and felt that sociobiological research threatened gay acceptance because it might equate homosexuality with futility. That they had internalised the strictures of a world that equated homosexuality with degeneracy was, they felt, enough of a daily struggle without having to deal with the possibility that they were evolutionary misfits. This heartfelt concern prompted one dear friend to write an impassioned letter setting out the seven deadly sins of evolutionary theorising. I hope that this chapter will go some way to meet his concerns.

THE FIRST DEADLY SIN: WE ARE ANIMALS

Let us start with the proposition that we are animals. Our evolutionary descent from the rest of the animal kingdom is a mere six million years or so, a moment compared with the four billion years of life on Earth. Our immediate ancestors are only a million or so years removed and if the archaeological record is any guide, shared much in common with our current simian coevolutionists. Human life, such as we know it, has an immediate past of no more than 120,000 years. Given the brevity of human existence it is highly unlikely that we are far removed from the immediate concerns and influences which shaped creation. Given that we are animals, it follows that the same evolutionary logic so evidently at work among other animals applies equally to ourselves. It is absolutely uncontroversial to see the forces of evolution shaping and moulding animal life and evolution is the most fundamental theory of modern biology. Ethology, the study of animal behaviour, is an honoured part of the biosciences and has led to many profound insights into our anatomy, growth and development, genetics and other areas. By the same logic, insights gained from animal studies should aid our understanding of human social behaviour. Yet we are reluctant to equate ourselves with animals and apply these insights to ourselves. This is a curious and particular blindness that limits the growth of the social sciences and restricts our vision.

Why this is so is one of the mysteries of creation. We are ready enough to anthropomorphise animals, transmogrifying them into our own image, but this is a rather one-way street. It would appear that explaining animal social evolution is a relatively uncontroversial occupation, however controversial its findings; yet human social evolution until recently was a closed book. It is sufficient here to assert that this is a nonsense. As with all the animal kingdom we obey the same blind laws of evolution that ultimately set the bounds of our activity. Within those bounds our behaviour is lawful and, at least in principle, explicable. A critic, such as Roger Scruton, who dismisses animal–human social comparisons as: 'small leap(s) of the imagination' if not 'the leap of a small imagination' (Scruton, 1986, cited in Ruse, 1988) ignores the possibility that human social behaviour is probably rather more and, at the same time, rather less complicated than he might imagine. A biology of social behaviour may well expand the reach and utility of the social sciences, while at the same time simplifying many of the puzzles with which it currently grapples. In any case, on purely epistemological grounds alone: 'we should be wary of critics, whatever their political persuasion, who confidently tell us that the extension of Darwinism to the social world is bound to be flawed or inadequate' (Ruse, 1988).

This leads us directly to the question of homosexuality. If it is the case that our behaviour is an analogue of animal behaviour we face two immediate difficulties in explaining homosexuality. First there are no real animal analogues of human homosexuality. Such homosexual acts that do occur are either pathological (Calhoun, 1962), or serve purposes clearly unrelated to human behaviour (Ridley, 1994). As many have said, it is a bit of a nonsense to talk of one rat loving another. Second, we need to account for a behaviour which on the surface at least seems a negation of evolutionary reproductive success. Both difficulties hearten those who would argue that homosexuality is a purely social behaviour, an artefact of human culture inexplicable in evolutionary terms; to explain homosexuality, they would argue, is misguided and probably unwise (Kitcher, 1985; Murphy, 1990).

At the heart of this difficulty of seeing ourselves as animals is the question 'How animal-like are we?' We immediately become embroiled in methodological debate. Underlying most challenges to an evolutionary analysis of human behaviour are concerns about the appropriateness of method and no more fundamental an issue arises than the appropriateness of using animals to model human behaviour. That animals may be simpler and less complex social beings is the hardest barrier to breach in the incredulity of social qua social science. Paper after paper raises the supposed inadequacy of animal models to explain human behaviour. What is the value of animal analogy?

There are a number of points to be made here.

First, that animal investigation is useful is immediately apparent when we look at the biochemistry of homosexuality and its precursors. If homosexuality is a matter of sexual orientation rather than preference then we are less concerned with animal social behaviour than with the biochemistry of sexuality. What is quite annoying is the sometimes mischievous inability of critics to acknowledge that causal explanation proceeds on many levels. Animals that have sex with other same-sexed animals do so for a reason. Critics of biosocial explanations delight in pointing out the rigidity of a rat's sexual responses and the sheer folly of comparing the intention of the act with the behavioural plasticity of humans (Vanwyk and Geist, 1995). While I am unsure just what degree of behavioural intentionality rats enjoy, I am sure that the rat's intentions is the least important part of the comparison. Rat brains and human brains do control behaviour and while informed critics point to the enormous structural differences between various mammalian brains, what is often conveniently ignored is that their biochemistry is remarkably similar. One of the plausible arguments for a biological basis for homosexuality is the similarity of mammalian sexual triggers. What turns you on and triggers the triggers depends on whether you are a rat or human but the triggers have a common biochemistry. Were they moulded for a common evolutionary purpose?

Second, those committed to biosocial perspectives are not relying on animal analogies to model human homosexuality. Rats do not love each other, so this criticism is misguided. We are less interested in finding homosexual animals than in asserting a similar ancestry for animals and humanity. We share a common evolution with animals, and behaviour is shaped by similar processes even if it serves dissimilar purposes. Homosexual love may not be part of animal life but animal sexuality is. Recall throughout this book how often explanation of some obscure point of homosexuality was clarified by observing similarities in human and animal sexuality. We may then legitimately ask if there is a common evolutionary logic underlying similar mammalian behaviour. To make the point clearer, it would be a nonsense to claim that animals are homosexual as we understand it, given the complexities that human consciousness brings, but in experiencing the same evolutionary pressures, species may arrive at similar solutions. Skua gull nest helpers may be as much victims of parental manipulation as are kin selective homosexuals and the gulls do not need to be gay to provide an insight into why Skua and human parents might benefit from nest helpers. To the extent that these pressures contribute to sexual orientation, animal analogies are useful. Of course this defence immediately raises issues of what we mean by sexual orientation but we will park that debate for the moment.

Let me give an example. In grappling with the finer points of frequency-dependent sexual selection I was puzzled by the paradox of gay men signalling excessive virility as part of their mating displays (Lumby, 1978; Deaux and Hanna, 1984; Buss, 1994), yet such hypervirility was seemingly at odds with a behaviour which had limited reproductive value. Then I reread Trivers' (1985) *Social Evolution*, where he makes the point that we are selected for deceit and gave a range of behaviours where birds and animals gained copulation by deception. This recalled to mind Darwin's 1871 discussion of hypervirility and secondary sexual characteristics. As I am a social psychologist, the corollary should have been obvious to me as a member of a species where men and women invest billions of dollars each year on cosmetics, cosmetic surgery and artful tailoring to deceive each other as to their genetic potential. I then recalled Richard Alexander (1975) saying, over twenty years ago, that we are a species dedicated to lying to each other. The selective advantage of such deceptions when used by straight men is obvious in retrospect, as is the reason why homosexual men use a more extreme form in their own displays, but it took an animal behaviour to make the connection.

Third, there is another very important point to animal analogues, one that social constructivists seem incapable of grasping, or unwilling to grasp. Human beings, at least over the last 10,000 years of our evolution, have not lived in natural environments (Symons, 1979; Irons, 1983; Badcock, 1991). Since the invention of agriculture, human social evolution and no doubt a rising self-consciousness have made it almost impossible to decide what are the ultimate 'real' causes of our behaviour. You will recall our discussion in Chapter 1 about whether homosexuality is natural and about the difficulties of distinguishing between proximate and ultimate explanations of human behaviour. Given that we live in unnatural environments, environments that are atypical of those long slow years that shaped our hominid evolution, it is difficult in the extreme to give more than proximate answers to such deceptively simple questions as why are there homosexuals? I am already on record as being dissatisfied with social constructivist theories which are simply long-chained descriptive explanations of surface phenomena. Given that our species is far from its roots, it is doubly difficult to arrive at the ultimate causes of our behaviour. Perhaps the way ahead is to seek the relative clarity that comes from observing natural behaviour in natural environments. That is, behaviour which obeys the evolutionary logic which gave it life. Perhaps the clearest examples lie in the animal kingdom, although this does not stop us from constantly drawing parallels from today's tribal cultures in the mistaken belief that they are somehow simpler, more natural forms of humanity, as Symons (1979) put it, 'fantasies of ancestral utopias and matriarchies'.

There are many other defences of using animals as models of human behaviour but these in one form or another amount to a rebuttal of charges of reductionism. We will return to these later. This brings us to the second deadly sin.

THE SECOND DEADLY SIN: EXPLAINING
HOMOSEXUALITY IS UNNECESSARY AND MISGUIDED

Evolutionary theory and its sociobiology attempts 'the systematic study of the biological basis of all social behavior' (Wilson, 1975). *All* social behaviour. It is a fundamental tenet of sociobiological theory that all social behaviour rests on an evolutionary footing and that important social behaviours such as homosexuality should be explicable in these terms. So for an evolutionist, homosexuality presents an immediate challenge, but sadly few commentators see the need. Most see homosexuality as purely a product of social learning, not biology. In this enlightened age, this inevitably leads one to see homosexuality as a sexual *preference* rather than an *orientation* – just another variant of human sexuality. From this viewpoint, critics such as Futuyma and Risch (1984) argue it is irksome to be confronted with a steady diet of biologically oriented researchers trying to uncover the causes of a behaviour which seems as obvious as heterosexuality: 'For us, homosexuality is one example of the immense flexibility of human behavior. It requires no more explanation than a preference for blondes or brunettes or for music or sports' (Futuyma and Risch, 1984). Such research is then at best ill-considered and at worst a lingering afterglow of a worldview which saw homosexuality as a pathological deviation in need of urgent remedy. Nor are theorists alone in this view, as it is a major irritant to homosexuals themselves that their behaviour is constantly under the spotlight.

Common to all of these challenges are clear doubts as to the necessity of explaining homosexuality. The most basic challenge faced is the perennial one of defending an evolutionary view of social behaviour. One becomes inured to the unpopularity of the evolutionary viewpoint and the fact that it is far from being a respected paradigm in the social sciences. However, there seems to be a particular resistance to examining homosexuality this way (Ruse, 1988). Critics assert that sociobiology lacks a method for evaluating sexual orientation; is over-inclusive and explains homosexuality at a level of generality that makes testing of competing hypotheses impractical; that it is so circular in explanation that it readily falls into the fallacy of affirming the consequent; and that, in any case, an evolutionary proof is impossible (Kitcher, 1985; Fausto-Sterling, 1992; Hubbard and Wald, 1993b; Lewontin, 1993; Kaplan and Rogers, 1994; McGuire, 1995). How plausible are these critiques?

Critics argue that much evolutionary theory is circular in nature and that often such explanation is simply reification, giving a behaviour a name and hoping that is sufficient explanation (Tobach and Rosoff, 1994). As an alternative, they propose that homosexuality is merely part of the immense flexibility of human behaviour and requires little explanation (Futuyma and Risch, 1984). However, purely social accounts of homosexuality are themselves circular in nature and largely *ad hoc*. For example: what is homosexuality? It is part of the plasticity of our sexual repertoire. How do we know? Because there are a variety of sexual preferences. A cursory inspection of this explanation shows an equal circularity to that claimed for evolutionary accounts. Moreover, as Seaborg (1984) noted, such arguments in effect dismiss the question of why homosexuality evolved in the first place and what is the ultimate basis of such behavioural plasticity. More to the point, is sociobiology fuzzy thinking?

Evolutionary biology posits two things in establishing the antecedents of social behaviour. If homosexuality has a biological basis then it must have genes that 'under suitable environmental conditions program individuals to develop the trait', and in addition that 'over the course of generations, these genes have replaced alternative genes, which do not code for that trait' (Futuyma and Risch, 1984). Such an explanation is not *ad hoc* and provides a causal mechanism which, at the very least, set predispositions that may become the building blocks of later phenotypic behaviour. Finding such genetic mechanisms provides sites for sexual orientation and for subsequent differences within the human population. In the absence of identifying sites on the genome (the ultimate hope of every evolutionist) we have to infer the actions of these genes by indirect means. These include estimates of heritability by correlational and twin studies; searching for morphological differences in brain sites and hormonal control mechanisms; insights from animal analogues and developmental psychology; *and* analyses of social behaviour. Subsequent theorising as to the evolutionary mechanisms underlying the behaviour is postulational-deductive rather than exclusively empirical but should be rigorous and predictive (Wilson, 1975). For an example of such an approach leading to several testable propositions recall the approach described in Chapter 3.

It *is* a problem that the very comprehensiveness of evolutionary theory lends it the appearance of explaining everything too simply. As E.O. Wilson acknowledged 'Paradoxically, the greatest snare in sociobiological reasoning is the ease with which it is conducted' (Wilson, 1975). Wilson argues that modern evolutionary theorising follows the procedures of 'strong inference' (hypothesis testing in field studies) characteristic of biological science, rather than the older naturalistic observation methods which, although useful, are difficult to replicate. It must be realised that proof within an evolutionary account is often a matter of what will be accepted as a reasonable level of coincidence of variables. The difficulty faced by empirical researchers is that proof is often a matter of generational change and experimental manipulations may take millennia to work themselves to a conclusion, even if procedural constraints are first overcome. For this reason what experimental proof we do have is conducted on fast-breeding simple animals such as *Drosophila*, which then brings us up against charges of false animal analogies again.

In the event that we identify possible genetic markers, manipulation of the genes for sexual orientation would not be possible for ethical reasons. Nor are animal analogies always acceptable models for human functioning, as their behavioural repertoire is often limited and generalisation is difficult. These difficulties make scientific falsification quite hard to achieve but possibly less so than in most other social sciences. In any case, it is not true that evolutionary explanation lacks scientific rigour or a method. In principle, it should be relatively easy to set a standard of proof that will satisfy the sharpest critic.

Perhaps it would be unkind to suggest that these criticisms have more to do with a failure to appreciate the thoroughness of genetic and endocrinological research than any failure of evolutionary theory but in any case, as described in Chapter 2, anatomists and molecular biologists are proving awkwardly indigestible of late. The recently identified markers for male homosexuality and several studies finding discrete differences between the brains of straight men and gay men make a strong essentialist case for homosexuality and necessitate an evolutionary account. And so to the third deadly sin.

THE THIRD DEADLY SIN: TRIVIAL PURSUITS

Other critics assert that such an investigation is trivial and even if you can make a case for a biological basis for homosexuality an evolutionary account is unnecessary. If you assume that *expressed* homosexuality is socially constructed then you inevitably need to question the relative worth of studies which examine the seminal causes of behaviour. Is the aetiology of homosexuality any more intrinsically interesting than that of heterosexuality? Why bother to study a given? Is some other subject more worthy of scarce time and resources? Murphy (1990), in his review of an earlier biology of homosexuality, cogently argued this view.

> It is hard to see that there is any ... reason to study the origins of behavior that is morally, medically, psychologically (and perhaps even religiously) aproblematic. Where after all, are the psychological and physiological accounts of devoted and monogamous spouses? Where are the hormonal studies of dedicated scientists? Where are the evolutionary accounts of fervent patriots, saints and heroes? That no one is interested in the causes of these behaviors suggests that it is anything but a disinterested desire to know that guides the hands of scientific research and grant foundations.
>
> (Murphy, 1990: 134)

Clearly the test of scientific worth assumes that such research has a hidden agenda. While it was reasonably easy to justify enquiry based on the inclusiveness principles of scientific curiosity, it is less easy to defend against charges of bias. Even in writing this account, pursuing the causality of homosexuality led several colleagues to an *ad hominem* questioning of motives. If it is unnecessary to explain homosexuality then any attempt to do so must have ulterior motives. Again Murphy neatly summarises these views:

> the incentive to discover the origins of homosexuality seems to belong to those who find homosexuality a pathological, sinful, immoral or criminal condition. At least on the basis of these views there is reason to try and understand the origins of homosexual behavior if only to prevent and eliminate it. It is ordinarily some deficit which prompts medicine, psychology and the rest to reach for a causal explanation of behavior.

> (Murphy, 1990: 134)

These challenges then enter the speculative area of morality. If the putative differences are trivial and the motives are suspect, then clearly the investigator is morally culpable, or at least on the slippery slope to cruel and unusual experimentation! I was impressed by the number of references in the literature to Nazi concentration camp experimentation in reviews of the merits of looking for the biology of homosexuality (Lang, 1940; Moir and Jessel, 1989; Lerner, 1992; Hubbard and Wald, 1993b; Stein, 1994; Haynes, 1995). No less prevalent were suggestions that such enquiries were disguised heterosexism. At best, writers from this perspective warn that curiosity is an insufficient rationale and that such enquiries should 'pass moral muster'. In line with the social constructivist view, kinder critics argue that such enquiries are not morally neutral and are unfortunate because we become preoccupied with the causality of homosexuality and this obscures the more pressing issues of the social climate which foster homophobia and discrimination towards homosexuals. From this view, concern with causes obscures or condones: 'the condition of their servitude' (Murphy, 1990).

In light of these and other challenges, to assert that homosexuality is an interesting theoretical puzzle is to immediately label oneself as suspect. Nevertheless the puzzle remains. While it is not my intention to set up stalking horses to be immediately knocked down, such arguments present major obstacles to an evolutionary analysis of behaviour and to homosexuality in particular, and need to be addressed. In answering this third challenge, let me start by observing that there is an immense literature on the causation of homosexuality and this in itself suggests the question is hardly trivial. However, as we have seen, those opposed to biological investigations claim that such studies are unnecessary and do little to advance the cause of homosexuals. Each new study piecing together homosexuality's biological antecedents is greeted by attacks on method and disputed conclusions. While this is the very core of scientific discourse and is to be encouraged, an overview of the debate reveals several subtexts. It might be interesting to address the question of triviality by examining these subtexts.

Let us start with 'trivial equals maladaptive'. From an evolutionary viewpoint behaviours which are durable and widespread are probably adaptive. Contrary to Freudian and medical accounts which see homosexuality as a pathological inversion, the evolutionist is challenged to account for homosexuality in positive terms (Weinrich, 1995). If homosexuality is adaptive, then it aids the evolution of a species and assists individual reproductive success. The challenge is to build theory to explain how this might happen. Clearly, homosexuality has had a bad press in the past and seems at first glance to be at odds with natural selection. However, as E.O.Wilson noted, sociobiological research often yields nonobvious and counterintuitive findings. If a homosexual gene can be demonstrated to be adaptive then evolutionary theory will have helped to reverse negative views of homosexuality. If it can be demonstrated that homosexuality is an adaptive variation, then a new generation will hopefully grow to be more tolerant and accepting than before. However, to put the negative case, homosexuality may well prove to be a byproduct of evolution, as not all social behaviours are adaptive. Even if homosexuality is the end of an evolutionary process rather than a link in an ongoing chain, this in itself is useful information. In either case, research into homosexuality's causality is hardly trivial.

There is another subtext underlying the charge of triviality, that evolutionary explanation is essentially facile 'pop sociobiology' (Kitcher, 1985). More enlightened critics like Lewontin (1993) acknowledge the impact of genetics on behaviour but dispute the reliability of evolutionary explanation, given the variability of individual accommodations to genetic predispositions and the consequent global nature of biosocial theory. This is a more subtle challenge. A rebuttal of this position is difficult and would involve establishing that an evolutionary analysis provides more favourable theoretical outcomes than other social science methods, a position advocated by Wilson (1975) in his *Sociobiology*. Wilson argues that this will eventually lead sociobiology to cannibalise and subsume other social sciences like psychology, a position not calculated to endear sociobiology to its critics. However, perhaps a more considered view sees evolution explaining behaviour at several quite different levels (Barkow, 1989). Rather than being trivial in its global approach, critics ignore the other levels of evolutionary theorising. Sociobiology makes hard predictions at a biological (micro) level and global explanations at a societal (macro) level, neatly bracketing the other social sciences. This is confusing to those of a more reductionist view of science, which leads us to the fourth deadly sin.

THE FOURTH DEADLY SIN: A CREEPING REDUCTIONISM

As Michael Ruse has noted the sociobiology of homosexuality 'lies more in the realm of the hypothetical than the proven' (Ruse, 1981) and fifteen years later this is still the case, despite an avalanche of biosocial studies. Perhaps the largely untested nature of much homosexual theorising has generated an enormous press opposed to the endeavour. The pages of the *Journal of Homosexuality* for the last decade have provided a forum for article after article castigating the sociobiological enterprise and the popular press was no less vehement. When aspects of Jim Malcolm's and my research percolated their way into the media consciousness we drew sharp reactions from the straight press like 'Heresies: The potent myth of the gay deceiver' (*Sydney Morning Herald*, 23 November 1995), and gay media like 'Biological bunkum' (*Sydney Star Observer*, 21 December 1995). When we mildly protested that we were simply taking pedigrees to establish rates of homosexuality within gay and straight families, fairly mundane research, our interest was labelled 'An abnormal sexual obsession' (*Sydney Star Observer*, 18 January 1996). Why is this area so controversial?

The clue came from my gay colleague who graciously supplied me with this list of sociobiology's sins in the hope that I would repent. He ended his five pages of fairly impassioned rhetoric saying that of all the sins I might commit if I wrote this book, the worst would be 'to degrade social theory into trite and unhelpful biologising'. It seems that at the heart of the social constructivist disquiet with evolutionary theorising is a worry that the knowledge base of the social sciences would be eroded by 'biologising' social phenomena. Ruse, in his usual penetrating style, goes right to the core of the matter:

> Social scientists tend to be horrified of and hostile towards biological science. Insecure at the best of times, they spend troubled nights dreaming of the bogey of 'reductionism', of the rape of the social sciences as biologists move into the human domain.
>
> (Ruse, 1981: 29)

This is an entirely well-founded worry. Unlike the early 1980s when Ruse made this observation, we are in the midst of a biological revolution that is rapidly pushing back the frontiers of our ignorance of genetics and shining a revealing light on many formerly obscure golden ghettos of theorising such as homosexuality. The 20th century has been the century of the physical sciences but the 21st will be biology's, and that this revolution is having an impact on the social sciences is an understatement! In a review of the social psychological literature, for example, there has been a 40 percent increase in biological/evolutionary theorising in such journals as *Personality and Social Psychology Bulletin* and *Journal of Personality and Social Psychology*, formerly bastions of social construct-ivist explanation (McKnight and Sutton, in press). This is no less the case with an explosion of articles and books on homosexuality that has on my count doubled every year between 1990 and 1993 and continued at a high level through 1994–1996. Social psychologists who have long owned the preserve of explaining human attraction, attitudes, sexual behaviour, aggression, helping, competition and the like, have suddenly discovered that population and behavioural geneticists, molecular biologists and zoologists are writing far more eruditely on aspects of social psychology that were formerly only trespassed on by anthropologists and sociologists! Here we must leave homosexuality for a moment and consider the nature of scientific explanation.

There are any number of reasons why social scientists might fear a reduction of their area but we will mention three. Let us start with psychology's lack of a grand theory. As long ago as 1933 J.R. Kantor, in *A Survey of the Science of Psychology*, lamented that psychology lacked a unifying theory and was an interesting collection of information and approaches but hardly a science. The nature of a science is that it collects information and synthesises it by connecting all the information in all its parts, and generates grand theory. Science by this definition is the art of interrelation of disparate information. Now while this is a task which is incomplete and perhaps never to be completed, at least the skeleton of the enterprise should be becoming obvious and this is not yet evident in psychology. Yet psychology does have an armature, a skeleton that will interrelate all the parts and provide a grand theory: it is synthetic Dar-winism, and this is only gradually becoming obvious to psychologists and other social scientists despite being available for at least the last sixty years (Crawford, 1989).

Darwinism is not philosophy, or psychology, or anthropology, or soci-ology, or ethology, or ethnology, or economics but it underpins them all. Now the nature of grand theory is that it is a more fundamental, all-embracing level of explanation than that which it seeks to interrelate. It is not that it is psychological in explaining psychology but that it embraces all that is psychological and gives it order and relates it to other sciences. To underpin a discipline may be seen as reductionism and there is no doubt that sociobiology, which seeks to integrate all social sciences within a biological framework, is a more fundamental level of explanation. The quite realistic fear then of social scientists is that, being without a grand theory, they are not yet sciences and, being protosciences at best, they are at risk of being colonised by some other science's meaning system with a superior, or at least a grand theory.

The second concern of social scientists is that reductionism will erode the knowledge base of their discipline and over time disciplines such as psychology will become simply descriptive meta-languages for more fundamental levels of explanation. There is some truth in this, as knowledge is hierarchical or at least seems that way to the human mind, which automatically classifies and readily adopts taxonomies. What then is left for the practitioners of the subsumed knowledge system? This is a less sophisticated concern than the first, as all knowledge is hierarchical and the trend is reductive and all sciences are descriptive meta-languages for those more fundamental. Michael Ruse (1981) noted that social scientists were not alone in their fear of reductionism: 'biologists have much the same fears when faced with the physical sciences: "Every biologist suffers from physics envy" '. The intrusion of a more fundamental approach to ordering information is reductionist and does change the way we study and integrate information. For example, the advent of molecular biology into genetics caused such a profound change of direction that forty years after its advent I searched for six months to find a classical geneticist in Australia who felt competent enough to read this manuscript, where once the work of Fisher and Waddington and Haldane would have been common knowledge. Perhaps one of the ironies of the advent of sociobiology is that it is colonising areas abandoned by biology (and for that matter psychology and other social sciences).

However, change does not equal subsumption and the arrival of molecular genetics into the biosciences has vastly expanded the reach and grasp of biology.

The third concern flows from the first two. If biology makes better sense of psychology than does psychology (or anthropology, or sociology, or ethology, or ethnology, or economics) then what place is left for psychologists? Put another way, is psychology a biological rather than a social science and, if it is, should psychologists become biologists? Perhaps. On my reading, psychology has been rapidly transforming itself into a cognitive and biological science since the early 1980s and in my country most universities training psychologists now do so from a cognitive-behavioural perspective and as biological scientists, rather than as liberal arts, social sciences, or humanities graduates.

Perhaps worries over creeping reductionism are simply a misapprehension about evolutionary theorising. One of the purposes of this chapter is to use homosexuality as a thinly disguised vehicle to argue for a more profound approach to social theory than we currently have but it is not designed to devalue psychological explanation. Rather, it is to bolster psychological and other social explanation by showing how it all relates. Much of the current dissatisfaction with social theorising is that the sheer behavioural plasticity of human behaviour defeats meaningful explanation and this is why some social scientists hunger for the illusory simplicities of reductionism. There is always an exception to your rule and an obscure branch of human culture that does it differently. Within social psychology, for example, this led to such a crisis of confidence that for twenty years the profession self-destructed publicly with many onlookers predicting its imminent demise. We recovered, but this crisis did enormous damage to a valuable discipline and led to a haemorrhaging of researchers and research funds (McKnight and Sutton, 1994). Social psychology is not alone in the social sciences in having such a crisis of confidence. Perhaps the core of the problem was sheer human diversity. Homosexuality is one such behaviour; it is so variable and diverse that the literature is a vast confusion from which few clear answers emerge. Why is this so?

Perhaps part of the answer is that we keep asking the wrong questions about homosexuality. We seem preoccupied in asking how homosexuality came about rather than why it persists and the latter question is by far the more fundamental. Mayr, in a profound article in *Science*, about the nature of causation, distinguished between ultimate and proximate causative theories (Mayr, 1961). While both explanations are valuable, ultimate causative theories are far more important as they interrelate behaviour and lead to the grand theory characteristic of science. By continually asking why some men are homosexual we descend into a welter of developmental, genetic, social and cultural explanations which in the end are nothing more than a long chain of proximate descriptions of causality. While understanding that a gene for homosexuality may exist on the long arm of the X chromosome (Hamer et al., 1993), and that it might be a hypervariable site in the genome (Turner, 1995), and that such variability is imprinted prior to conception (Pollard, 1996), and probably because a parent was stressed (Dorner et al., 1991), and that this led to hormonal changes in the foetal brains of homosexuals (Ellis and Ames, 1987), which may have led to anatomical differences in the hypothalamus underpinning sexual orientation (LeVay, 1991), may sound like a reasonable explanation of the aetiology of homosexuality, it still has not answered why are there gay men? Donald Symons (1979) observed that with proximate explanations 'it is possible to provide a complete proximate explanation of a behavior pattern without reference to, or knowledge of, evolution or evolutionary processes'. While we do so we ignore the basis of a truly predictive psychology of human sexuality.

This is not a partisan approach to the question but rather a sober evaluation of the explanatory power of each approach. Ultimate, or evolutionary, explanations relate to the grand theory which underpins them and in so doing interrelate all the elements that provide an answer to the 'why' question not addressed above. To return for a moment to what is possibly the longest sentence in this book, you need to ask yourself if the causal chain in the last paragraph was a sufficient explanation of homosexuality? If it seems okay, ask yourself why such a hypervariable site arose and why it continues to exist if it is deleterious to the person who has it. Ultimate explanations provide answers in terms of the evolution of the behaviour and its adaptive fitness. This is not just another type or level of question but a more fundamental answer to why we have the biochemistry, or stress, or imprinting or whatever causes the homosexuality. Alexander wrote that:

> Although proximate and ultimate causations are separate – and equal in the sense that each provides challenging scientific problems – they are not equal in their potential for providing a general theory of behavior: no theory of behavior remotely compares in usefulness or generality to evolutionary theory.
>
> (Alexander, 1975, cited in Symons, 1979: 8)

Now all of the above is not designed to denigrate psychology or the other social sciences, but to set boundaries to their existential and epistemological reach. Proximate and ultimate explanations are coextensive but different. Social psychology tells us how the homosexual thinks, feels and acts, and evolutionary psychology tells us why he does so. Each has their place. That one is more fundamental and has broader explanatory power necessarily means that the other is superior in the fine-grained detail.

THE FIFTH DEADLY SIN: SLY DETERMINISM

Perhaps at the bottom of resistance to biological research on the causes of homosexuality are deeper fears. Whether homosexuality is adaptive or otherwise, many commentators suggest that biological research may absolve us from changing prejudicial attitudes and behaviour (Gould, 1982). Rather, we should just abort homosexual foetuses and then genetically engineer a heterosexual tranquillity for those unlucky in life's lottery. Then again, if homosexuality is innate, perhaps our prejudices are too, and once again intolerance is excused as we are simply reacting to a biological reality (Gallup, 1995). As Ruse (1985) noted, resistance to biological theories of homosexuality ultimately boils down to concern that such explorations will reduce human freedom. Irrespective of the reasoning, sociobiological theory is viewed as a retrograde step, dragging homosexuality research back into a determinist ghetto it has long struggled to escape. Two points might be made here.

First, many feel that biology equals determinism, indeed that the terms are synonyms. However, this is not the case and in saying this I am expressing an opinion. All controversial views have adherents who take a harder or softer line to add emphasis to their views. In a multidisciplinary area like evolutionary theory (or indeed sexuality) this is particularly true. There are hard sociobiologists, like Wilson, usually from the zoological end of the profession, who are quite determinist. However, on my reading of the discipline as it unfolds, few theorists or researchers would be so definite, particularly as one's theorising deals with more complex organisms. The most that a moderate sociobiologist would claim is that homosexuality has a genetic basis. This does not mean that an individual possessing those genes will become a homosexual. Our genes set predispositions from which the individual constructs their life. All other factors being equal, if an individual has homosexual genes then they will identify as homosexuals. However, it is rarely the case that all things are equal and many environmental factors influence our sexual orientation. Given a genetic basis to homosexuality, it will probably be polygenic in nature. So the strongest prediction a sociobiologist would make is that the degree of genetic predisposition will be reflected in the degree of homosexual identification. This is a considerable source of confusion among critics of sociobiology and shows an incomplete appreciation of evolutionary theory. Sociobiologists do not claim a biological determinism. Evolution is both a social and biological process. The individual is nothing without a genetic basis and nothing without a phenotypic expression which includes behaviour. As one goes up the phylogenetic tree, instinct, or routinised behavioural responses, are less controlled by an individual's genes and more so by their environment. Ultimately it is the sheer plasticity of our responses to our genetic heritage that has enabled the rapid evolutionary advances made by human beings.

Second, even if it were the case, as Napoleon suggested, that biology equals destiny, human beings are a perverse lot and our history is one of transcending the limits set by our biological nature. As Katherine Hepburn said in the film *The African Queen* to Humphrey Bogart: 'Nature, Mr Allnut, is what we are put into this world to rise above' (quoted in Ridley, 1994). In a trite example, evolution has not equipped us with wings, so we go hang-gliding or build jumbo jets. In a similar way the genetics of our sexual orientation are not determinist. A strong predisposition towards homosexuality may meet and be overcome by a stronger desire for social conformity in a climate hostile to homosexuality. We do not have to perpetuate ourselves nor obey the dictates of our genes, although obviously some limits are harder than others. All that a sociobiologist would argue is that you may discern the evolutionary logic of our behaviour by analysing its functional significance. Sociobiologists fashion hypothetical-deductive postulates by building and testing mathematical models as do other sciences. They determine the impact of genes and behaviour by looking for trend lines through the middle of all the individual accommodations human beings make to their genetic endowment. In this sense, sociobiology is globally predictive even if it is not individually determinist.

THE SIXTH DEADLY SIN: SOCIOBIOLOGY IS MORALLY BANKRUPT

My answer to this is an unqualified yes and we will not waste much time on it! Sociobiologists may not be morally neutral, the uses sociobiology findings are put to may not be morally neutral, and the interpretations of others including the critics may not be morally neutral, but the truth always is. At the risk of digressing at this point, an enormous amount of time is wasted debating the morality of science. Science is, of necessity, value-free. Too much fuzzy thinking asserts that science is what scientists do, and because scientists are human, science is a fallible process and hence must be value-laden. All of this is true. Unfortunately, by the same logic, theorists and critics alike must be equally tainted. Therefore, if we accept that science is impossible to do without a human element, then it is a moot point who has the superior insight, the theorist or the critic. Let the research speak. Equally, one of the most contentious areas of human endeavour is – what is moral? A casual glance at history shows there is no absolute morality slowly trying to reveal itself. Five decades of trying to interpret and apply the United Nations Universal Declaration of Human Rights would be sufficient to highlight the difficulties. Morality is relative to time and place.

Homosexuality is one area where the morality of scientific enquiry is hotly contested. This demonstrates the importance of sexual orientation to the community and, incidentally, the importance of the evolutionary viewpoint. This is not to say that all evolutionary theorising is sane. As Symons observes:

> The search for morality in nature has led [sociobiologists] to sentimentalizing and romanticizing nonhuman animals and preliterate peoples, to unsupported implications that selection favors groups, populations, cultures, societies, and ecosystems at the expense of the constituent individuals, to fantasies of ancestral utopias and matriarchies.
>
> (Symons, 1979: 61)

Still sensible sociobiologists, like other scientists, are simply trying to bring their own peculiar insights derived from evolutionary biology and the social sciences to an understanding of homosexuality. In this they should be encouraged, as this will ultimately prove to be the quickest way to precipitate the debate if they are mistaken. Self-righteous indignation about the ultimate purposes of sociobiological enquiry into homosexuality is not only ponderous but also counterproductive. By all means, critique sociobiological insights as this will hasten its demise if it is fallacious, but second-guessing the morality of theorists' intentions will only waste time. In the absence of agreement as to what is moral, the only solution is to encourage scientific debate.

On rereading my last few paragraphs it is obvious that my disquiet about critics' *ad hominem* attacks has led to naked special pleading for the freedom of sociobiological enquiry. Still, I think a bit of special pleading is necessary, for there is too much righteous indignation apparent in these criticisms and, in my view, too little science. One even detects a note of febrile anger in some criticism that sociobiologists persist in trying to explain homosexuality (see for example Ricketts, 1984, or Murphy, 1990). Michael Ruse's (1984) comment that critics see 'sociobiology's persistence in trying to relate human to evolutionary biology [as] proof that their real motivation is underhand and not genuinely scientific' sums this up. What a nonsense! Surely the question is one of good or bad science. Whether it is, or not, is not decided by questioning motives, or even worrying about possible applications, but by determining if homosexuality has a biological basis. Sociobiologists think so. It is the task of critics to dispute this with better science, not impute motives.

This of course will alarm those cautious thinkers who write on the morality of science and worry about its applications. Yet my reading in the sociology of scientific enquiry shows that too often scientific enquiry is vitiated by a too passionate moral scrutiny. Nonsensical? Two analogies will suffice. First, it might be instructive to count the number of times sociobiological enquiry is linked by analogy to Nazi experimentation in articles by sociobiology's friends and foes. This is a non sequitur. It seems implicit in much critical comment that to acknowledge a biological basis to homosexuality is to start on the slippery slope to eugenics and the gas chambers. A second analogy points to the importance of pursuing theory not motives. It might be instructive to examine the race–IQ debate, particularly as it developed in its later years as an evolutionary issue. The hostility of ill-considered assignations of motives and *ad hominem* attacks may well have made the truth unreachable and there are many uncomfortable parallels between the race–IQ debate and the search for the biological roots of homosexuality. As more evidence accumulates that sexual orientation is biological, it would be unfortunate if we went down a similar path.

Before we leave morality it might be instructive to examine the gene's morality. Books like Richard Dawkins' *The Selfish Gene* (1976) and *The Blind Watchmaker* (1986) have done a fair bit to anthropomorphise the gene in the public mind. From recent radio talks one is left with an impression of a gene plotting to ensure its survival and using all manner of underhand and devious tricks to get its way. This is certainly the impression in my students' minds. However, fact is far from fancy. Natural selection is a non-conscious, cold, impersonal and even ruthless process. While not quite a matter of 'nature red in tooth and claw', as human emotion certainly underlies sexual orientation (and its study), the underlying mechanics of evolution admit to no emotions. As Wilson (1975) noted in his opus, the gene knows no morality, and perhaps nor does the truth.

THE SEVENTH DEADLY SIN: SOCIOBIOLOGY IS SEXIST

To end on an even more controversial note, many like Fausto-Sterling (1992), Hubbard and Wald (1993b), Kaplan and Rogers (1994), and Ardill (1996) find an evolutionary analysis of homosexuality sexist. This critique flows two ways. One branch notes that most of the studies concentrate on male homosexuality and see this as evidence of entrenched male gender bias, even among those who are its victims; and the second more sustained attack notes that evolutionary accounts of homosexuality support patriarchal views of sexuality.

To tackle the second criticism first it would be sufficient to rely on the freedom of enquiry defence we discussed under the sixth deadly sin. However, I know this will not suffice, so may I further risk my credibility by saying that I think human sexuality is inherently, quite naturally, sexist. When viewed from an evolutionary perspective, sexuality is neither fair nor equitable. Men and women follow quite different reproductive strategies and several fairly hard findings emerge when we consider the massive literature on human mating and sexual selection. As Gordon Gallup and Susan Suarez (1983) note in their summary of these findings:

> Males ... have the capacity to father many offspring and are largely exempt from having to contend directly with the biological conse- quences of conception. Thus lacking genetic assurance as to their relatedness to offspring, males should be selected for high frequency sex with a large number of females. Whereas the optimal female strategy would be to postpone copulation for purposes of assessing mate quality and signs of commitment, males should be motivated by concerns of relatively immediate sexual gratification. Similarly, since males can be cuckolded, males should be more prone to commit adultery, and at the same time, more offended than females by an adulterous mate.
>
> (Gallup and Suarez, 1983: 317)

For these reasons, childrearing is also a female-linked behaviour: it reflects women's greater need to protect their relatively few offspring. Matriarchy as we understand it is a direct consequence of these differing sexual strategies. Only since we have had reliable contraception have we had the possibility of revising these roles. The feminist revolution which freed women from large families has paradoxically intensified this pres- sure by reducing even further the number of chances women have to pass on their genes. By the same logic, men now have even more sexual freedom and the much higher rates of male extramarital infidelity, incest, infanticide, neglect of step-children (and children), and indeed patriarchy itself, reflect a clear, if unpalatable evolutionary logic. I suggest that if anyone needs to be convinced of the inherently sexist nature of sex they should read David Buss's (1994) *The Evolution of Desire* or Robin Baker's (1996) *Sperm Wars*, two excellent popular accounts of the inequities of sexual selection. At this point I would like to repeat what was said when discussing the fifth deadly sin. Biology is only destiny to the degree that human ingenuity has so far failed to bend its rules!

What has this to do with homosexuality? Let us start with semantics. In a moment we will return to considering why gay men might collude in their oppression. However, if in the unlikely event that it were true that evolutionary outcomes such as homosexuality are patriarchal, is this necessarily a bad thing? Patriarchy is a descriptive label for a system which vests control of resources and reproduction in male hands. Lately it has become a pejorative word but it still retains all of its descriptive power. To label an explanation as patriarchal may be a fairly pointless exercise if we shift the baseline on its use. Evolutionary explanation seeks not to explain or pass judgement on current behaviour but to decide its adaptive value. To do this it compares the behaviour to the natural environment in which it arose. A current behaviour is adaptive if it reflects the evolutionary logic that gave rise to it over the long haul of our primate evolution. As Symons (1979) notes, any behaviour today that is judged maladaptive may be 'a byproduct of an adaptive behavior' or 'it may be a relic of a formerly adaptive character in the process of being lost'. What is important in deciding this question is not whether it is beneficial but its function (Williams, 1966). To say that a homosexual scenario is patriarchal may just be a neutral description of the conditions under which it arose. As we no longer live in natural environments (recall the discussion of novel environments in Chapter 4) all our behaviour may be functionally maladaptive (unlikely). Deciding if homosexuality is adaptive or maladaptive is not an example of patriarchy at work but a comparative judgement. I think critics who would see evolutionary explanation as unconscious patriarchy are using too short a baseline. 'Patriarchal' is a pejorative adjective only if the critic assumes the theorist describing a patriarchal system commends it as a lifestyle to be followed by all.

Then of course we need to decide if male sexual agendas and homosexual variants *are* patriarchal in natural environments. This is unlikely. As long ago as 1951 Ford and Beach demonstrated that while power and resources may be held by men in most but not all cultures, women were firmly in control of reproduction and this is the most fundamental aspect of patriarchy. Women's fertility is the limiting variable in the human mating system and, as Baker (1996) demonstrates, women have evolved an impressive and extensive armoury of tactics to ensure that reproduction occurs on their terms. It may be that a historical analysis of patriarchy's oppression of Western women is epiphenomenal when judged against a long prehistory of 'wimmin's business'.

Evidence either way is speculative but Gallup and Suarez (1983) advanced a theory of male homosexuality which has enjoyed some considerable interest and supports this contention. They argue that homosexuality arose as a consequence of women's control of the reproductive agendas in our natural environments. Because women are selected to be cautious and to delay sex, men are counterselected to become seductive, urgent and demanding. As the resolution of this basic impasse requires patience, skill and tactics on the part of the seducer, this inevitably advantages those experienced in the seduction game. As young males are neither patient nor skilled and have poor access to females, they may turn from frustration to their own sex for sexual relief. This theory has much going for it as it amplifies our understanding of the early adolescent homosexual phase so characteristic of male development. Baker and Bellis (1995) have used this prehomosexual frustration as one of the bases of their sperm competitive advantage theory of homosexuality. What is important here is that Gallup and Suarez argue a different case for lesbianism. Sexual selection is essentially a matriarchal system, so lesbians are little different from their heterosexual sisters and lead relatively quiet and inconspicuous lives compared to their gay peers.

This brings us back to the first criticism: why are theorists ignoring lesbianism in our discussion of homosexuality? Probably because gayness and lesbianism are unrelated phenomena. Because each orientation prefers its own sex we assume a similarity. This may be mistaken. Irrespective of the political correctness of having a combined homosexual lobby, the evidence is fairly clear that gay men and lesbians are dissimilar and that each has more in common with their heterosexual counterparts than with each other. If there is one clear finding to emerge from research on homosexuality it is that gay men share more in common with straight men than they do with lesbians or heterosexual women in their attitudes, feelings, fantasies and behaviours. To put this another way, gay men are men first and homosexuals second and it seems the same for lesbians as women. What is the evidence for this?

Male and female homosexual behaviour is quite different and obeys a different evolutionary logic. Male homosexuals are much more preoccupied with the sex act than are lesbians and this suggests they are following the logic of their sex, not that of their orientation. In surveys from the two early Kinsey studies (Kinsey et al., 1948, 1953), through the two Kinsey Centre reports (Bell and Weinberg, 1978; Weinberg et al., 1994b), to the large UK survey of Johnson and her colleagues (Johnson et al., 1994), consistent differences between gay men and lesbians have been reported. Summarising these differences: gay men are markedly more promiscuous, with many reporting over 1,000 sexual partners whereas lesbians had a median range of 3–8. Gay men will engage in anonymous sex with complete strangers without concern for the other person, whereas lesbians seek love and commitment. Bell and Weinberg's (1978) sample found that over 90 percent of gay men had: 'routinely engaged in sexual contact with strangers'. Few lesbians have ever had sex with a stranger. While gay men spend a significant proportion of their time: ' "cruising" in homosexual bars or on the street' (Gallup and Suarez, 1983), lesbians do not and these women typically found their partners through mutual interests or friendship networks and unlike gay men tend to build long-term monogamous relationships based on love and commitment (Sharp, 1995).

These differences are evident when you study the content of contact advertisements placed by homosexual men and women. Gay men will advertise for sex and display a narcissistic list of their own physical attributes, while lesbians offer friendship, commitment and display their hobbies and interests (McKnight and Sutton, 1994). All of these findings reflect Gallup and Suarez's summary of the differences between heterosexual men and women's reproductive agendas, perhaps to a heightened degree. Not only are these differences indicative of the separate goals of lesbians and gay men but they are a source of some tension within these communities. As a lesbian colleague remarked, 'Gay men want to meet the meat, we want to meet the mate.'

Differences in attitudes and actions reflect the biological difference between the two groups. Hamer and his colleagues have found no causal link between the markers for male homosexuality, and female heterosexuality, or lesbianism (Hu et al., 1995). It seems the aetiology of lesbianism has different pathways than for homosexual men (Pattatucci and Hamer, 1995). To the extent that hormones in early development influence the brains of homosexual men and women (an open question) they are proposed to follow differentiation pathways opposite to their gender, leaving lesbian brains relatively masculinised and gay brains relatively feminised (Byne and Parsons, 1993), suggesting quite different developmental progressions. Perhaps the best evidence for a difference between gay men and lesbians is the penetrance of each phenotype in the community. Proband studies and wider community surveys regularly report a ratio of four to one in favour of gay men.

All the above suggests that male and female homosexuality are quite different orientations with little in common. So why are we ignoring lesbians? As we noted in the Preface, at present scientific studies of lesbianism are woefully inadequate. Not only are they fewer in number than gay men but they are a less visible population, hard to target and harder to characterise. The lesbian press avoids the 'gay' label and sharply differentiates each community. My suspicions are that lesbianism and male homosexuality have very little in common at an evolutionary level but this is simply a guess, no more. Nevertheless, it is a guess based on accumulating evidence.

CONCLUSIONS

Where are we then? At the conclusion of such a book the author should be able to offer a few erudite pronouncements on the state of homosexuality and provide directions for future research. While we have done the latter in many areas, unfortunately the evidence is far from complete and the problem with which we started remains. Why there are homosexuals, and why does homosexuality survive, are still questions to be answered. Yet our analysis has not been a futile enterprise and several trends are gradually emerging.

- Male homosexuality is a separate sexual orientation from lesbianism and has a different aetiology.
- There are a range of male homosexualities with at least five types of homosexual aetiology.
- There is a substantial biological basis to at least two forms of male homosexuality and a genetic basis to at least one type.
- Genetics merely provide a predisposition towards homosexuality rather than mandating it. That is, the gene/s are variable in penetrance.
- Nevertheless, in aggregating these predispositions, it is clear that gayness is as much a matter of orientation as of preference.
- Therefore, human variation both genetic and behavioural will ensure a range of sexual behaviours, fantasies and emotional attachments ranging from exclusively homosexual to exclusively heterosexual.
- The genetics of male homosexuality are variable in penetrance and are likely to be modified by other genes (polygenic transmission).
- The genes for homosexuality cause differential development between gay men and straight men at stages following conception and at puberty.
- The homosexual genotype's phenotypic expression is influenced by environmental factors.

Explaining these conclusions from an evolutionary perspective is problematic. It is fairly certain that exclusive homosexuality in itself is an evolutionary byproduct and that the genes for homosexuality are transmitted in a heterozygous condition where they advantage heterosexually oriented men and women. That is, homosexuality provides a heterotic advantage which balances the genes in the population via a benefit conferred on straight men rather than being adaptive in its own right. The literature provides reasonably clear evidence that homosexuals, exclusive or otherwise, have reduced reproductive rates and face the extinction of their special contribution unless bolstered by such a heterotic advantage. None of the models we review provides a clear benefit to homosexuality in a homozygous form. Therefore, summarising this book in a sentence: homosexuality is an evolutionary byproduct, part of our variable sexual orientation and held in balance against its deleterious consequences by selecting for enhanced heterosexuality.

These are fighting words and this summary will not endear me to sectors of the gay community, which have an agenda of acceptance predicated on homosexuality being part of normal, that is, expected human variability. We started this chapter with a quotation from a lesbian activist who characterised our research as having an obsession with heterosexuality as 'normality'. Yet is natural normal? As Futuyma and Risch (1984) observed, such an appeal 'is based on the untenable presumption that what is biologically "natural" is also good'. Ardill, and researchers who are her ideological companions, are keen to argue a statistical normality. That if you can demonstrate a substantial percentage of the population follow some practice such as masturbation it must be normal, that is, expected. On this basis they argue that homosexuality be accepted as a common human behaviour. This seems misguided to me. Too many nasty behaviours such as rape and child abuse are more common than homosexuality, yet we would not include them as normal human sexual variation, or should we? This seems a dangerous line to take in arguing for gay rights. To follow this line of argument is to have to rely on morality to decide normality and, as we have seen, morality is as shaky a concept as is statistical normality.

Perhaps a cleverer way forward with the natural-is-good argument is to rely on the defence that homosexuality is unchosen. Despite all the problems it has given us, the triumph of psychiatry over the last 150 years was to afford the protection of labelling to those who are different and who were made that way. We no longer torture schizophrenics, because they have the protection of having an unchosen illness. By analogy, we may argue that many areas of human activity have similar protections today. We no longer punish the unemployed for cyclical economic downturns, the exceptionally bright child for being unable to fit into class, and so on. If we can move the argument forward just a little to an acceptance that for some gay men there was little choice in the way they are, then we can move on to the more important question of whether homosexuality is a behaviour needing remediation as with the schizophrenic, or special support and encouragement as with the exceptional child. In the argument that homosexuality is a net benefit to mankind, an evolutionary analysis of its adaptive potentials will make a significant contribution.

Even so, I think an even better argument is that homosexuality *is* part of our nature and that a substantial percentage of the human community shares genes that confer advantages on those lucky enough to have them.

We are a species with a close genome. Differences between you and me are less than 0.1 percent, about three million base pairs, and much of that is just noise – a trivial difference. So all genetic variation is priceless. In this sense, homosexuality is as precious as any obscure miracle cure hidden in a Brazilian rain forest. Yet to be clear about this, their disposition is really ours too. As much as the gay community is a reservoir for these genes and may aid their perpetuation, if what we have seen here is any indication, straight men (or women) carry them forward from generation to generation and this is the final answer to homophobia. Contrary to what Ardill and others might think, this does not argue that 'Normal requires abnormal' and, by implication, that gay men are losers in life's reproductive lottery. Rather, it acknowledges that there are many ways to play the evolutionary game in a rapidly changing species. Viewed this way, questions of normality become issues of adaptiveness and, as we have seen, usefulness changes as quickly as our times. Gay men, rather than being abnormal, are reservoirs of adaptive variation. Our species shares too much in common to be excluding anyone.

Glossary

allele (ic) for most genetic characteristics we have at least two sets of information (alleles), one set from each parent.

ambisexuality a *sexual orientation* or *sexual preference* towards members of both sexes. See also *bisexuality*.

androgen insensitivity syndrome a rare *autosomal, recessive* genetic condition in which genetic male foetuses are insensitive to the male hormone *testosterone* and as a consequence develop partial or complete female sexual characteristics. See also *pseudohermaphroditism*, *5-alpha reductase deficiency* and *congenital adrenal hyperplasia (CAH) syndrome*.

androgen receptor gene a neuronal site in the brain which is triggered by male sex hormones.

assortative mating choosing mates who are similar to ourselves minimising potential sources of conflict. See also *matching principle*.

autosomal a gene carried on other than the sex chromosomes.

balance polymorphism the situation where two or more forms of a gene or its *phenotype* become balanced in the *gene pool*. See also *balanced superior heterozygotic fitness*.

balance theory of population structure to ensure adaptability, natural selection may either favour a range of *optimum genotypes* within a species, or versatile individuals with a more heterogeneous *genotype*, or use both strategies. See also *directional or 'normalising' natural selection*.

balanced superior heterozygotic fitness a variant of *balance polymorphism* in which a deleterious *recessive* gene is kept in the *gene pool* by the advantage it provides to the *heterozygote* who carries it.

balancing selection see *stabilising selection*.

bisexuality loosely, a *sexual orientation* or *sexual preference* towards members of both sexes. The more correct usage is *ambisexuality*; bisexuality is also used to denote being of intermediate or of both sexes.

coevolution the mixture of genetic, biological, developmental, environmental, social and cultural factors which interact to determine one's *fitness*.

concordance the degree to which one trait correlates with another.

congenital adrenal hyperplasia (CAH) syndrome also known as *21-hydroxylase deficiency* a rare genetic condition in which the male sex hormone *testosterone* present in both sexes is secreted in abnormal amounts leading to partial or complete masculinisation of sexual characteristics in otherwise genetic females. See also *pseudohermaphroditism* and *5-alpha reductase deficiency.*

Coolidge Effect   flagging male sexual performance is boosted by the introduction of a new sex partner.

co-twin   the other twin of any particular twin pair under discussion.

cryptic ovulation theory   or *oestrus concealment theory* human females are continually sexually receptive yet show few signs of ovulation and this may be a deliberate evolutionary tactic to bond mates.

density-dependency   the numbers of a particular gene within the *gene pool*. See also *frequency-dependency.*

dihydrotestosterone (DHT)   a sex hormone derivative of *testosterone* which is present in both genetic sexes, has a primary role in masculinising male external genitalia.

directional or 'normalising' natural selection   occurs when one of the extremes of a phenotypic range becomes the most fit. This occurs when the environment changes and the *optimum type* is replaced by a new *mutation* or a previously less favoured *genotype*. See also the *balance theory of population structure.*

diversifying selection   also known as **disruptive selection**. Occurs when both extremes of a phenotypic range are selected for, often eventually leading to two new species. Opposite to *stabilising selection.*

dizygotic (DZ)   literally 'two eggs'. Usually applied to non-identical twins who come from two different zygotes. See also *monozygotic.*

dominant a gene (or its *allele*) whose action blocks *recessive* genes' (or alleles') *expression.*

double-mating   having sex with two males near the time of ovulation allowing *sperm competition* to occur.

DNA markers   are not a gene, but a region of a chromosome in which there is some observable characteristic, a mapped gene or a repeat sequence, that allows a genetic variation to be readily identified.

essentialism   the idea that all behaviour has biological or inherited predispositions. See also *social constructivism.*

euheterosis   the *hybrid vigour* resulting from an indirect reproductive advantage conferred by *outbreeding.*

expression   the action of a gene on a characteristic it controls.

extra-pair couplings (EPCs)   extramarital sex through adulterous relationships, or by consent as in group sex, spousal swapping or prostitution, or by forced intercourse as in rape. See also *sperm competition* and *double-mating.*

familiality   a characteristic, usually genetic, which runs through a family line.

fellatio   sexual stimulation of the penis by the mouth.

Fisher's theorem   British geneticist R.A. Fisher in 1930 noted that the rate of increase in fitness of any organism at any time is equal to its genetic variance of fitness at that time.

fitness   those genes, characteristics and behaviours which are not selected against by *natural selection*. In practice, those aspects which help individuals survive and prosper.

fitness-investment-potential of the recipient   a component of our decision as to which kin we will aid. The calculation measures the degree of reproductive fitness both realised and potential. We should aid younger kin who have a longer payback time.

5-alpha reductase deficiency   a rare genetic condition in which the hormone controlling the in-utero development of masculine sex characteristics is blocked leading to partial or full feminisation of genetic males. See also *pseudohermaphroditism* and *21-hydroxylase deficiency (congenital adrenal hyperplasia (CAH) syndrome)*.

fixity   or a complete homozygosity for a gene – the ultimate aim of *directional* or *'normalising' natural selection*.

frequency-dependency   the ratio of a particular gene within the *gene pool*. See also *density-dependency*.

fundamental postulate   Daniel Vining's challenge to sociobiology's main dictum – that we strive to increase our own genetic representation in subsequent generations. Vining noted that in all developed nations, individuals are voluntarily limiting their reproduction.

gene pool   the complete complement of genes theoretically available to all breeding members of a population or species. See also *genome*.

genetic load   every time a gene mutates the *optimum type* is challenged by the occurrence of another *allele* at the same locus creating a load through the reduction of average *fitness*.

genome   the complete genetic message of a species which includes all variant forms of genes characteristic of a species. See also *gene pool*.

genotype   an individual's set of genetic instructions as to how they should develop and respond. See also *phenotype*.

good genes theory   an explanation for selecting for *secondary sex characteristics* which are indirect clues for reproductive vigour.

guevedoces   (eggs (testes) at 12). Genetic males who do not develop masculine sexual characteristics until puberty. See also *pseudohermaphroditism* and *5-alpha reductase deficiency*.

heterosis   see *hybrid vigour*.

heterotic advantage   the reproductive advantage gained from *hybrid vigour*.

heterotic balancing selection   the *heterotic advantage* which leads to *optimum type* becoming balanced in the *gene pool*. See also *stabilising selection* or *balancing selection*.

heterozygote (ous, otic)   having two or more different *alleles* for a gene. See also *homozygote*.

homozygote (ous, otic)   having two similar copies (*alleles*) of a gene, one provided by each parent. See also *heterozygote*.

hybrid vigour   or more formally *heterosis*, is a very useful but imprecise concept in classical genetics. Often outbreeding produces bigger, stronger and more robust offspring than breeding close to one's kind. There are many actual mechanisms for this effect. See also *outbreeding*.

hypervariable mutation   the result of trinucleotide repeat sequences 'stuttering' at a hypervariable site on the *genotype* or *genome*.

inclusive fitness   any action which increases the prevalence of our genes in the next generation including the indirect reproductive benefits of selecting for *replicates* see also *kin selection*.

interstitial nuclei of the anterior hypothalamus (INAH)   a part of the hypothalamus implicated in regulating sexual orientation, that is substantially larger in men than women.

K strategy   a reproductive strategy that involves having fewer children but investing heavily in them to ensure their survival. See *R strategy.*

kin selection   practices which favour kin over unrelated members of one's social group. Such favouritism increases kin's chances of reproductive success and as they carry common genes *replicates* to our own they increase the likelihood of our genetic posterity. See also *inclusive fitness.*

Kinsey Scale   a widely used 7-point scale developed by Kinsey and his colleagues in 1948 which measures *sexual orientation* from exclusively heterosexual (0) to exclusively homosexual (6).

linkage analysis   estimating the presence or operation of a gene by observing variations in the trait compared to known markers, with which it is thought to be associated (linked) at *meiosis.*

luxuriance   a form of *hybrid vigour* resulting from *genetic loads* being masked by a *dominant* gene.

magnetoencephalograph (MEG)   a technology for measuring magnetic fields and activity in the brain.

matching principle   choosing mates who are similar to ourselves minimising potential sources of conflict. See also *assortative mating.*

meiosis   the splitting of genetic material to form the egg and sperm.

molecular imprinting   where a trait becomes more pronounced through successive generations because alterations to the gene are cumulative.

monozygotic (MZ)   literally 'one egg'. Usually applied to identical twins who come from the same zygote. See also *dizygotic.*

mutation   any change in the composition of a gene. Usually applied only to changes which are heritable and potentially permanent.

natural selection   chance processes which select against individuals of lesser *fitness.*

nature/nurture debate   the relative influence of genetic and social factors on our *phenotype.* See also *essentialism* and *social constructivism.*

novel environments defence   the suggestion that any behaviour which seems to defy evolutionary logic is a reflection of the atypical times in which we live and not characteristic of our evolutionary past.

oestrogen feedback effect (EFE)   surges in cyclic female sex hormones accompanying ovulation. High oestrogen levels stimulate a surge of luteinising hormone from the anterior pituitary prompting ovulation.

oestrus concealment theory   or *cryptic ovulation theory* human females are continually sexually receptive yet show few signs of ovulation and this may be a deliberate evolutionary tactic to bond mates.

optimum type   the best or optimal combination of alleles or genes matching environmental constraints. Characteristics that have not been selected against. What has actually happened. See *natural selection.*

outbreeding   see *hybrid vigour.*

overloving effect   a theory proposed to explain how a gene for male homosexuality located on the maternal X chromosome might be carried forward in a *homozygous* manner by women.

parental manipulation   the parent increasing their genetic representation in subsequent generations by requiring that some of their offspring forgo their own reproduction to aid other kin.

parliament of genes   when the phenotypic expression of a trait results from an averaging of a wide range of influences and triggers.

paternity certainty   the assurance that your offspring is your own, usually by female guarding or isolation tactics.

penetrance   the degree to which a gene expresses itself (see *expression*) in an individual or a population.

phenotype   the expressed characteristics of our *genotype* as modified by our personal development and environment. That is, the person as they are.

polygene (ic)   many genes acting together to regulate a characteristic.

probands   genetic relatives usually closer than second cousins.

pseudohermaphroditism   a hormonal condition which mimics hermaphroditism or having the genitalia and sexual characteristics of both sexes. See *5-alpha reductase deficiency* and *21-hydroxylase deficiency (congenital adrenal hyperplasia (CAH) syndrome)*.

R strategy   having many children but putting few resources into each. While reducing the chances of any one offspring reaching their own reproductive years, having more children should offset this disadvantage. See *K strategy*.

recessive   a gene (or its *allele*) whose action is blocked by other *dominant* genes (or alleles).

reciprocal altruism   a form of helping behaviour which is predicated on the help given, being returned at a later time.

replicates   close copies of our genes, held by near relatives, that are being passed on to future generations.

secondary sex characteristics   anatomical features such as antlers or beards, which are indirect clues to reproductive vigour. See also *good genes theory*.

sexual inversion   a view that all non-heterosexual orientations are an abnormal interruption of normal heterosexual development.

sexual orientation   an innate tendency toward one or other sexual expression. How nature has intended us to be. See also *sexual preference*.

sexual preference   how we choose to express ourselves sexually. See also *sexual orientation*.

sexual selection   choosing a mate for reasons other than direct reproductive vigour.

sissy-boy syndrome   gender-atypical behaviours and effeminate characteristics in young boys and adolescents which predict a higher than expected incidence of homosexuality in later life.

slippage   men habitually report having twice as many sexual partners than women, which leads to the problem of who is servicing these men.

social constructivism   the paradigm that behaviour is socially determined, subjective and culture bound. Social constructivist critique is directed at *essentialism*.

sperm competition   the sperm of one male will out-compete those of another male inseminated within a short time of each other. This *double-mating* is then a straight race for the ovum.

stabilising selection   also known as *balancing selection*. Selects for the elimination of phenotypic extremes. The *optimum types* that cluster around the population mean are well adapted to their environment. Opposite to *diversifying selection*.

substitution   is the most frequent kind of *mutation* and usually involves the swapping (substitution) of one base pair for another due to errors in replication.

suprachiasmatic nucleus (SCN)   a part of the hypothalamus, which is twice as large in homosexual, compared to heterosexual men. The SCN is involved in regulating sleep and activity cycles in the mammalian brain.

synthetic theory of evolution   the amalgamation of Darwin's theory of *natural selection* with modern genetics. Molecular biology provided a mechanism by which natural selection could work.

testosterone   the male sex hormone which, with its derivatives, governs many aspects of the development of male sexual characteristics. See also *dihydrotestosterone (DHT)*.

transsexuals   those individuals who feel their gender orientation is different from their gender. Usually applied to those undergoing sex-change operations.

21-hydroxylase deficiency   see *congenital adrenal hyperplasia (CAH) syndrome*.

vaginal phagocytosis   chemical and other mechanisms in the vaginal tract which destroy weak sperm promoting *sperm competition* and reproductive vigour.

wildtype genes   the dominant genes for a trait in the *gene pool*.

zygosity   the composition of the fertilised egg (zygote). Usually applied to either *monozygotic* and *dizygotic* twinning and to the *allelic* status of a trait. See also *heterozygotic, homozygotic*.

Bibliography

Aarskog D. (1971) Intersex conditions masquerading as simple hypadias. *Birth Defects: Original Articles Series*, 7, 122–130

Adam B. D. (1985) Age, structure and sexuality: Reflections on the anthropological evidence on homosexual relations. In E. Blackwood (Ed.) *Anthropology and Homosexual Behavior*, NY, Haworth Press

Aiman J. and Griffin J. E. (1982) The frequency of androgen receptor deficiency in infertile men. *Journal of Endocrinological Metabolism*, 54, 725–732

Alexander J. E. and Sufka K. J. (1993) Cerebral lateralization in homosexual males: A preliminary EEG investigation. *International Journal of Psychophysiology*, 15, 269–274

Alexander R. D. (1975) The search for a general theory of behavior. *Behavioral Science*, 20, 77–100

Allen K. R. and Demo D. H. (1995) The families of lesbians and gay men: A new frontier in family research. *Journal of Marriage and the Family*, 57, 111–127

Allen L. S. and Gorski R. A. (1992) Sexual orientation and the size of the anterior commissure in the human brain. *Proceedings of the National Academy of Science*, National Academy of Science, Washington, 89, 7199–7202

Allen L. S., Hines M., Shryne J. E. and Gorski R. A. (1989) Two sexually dimorphic cell groups in the human brain. *Journal of Neuroscience*, 9, 497–506

Allison A. C. (1954) Protection afforded by sickle-cell trait against subtertian malarial infections. *British Medical Journal*, 1, 250–294

Ardill S. (1996) An abnormal sexual obsession. *Sydney Star Observer*, Sydney, 286, 12

Arnold A. P. (1980) Sexual differences in the brain. *American Scientist*, 68, 165

Ashton G. C. (1980) Mismatches in genetic markers in a large family study. *American Journal of Human Genetics*, 32, 601–613

Badcock C. R. (1991) *Evolution and Individual Behaviour: An Introduction to Human Sociobiology*, Oxford, Basil Blackwell

Bailey J. M. (1995) Sexual orientation revolution. *Nature Genetics*, 11, 353–354

Bailey J. M. and Bell A. P. (1993) Familiality of female and male homosexuality. *Behavior Genetics*, 23, 313–322

Bailey J. M. and Pillard R. C. (1991) A genetic study of male sexual orientation. *Archives of General Psychiatry*, 48, 1089–1096

Bailey J. M. and Pillard R. C. (1993) Reply to a 'Genetic Study of Male Sexual Orientation.' *Archives of General Psychiatry*, 50, 240–241

Bailey J. M., Miller J. S. and Willerman L. (1993) Maternally rated childhood gender nonconformity in homosexuals and heterosexuals. *Archives of Sexual Behavior*, 22, 461–469

Bailey J. M., Willerman L. and Parks C. (1991) A test of the maternal stress theory of human male homosexuality. *Archives of Sexual Behavior*, 20, 277–293

Bailey J. M., Gaulin S., Agyei Y. and Gladue B. A. (1994) Effects of gender and sexual orientation on evolutionarily relevant aspects of human mating psychology. *Journal of Personality and Social Psychology*, 66, 1081–1093

Baker R. R. (1996) *Sperm Wars: Infidelity, Sexual Conflict and Other Bedroom Battles*, London, Fourth Estate

Baker R. R. and Bellis M. A. (1993) Human sperm competition: Ejaculate adjustment by males and the function of masturbation. *Animal Behaviour*, 46, 861–885

Baker R. R. and Bellis M. A. (1995) *Human Sperm Competition: Copulation, Masturbation and Fidelity*, London, Chapman and Hall

Banks A. and Gartrell N. K. (1995) Hormones and sexual orientation: A questionable link. *Journal of Homosexuality*, 28, 247–268

Barber N. (1995) The evolutionary psychology of physical attractiveness – sexual selection and human morphology. *Ethology and Sociobiology*, 16, 395–424

Barinaga M. (1991) Is homosexuality biological? *Science*, 253, 956–957

Barkow J. H. (1989) *Darwin, Sex and Status: Biological Approaches to Mind and Culture*, Toronto, University of Toronto Press

Barkow J. H. and Burley N. (1980) Human fertility, evolutionary biology, and the demographic transition. *Ethology and Sociobiology*, 1, 163–180

Baron M. (1993) Genetics and human sexual orientation. *Biological Psychiatry*, 33, 759–761

Barraclough C. A. and Gorski R. A. (1962) Studies on mating behaviour in the androgen-sterilised female rat in relation to the hypothalamic regulation of sexual behaviour. *Journal of Endocrinology*, 25, 175–182

Bateson P. P. G. (1983) Rules for changing the rules. In D. S. Bendall (Ed.) *Evolution from Molecules to Men*, Cambridge, Cambridge University Press

Beatty J. (1995) *Principles of Behavioral Neuroscience*, Madison, Wisconsin, Brown and Benchmark

Bell A. P. and Weinberg M. S. (1978) *Homosexualities: A Study of Diversity Among Men and Women*, NY, Simon and Schuster

Bellis M. A. and Baker R. R. (1990) Do females promote sperm competition? Data for humans. *Animal Behaviour*, 40, 997–999

Berenbaum S. A. and Snyder E. (1995) Early hormonal influences on childhood sex-typed activity and playmate preference: Implications for the development of sexual orientation. *Developmental Psychology*, 31, 31–42

Bermant G. (1976) Sexual behavior: Hard times with the Coolidge effect. In M. H. Siegal and H. P. Ziegler (Eds.) *Psychological Research: The Inside Story*, NY, Harper and Row

Birke L. I. (1982) Is homosexuality hormonally determined? *Journal of Homosexuality*, 6, 35–49

Blanchard R. and Bogaert A. F. (1996) Homosexuality in men and number of older brothers. *American Journal of Psychiatry*, 153, 27–31

Blanchard R. and Sheridan P. M. (1992) Sibship size, sibling sex ratio, birth order, and parental age in homosexual and nonhomosexual gender dysphorics. *Journal of Nervous and Mental Disease*, 180, 40–47

Blanchard R. and Zucker K. J. (1994) Re-analysis of Bell, Weinberg, and Hammersmith's data on birth order, sibling sex ratio, and parental age in homosexual men. *American Journal of Psychiatry*, 151, 1375–1376

Blanchard R. Dickey R. and Jones C. L. (1995) Comparison of height and weight in homosexual versus nonhomosexual male gender dysphorics. *Archives of Sexual Behavior*, 24, 543–554

Bone J. (1995) Gay gene claim thrown into doubt. *The Australian*, 11th July, 14

Boone J. L. (1986) Parental investment and elite family structure in preindustrial states: A case study of late mediaeval–early modern Portuguese genealogies. *American Anthropologist*, 88, 859–878

Brandon R. N. (1990) *Adaptation and Environment*, Princeton, Princeton University Press

Breedlove S. M. (1994) Sexual differentiation of the human nervous system. *Annual Review of Psychology*, 45, 389–418

Broude G. E. and Greene S. J. (1976) Cross-cultural codes on twenty sexual attitudes and practices. *Ethnology*, 15, 410–429

Buhrich N., Bailey J. M. and Martin N. G. (1991) Sexual orientation, sexual identity and sex-dimorphic behaviors in male twins. *Behavior Genetics*, 21, 75–96

Burley N. (1979) The evolution of concealed ovulation. *American Naturalist*, 114, 835–858

Buss D. M. (1989) Sex differences in human mate preferences: Evolutionary hypotheses tested in 37 cultures. *Behavioral and Brain Science*, 12, 1–49

Buss D. M. (1994) *The Evolution of Desire: Strategies of Human Mating*, NY, Basic Books

Buss D. M. (1996) Paternity uncertainty and the complex repertoire of human mating strategies. *American Psychologist*, 51, 161–162

Buss D. M. and Barnes M. (1986) Preferences in human mate selection. *Journal of Personality and Social Psychology*, 50, 559–570

Byne W. (1994) The biological evidence challenged. *Scientific American*, 270, 50–55

Byne W. and Parsons B. (1993) Human sexual orientation: The biologic theories reappraised. *Archives of General Psychiatry*, 50, 228–239

Calhoun J. B. (1962) Population density and social pathology. *Scientific American*, 206, 139–148

Campbell D. T. (1975) On the conflicts between biological and social evolution and between psychology and moral tradition. *American Psychologist*, 30, 1103–1126

Carrier J. M. (1995) Homosexuality – research implications for public policy: Gonsiorek J. C., Weinrich J. D. *Archives of Sexual Behavior*, 24, 98–102

Chagnon N. A. and Irons W. (1979) (Eds.) *Evolutionary Biology and Human Social Behavior: An Anthropological Perspective*, Mass, Duxberry Press

Churchill W. (1967) *Homosexual Behavior Among Males: A Cross-Cultural and Cross-Species Investigation*, NY, Hawthorne Books

Clarke B. (1975a) The causes of biological diversity. *Scientific American*, 233, 50–60

Clarke B. (1975b) Frequency-dependent and density-dependent natural selection. In F. M. Salzano (Ed.) *The Role of Natural Selection in Human Evolution*, NY, North-Holland/American Elsevier

Cloninger C. R., Adolfsson R. and Svrakic N. M. (1996) Mapping genes for human personality. *Nature Genetics*, 12, 3–4

Cohen J. (1977) *Reproduction*, London, Butterworths

Cole S. O. (1995) The biological basis of homosexuality: A Christian assessment. *Journal of Psychology and Theology*, 23, 89–100

Cooper E. (1994) *The Sexual Perspective: Homosexuality and Art in the Last 100 Years in the West*, London, Routledge

Crawford C. B. (1989) The theory of evolution: Of what value to psychology? *Journal of Comparative Psychology*, 103, 4–22

Cunningham M. R., Barbee A. P. and Pike C. L. (1990) What do women want?

Facialmetric assessment of multiple motives in the perception of male facial physical attractiveness. *Journal of Personality and Social Psychology*, 59, 61–72

Dalhof L. G., Hard E. and Larsson K. (1977) Influence of maternal stress on offspring sexual behaviour. *Animal Behaviour*, 25, 958–963

Daly M. and Wilson M. (1978) *Sex, Evolution and Behavior*, North Scituate, Mass, Duxbury Press

Darke R. A. (1948) Heredity as an etiological factor in homosexuality. *Journal of Nervous and Mental Disease*, 107, 251–268

Darwin C. (1859) *The Origin of Species by Means of Natural Selection*, Britannica Great Books, Chicago, Encyclopaedia Britannica

Darwin C. (1871) *The Descent of Man and Selection in Relation to Sex*, Britannica Great Books, Chicago, Encyclopaedia Britannica

Dawkins R. (1976) *The Selfish Gene*, Oxford, Oxford University Press

Dawkins R. (1982) *The Blind Watchmaker*, Harmondsworth, Penguin

Deaux K. and Hanna R. (1984) Courtship in the personal columns: The influence of gender and sexual orientation. *Sex Roles*, 11, 363–375

De Cecco J. P. and Parker D. A. (1995) The biology of homosexuality: Sexual orientation or sexual preference? *Journal of Homosexuality*, 28, 1–27

Demb J. (1992) Are gay men artistic? A review of the literature. *Journal of Homosexuality*, 23, 83–92

Derry P. S. (1996) Buss and sexual selection: The issue of culture. *American Psychologist*, 51, 159–160

Dickemann M. (1993) Reproductive strategies and gender construction: An evolutionary view of homosexualities. *Journal of Homosexuality*, 24, 55–71

Dickemann M. (1995) Wilson's panchreston: The inclusive fitness hypothesis of sociobiology re-examined. *Journal of Homosexuality*, 28, 147–183

Dittmann R. W., Kappes M. E. and Kappes M. H. (1992) Sexual behavior in adolescent and adult females with congenital adrenal hyperplasia. *Psychoneuroendocrinology*, 17, 153–170

Dobzhansky T. H (1952) The nature and origin of heterosis. In J. W. Gowen (Ed.) *Heterosis*, Des Moines, Iowa, Iowa State College Press

Doell R. G. (1995) Sexuality in the brain. *Journal of Homosexuality*, 28, 345–354

Dorner G. (1976) *Hormones and Brain Sexual Differentiation*, Amsterdam, Elsevier Scientific

Dorner G. (1979) Psychoneuroendocrine aspects of brain development and reproduction. In L. Zichella and E. Pancheir (Eds.) *Psychoneuroendocrinology and Reproduction*, Amsterdam, Elsevier

Dorner G. (1989) Hormone-dependent brain development and neuroendocrine prophylaxis. *Experimental and Clinical Endocrinology*, 94, 4–22

Dorner G. and Docke F. (1964) Sex-specific reaction of the hypothalamo-hypophysia system of rats. *Journal of Endocrinology*, 30, 265–266

Dorner G. and Hinz G. (1968) Induction and prevention of male homosexuality by androgens. *Journal of Endocrinology*, 40, 387–388

Dorner G., Schenck B., Schmiedel B. and Ahrens L. (1983) Stressful events in prenatal life of bi- and homosexual men. *Experimental and Clinical Endocrinology*, 81, 83–87

Dorner G., Geier T., Ahrens L. et al. (1980) Prenatal stress as a possible aetiogenetic factor of homosexuality in human males. *Endokrinologie*, 75, 365–368

Dorner G., Poppe I., Stahl F. et al. (1991) Gene- and environment-dependent neuroendocrine etiogenesis of homosexuality and transsexualism. *Experimental and Clinical Endocrinology*, 98, 141–150

Dorner G., Rohde W., Stahl F. et al. (1975) A neuroendocrine predisposition for homosexuality in men. *Archives of Sexual Behavior*, 4, 1–8

Dray W. (1957) *Laws and Explanation in History*, Oxford, Oxford University Press

Durham W. H. (1991) *Coevolution: Genes, Culture and Human Diversity*, Stanford, Stanford University Press

Eckert E. D., Bouchard T. J., Bohlen J. and Heston L. L. (1986) Homosexuality in monozygotic twins reared apart. *British Journal of Psychiatry*, 148, 421–425

Edwards J. H. (1957) A critical examination in the reputed primary influence of ABO phenotype on fertility and sex ratio. *British Journal of Preventative Social Medicine*, 11, 79–89

Ehrhardt A. A. (1975) Prenatal hormonal exposure and psychosexual differentiation. In E. Sachar (Ed.) *Topics in Psychoendocrinology*, NY, Grune and Stratton

Ehrhardt A. A. (1978) Behavioral sequelae of perinatal hormonal exposure in animals and man. In M. A. Lipton, A. DiMascio and K. F. Killam (Eds.) *Psychopharmacology: A Generation of Progress*, NY, Raven Press

Ehrhardt A. A. and Meyer-Bahlburg H. F. L. (1981) Effects of prenatal sex hormone on gender-related behavior. *Science*, 211, 1312–1318

Ehrman L. (1970) The mating advantage of rare males in *Drosophila*. *Proceedings of the National Academy of Science*, 65, 345–348

Einon D. (1994) Are men more promiscuous than women? *Ethology and Sociobiology*, 15, 131–143

Ellis H. (1915) *Studies in the Psychology of Sex: Sexual Inversions* (Vol. 2) (3rd Edn), Philadelphia, Davis

Ellis L. and Ames M. A. (1987) Neurohormonal functioning and sexual orientation: A theory of homosexuality–heterosexuality. *Psychological Bulletin*, 101, 233–258

Erickson R. P. and Lewis S. E. (1995) The new human genetics. *Environmental and Molecular Mutagenesis*, 25, 7–12

Ernulf K. E. and Innala S. M. (1995) Sexual bondage – a review and unobtrusive investigation. *Archives of Sexual Behavior*, 24, 631–654

Essock-Vitale S. M. and McGuire M. T. (1985) Women's lives viewed from an evolutionary perspective: Sexual histories, reproductive success, and demographic characteristics of a random subsample of American women. *Ethology and Sociobiology*, 6, 137–154

Farber S. L. (1981) *Identical Twins Reared Apart: A Re-analysis*, NY, Basic Books

Fausto-Sterling A. (1992) *Myths About Gender: Biological Theories about Men and Women*, NY, Basic Books

Feder H. H. (1984) Hormones and sexual behavior. *Annual Review of Psychology*, 35, 165–200

Fiet J., Gueux B., Raux-Demay M. C. et al. (1989) Le 21 desoxychortisol un noveau marqueur de l'hyperandrogenie surrenalienne par deficit en 21 hydroxylase. *Presse Medicale*, 18, 1965–1969

Fisher R. A. (1930) *The Genetical Theory of Natural Selection*, Oxford, Clarendon Press

Fisher R. A. (1958) *The Genetical Theory of Natural Selection* (2nd Edn), NY, Dover

Ford C. S. and Beach F. A. (1951) *Patterns of Sexual Behavior*, NY, Harper & Row

Ford J. J. (1983) Postnatal differentiation of sexual preference in male pigs. *Hormones and Behavior*, 17, 152–162

Forel A. (1924) *The Sexual Question*, NY, Physicians and Surgeons Book Company

Friedman R. C. and Downey J. I. (1993) Psychoanalysis, psychobiology and homosexuality. *Journal of the American Psychoanalytic Association*, 41, 1159–1198

Friedman R. C. and Downey J. I. (1994) Homosexuality. *New England Journal of Medicine*, 331, 923–930

Friere-Maia N. (1975) Adaptation and genetic load. In F. M. Salzano (Ed.) *The Role of Natural Selection in Human Evolution*, NY, North-Holland/American Elsevier

Futuyma D. J. and Risch S. J. (1984) Sexual orientation, sociobiology and evolution. *Journal of Homosexuality*, 9, 157–168

Gallagher B. J., McFalls J. A. and Vreeland C. N. (1993) Preliminary results from a national survey of psychiatrists concerning the etiology of male homosexuality. *Psychology – A Quarterly Journal of Human Behavior*, 30, 1–3

Gallup G. G. (1995) Have attitudes toward homosexuals been shaped by natural selection? *Ethology and Sociobiology*, 16, 53–70

Gallup G. G. and Suarez S. D. (1983) Homosexuality as a by-product of selection for optimal heterosexual strategies. *Perspectives in Biology and Medicine*, 26, 315–322

Garrett L. (1994) *The Coming Plague: Newly Emerging Diseases in a World Out of Balance*, London, Virago Press

Gayley T. (1993) Genetics of kin selection: The role of behavioral inclusive fitness. *American Naturalist*, 141, 928–953

Getz W. M. (1993) Invasion and maintenance of alleles that influence mating and parental success. *Journal of Theoretical Biology*, 162, 515–537

Gladue B. A. and Bailey J. M. (1995) Aggressiveness, competitiveness and human sexual orientation. *Psychoneuroendocrinology*, 20, 475–485

Gladue B. A., Green R. and Hellman R. E. (1984) Neuroendocrine response to estrogen and sexual orientation. *Science*, 225, 1496–1499

Gomila J. (1975) Fertility differentials and their significance for human evolution. In F. M. Salzano (Ed.) *The Role of Natural Selection in Human Evolution*, NY, North-Holland/American Elsevier

Goodenough U. (1984) *Genetics* (3rd Edn), NY, Holt Saunders

Gooren L. J. G. (1986a) The neuroendocrine response of luteinizing hormone to estrogen administration in the human is not sex-specific but dependent on the hormonal environment. *Journal of Clinical Endocrinology and Metabolism*, 63, 588–593

Gooren L. J. G. (1986b) The neuroendocrine response of luteinizing hormone to estrogen administration in heterosexual, homosexual and transsexual subjects. *Journal of Clinical Endocrinology and Metabolism*, 63, 583–588

Gooren L. J. G. (1995) Biomedical concepts of homosexuality: Folk belief in a white coat. *Journal of Homosexuality*, 28, 237–246

Gorski R. A., Gordon J. H., Shryne J. E. and Southam A. M. (1978) Evidence for a sex difference in the medial preoptic area of the rat brain. *Brain Research*, 148, 333–346

Gould S. J. (1976) Grades and clades revisited. In R. B. Masterton, W. Hodos and H. Jerison (Eds.) *Evolution, Brain and Behavior: Persistent Problems*, Hillsdale, NJ, Lawrence Erlbaum Associates

Gould S. J. (1982) *The Mismeasurement of Man*, NY, Norton

Goy R. W. and McEwen B. S. (1980) *Sexual Differentiation of the Brain*, Cambridge, Mass, MIT Press

Grafen A. (1982) How not to measure inclusive fitness. *Nature*, 298, 425–426

Green R. (1987) *The 'Sissy-boy Syndrome' and the Development of Homo-sexuality*, New Haven, Yale University Press

Green R. and Stoller R. J. (1971) Two monozygotic (identical) twin pairs discordant for gender identity. *Archives of Sexual Behavior*, 1, 321–327

Grellert E. A., Newcomb M. D. and Bentler P. M. (1982) Childhood play activities of male and female homosexuals and heterosexuals. *Archives of Sexual Behavior*, 11, 451–478

Gribbin M. and Gribbin J. (1993) *Being Human: Putting People in an Evolutionary Perspective*, London, J. M. Dent

Haas O. A. (1996) Genomic imprinting – molecular basis for an important new genetic concept and its role in the pathogenesis of neoplastic diseases [Review]. *International Journal of Pediatric Hematology/Oncology*, 3, 5–27

Haldane J. B. S. (1932) *The Causes of Evolution*, London, Harper

Haldeman D. C. (1994) The practice and ethics of sexual orientation conversion therapy. *Journal of Consulting and Clinical Psychology*, 62, 221–227

Hall J. A. Y. and Kimura D. (1995) Sexual orientation and performance on sexually dimorphic motor tasks. *Archives of Sexual Behavior*, 24, 395–407

Halley J. E. (1994) Sexual orientation and the politics of biology: A critique of the argument from immutability. *Stanford Law Review*, 46, 503–568

Halperin D. (1990) *One Hundred Years of Homosexuality: and Other Essays on Greek Love*, London, Routledge

Hamer D. H. and Copeland P. (1994) *The Science of Desire: The Search for the Gay Gene and the Biology of Behavior*, NY, Simon and Schuster

Hamer D. H., Hu S., Magnuson V. L., Hu N. and Pattatucci A. M. L. (1993) A linkage between DNA markers on the X chromosome and male sexual orientation. *Science*, 261, 321–327

Hamilton W. D. (1964) The evolution of social behavior. *Journal of Theoretical Biology*, 7, 1–52

Hastie P. (1994) Just genes? *Good News Australia*, 1, 10–14

Haumann G. (1995) Homosexuality, biology and ideology. *Journal of Homosexuality*, 28, 57–77

Haynes J. D. (1995) A critique of the possibility of genetic inheritance of homosexual orientation. *Journal of Homosexuality*, 28, 91–113

Henderson N. (1982) Human behavior genetics. *Annual Review of Psychology*, 33, 403–440

Henry G. D. (1941) *Sex Variants: A Study of Homosexual Patterns*, NY, Hoeber

Herek G. M. and Capitanio J. P. (1996) Some of my best friends – intergroup contact, concealable stigma, and heterosexuals' attitudes toward gay men and lesbians. *Personality and Social Psychology Bulletin*, 22, 412–424

Heston L. L. and Shields J. (1968) Homosexuality in twins. *Archives of General Psychiatry*, 18, 149–160

Hewitt C. (1995) The socioeconomic position of gay men – A review of the evidence. *American Journal of Economics and Sociology*, 54, 461–479

Hirschfeld M. (1920) *Homosexuality in Men and Women*, Berlin, Marcus

Hodson A. (1992) *Essential Genetics*, London, Bloomsbury

Hooper C. (1992) Biology, brain architecture and human sexuality. *Journal of NIH Research*, 4, 53–59

Hoult T. F. (1984) Human sexuality in biological perspective: Theoretical and methodological considerations. *Journal of Homosexuality*, 9, 137–155

Howard J. A., Blumstein P. and Schwartz P. (1987) Social or evolutionary theories? Some observations on preferences in human mate selection. *Journal of Personality and Social Psychology*, 53, 194–200

Hrdy S. B. (1981) *The Woman that Never Evolved*, Cambridge, Mass, Harvard University Press

Hu S., Pattatucci A. M. L., Patterson C., Li L., Fulker D. W., Cherny S. S., Kruglyak L. and Hamer D. H. (1995) Linkage between sexual orientation and chromosome Xq28 in males but not in females. *Nature Genetics*, 11, 248–256

Hubbard R. and Wald E. (1993a) The eugenics of normalcy: The politics of gene research. *The Ecologist*, 23, 185–191

Hubbard R. and Wald E. (1993b) *Exploding the Gene Myth*, Boston, Beacon Press

Hudson J. W. and Henze L. P. (1969) Campus values in mate selection: A replication. *Journal of Marriage and the Family*, 31, 772–778

Hughes D. L. (1988) *Evolution and Human Kinship*, NY, Oxford University Press

Hull E. M., Franz J. R., Snyder A. M. and Nishita J. K. (1980) Perinatal progesterone and learning, social and reproductive behavior in rats. *Physiology and Behavior*, 24, 251

Hull E. M., Nishita J. K., Bitran D. and Dalterio S. (1984) Perinatal dopamine-related drugs demasculinize rats. *Science*, 224, 1011–1013

Hutchinson G. E. (1959) A speculative consideration of certain possible forms of sexual selection in man. *American Naturalist*, 93, 81–91

Huxley A. F. (1983) How far will Darwin take us? In D. S. Bendell (Ed.) *Evolution from Molecules to Men*, Cambridge, Cambridge University Press

Huxley J. (1942) *Evolution: The Modern Synthesis*, London, Harper

Imperato-McGinley J., Guerrero L., Gauthier T. and Peterson R. E. (1974) Steroid 5-alpha-reductase deficiency in man: An inherited form of male pseudohermaphroditism. *Science*, 186, 1213–1215

Imperato-McGinley J., Peterson R. E., Gauthier T. and Sturla E. (1979) Androgens and the evolution of male-gender identity among male pseudohermaphrodites with 5-alpha-reductase deficiency. *New England Journal of Medicine*, 300, 1233–1239

Imperato-McGinley J., Pichardo M., Gauthier T., Voyer D. and Bryden M. P. (1991) Cognitive abilities in androgen-insensitive subjects: Comparison with control males and females from the same kindred. *Clinical Endocrinology*, 34, 431–447

Irons W. (1979) Investment and primary social dyads. In N. A. Chagnon and W. Irons (Eds.) *Evolutionary Biology and Human Social Behavior: An Anthropological Perspective*, Mass, Duxberry Press

Irons W. (1983) Human female reproductive strategies. In S. K. Wasser (Ed.) *Social Behavior of Female Vertebrates*, NY, Academic Press

Irons W. (1986) Social and reproductive success: Useful data but rethink the theory. *The Behavioral and Brain Sciences*, 9, 197–198

Johnson A. M., Wadsworth J., Wellings, K. and Field J. (1994) *Sexual Attitudes and Lifestyles*, Oxford, Blackwell Scientific

Johnstone R. A. (1994) Female preference for symmetrical males as a by-product of selection for mate recognition. *Nature*, 372, 172–175

Jordan K. M. and Deluty R. H. (1995) Clinical interventions by psychologists with lesbians and gay men. *Journal of Clinical Psychology*, 51, 448–456

Kallmann F. J. (1952) Comparative twin study on the genetic aspects of male homosexuality. *Journal of Nervous and Mental Disease*, 115, 283–298

Kallmann F. J. et al. (1960) Homosexuality and heterosexuality in identical twins. *Psychosomatic Medicine*, 22, 251–259

Kantor J. R. (1933) *A Survey of the Science of Psychology*, Bloomington, Indiana, The Principia Press

Kaplan G. and Rogers L. J. (1994) Race and gender fallacies: The paucity of biological determinist explanations of difference. In E. Tobach and B. Rosoff (Eds.) *Challenging Racism and Sexism: Alternatives to Genetic Explanation*, NY, Feminist Press, The City University of New York

Kennedy H. C. (1980/81) The 'third sex' theory of Karl Heinrich Ulrichs. *Journal of Homosexuality*, 6, 103–111

Kenrick D. T. and Trost M. (1989) A reproductive exchange model of heterosexual relationships: Putting proximate economics in ultimate perspective. In C. Hendrik (Ed.) *Close Relationships*, Newbury Park, Ca, Sage

Kenrick D. T., Groth G. E., Trost M. R. and Sadalla E. K. (1993) Integrating evolutionary and social exchange perspectives on relationships: Effects of gender, self-appraisal, and involvement level on mate selection criteria. *Journal of Personality and Social Psychology*, 64, 951–969

King M. and McDonald E. (1992) Homosexuals who are twins: A study of 46 probands. *British Journal of Psychiatry*, 160, 407–409

King M.-C. (1993) Sexual orientation and the X. *Nature*, 364, 288–289

Kinsey A. C., Pomeroy W. B. and Martin C. E. (1948) *Sexual Behavior in the Human Male*, Philadelphia, Saunders

Kinsey A. C., Pomeroy W. B., Martin C. E. and Gebhard P. H. (1953) *Sexual Behavior in the Human Female*, Philadelphia, Saunders

Kirsch J. A. W. and Weinrich J. D. (1991) Homosexuality, nature, and biology: Is homosexuality natural? Does it matter? In J. C. Gonsiorek and J. D. Weinrich (Eds.) *Homosexuality: Research Implications for Public Policy*, Newbury Park, Ca, Sage

Kitcher P. (1985) *Vaulting Ambition*, Cambridge, Mass, MIT Press

Kite M. E. and Whitley B. E. (1996) Sex differences in attitudes toward homosexual persons, behaviors, and civil rights – a meta-analysis. *Personality and Social Psychology Bulletin*, 22, 336–353

Klintworth G. K. (1962) A pair of male monozygotic twins discordant for homosexuality. *Journal of Nervous and Mental Disease*, 135, 113–125

Kraft-Ebbing R. (1886) *Psychopathia Sexualis*, Reprinted by Stein and Day, NY, 1965

Lang S. (1990) *Männer als Frauen-Frauen als Männer: Geschlechtsrollenwechsel bei den Indianern Nordamerikas*. Hamburg, Wayasbah Verlag

Lang T. (1940) Studies on the genetic determination of homosexuality. *Journal of Nervous and Mental Disease*, 92, 55–64

Lavrakis P. J. (1975) Female preferences for male physiques. *Journal of Research in Personality*, 9, 324–334

Lerner R. M. (1992) *Final Solutions: Biology, Prejudice, and Genocide*, University Park, Pa, Pennsylvania State University Press

LeVay S. (1991) A difference in hypothalamic structure between heterosexual and homosexual men. *Science*, 253, 1034–1037

LeVay S. (1993) *The Sexual Brain*, Cambridge, Mass, MIT Press

LeVay S. and Hamer D. H. (1994) Evidence for a biological influence in male homosexuality. *Scientific American*, 270, 44–49

Lewontin R. C. (1993) *The Doctrine of DNA: Biology as Ideology*, Harmondsworth, Penguin Books

Lidz T. (1993) Reply to 'A genetic study of male sexual orientation'. *Archives of General Psychiatry*, 50, 240

Lumby M. F. (1978) Men who advertise for sex. *Journal of Homosexuality*, 4, 63–72

Lumsden C. and Wilson E. O. (1981) *Genes, Mind, and Culture: The Coevolutionary Process*, Cambridge, Mass, Harvard University Press

McConaghy N. and Blaszczynski A. (1980) A pair of monozygotic twins discordant for homosexuality, sex-dimorphic behaviour and penile volume responses. *Archives of Sexual Behavior*, 9, 123–131

McCormick C. M. and Witelson S. F. (1991) A cognitive profile of homosexual men compared to heterosexual men and women. *Psychoneuroendocrinology*, 16, 459–473

McCreary D. R. (1994) The male role and avoiding femininity. *Sex Roles*, 31, 517–531

McGuire T. R. (1995) Is homosexuality genetic? A critical review and some suggestions. *Journal of Homosexuality*, 28, 115–145

MacIntyre F. and Estep K. W. (1993) Sperm competition and the persistence of genes for male homosexuality. *Biosystems*, 31, 223–233

Macintyre S. and Sooman A. (1992) Non-paternity and prenatal genetic screening. *Lancet*, 338, 839

Macke J. P., Hu N., Hu S., Bailey M., King V. L., Brown T., Hamer D. and Nathans J. (1993) Sequence variation in the androgen receptor gene is not a common determinant of male sexual orientation. *American Journal of Human Genetics*, 53, 844–852

McKnight J. and Sutton J. E. (1994) *Social Psychology*, Sydney, Prentice Hall

McKnight J. and Sutton J. E. (in press) *Social Psychology*, (2nd Edn), Sydney, Prentice Hall

McPhaul M. J., Marcelli M., Zoppi S., Griffin J. E. and Wilson J. D. (1993) Genetic basis of endocrine disease: The spectrum of mutations in the androgen receptor gene that causes androgen resistance. *Journal of Clinical Endocrinology and Metabolism*, 76, 17–23

Maddox J. (1993) Editorial: Wilful public misunderstanding of genetics, *Nature*, 364, 281

Malcolm, J. (1997) *Internalised Homophobia in Formerly Married Gay Men*, Unpublished manuscript, Sydney, University of Western Sydney, Macarthur

Manning J. T. (1995) Fluctuating asymmetry and body weight in men and women – implications for sexual selection. *Ethology and Sociobiology*, 16, 145–153

Margulis L. and Sagan D. (1991) *Mystery Dance: On the Evolution of Human Sexuality*, NY, Summit Books

Marshall E. (1995) NIH's 'Gay Gene' study questioned. *Science*, 268, 1841

Masters W. H. and Johnson V. E. (1966) *Human Sexual Response*, Boston, Mass, Little Brown

Masters W. H. and Johnson V. E. (1979) *Homosexuality in Perspective*, Boston, Mass, Little Brown

Mayr E. (1961) Cause and effect in biology. *Science*, 134, 1501–1506

Meyer-Bahlburg H. F. L. (1984) Psychoendocrine research on sexual orientation: Current status and future options. *Progress in Brain Research*, 61, 375–398

Meyer-Bahlburg H. F. L., Ehrdardt A. A., Rosen L. R. et al. (1995) Prenatal estrogens and the development of homosexual orientation. *Developmental Psychology*, 31, 12–21

Midgley M. (1985) *Evolution as a Religion*, London, Routledge

Midgley M. (1994) *The Ethical Primate: Humans, Freedom and Morality*, London, Routledge

Mihalik G. J. (1988) Sexuality and gender: An evolutionary perspective. *Psychiatric Annals*, 18, 40–42

Mihalik G. J. (1991) From anthropology: Homosexuality, stigma, and biocultural evolution. *Journal of Gay and Lesbian Psychotherapy*, 1, 15–30

Moir A. and Jessel D. (1989) *Brain Sex: The Real Difference Between Men and Women*, London, Michael Joseph

Moller A. P. (1990) Fluctuating asymmetry in male sexual ornaments may reliably reveal male quality. *Animal Behaviour*, 40, 1185–1187

Money J. (1969) Sexually dimorphic behavior, normal and abnormal. In N. Kretchmer and D. N. Walcher (Eds.) *Environmental Influences on Genetic Expression*, Washington, DC, US Government Printing Office

Money J. (1990) Agenda and credenda of the Kinsey scale. In D. P. McWhirter, S. A. Sanders and J. M. Reinisch (Eds.) *Homosexuality/Heterosexuality: Concepts of Sexual Orientation: The Kinsey Institute Series* (Vol. 2), NY, Oxford University Press

Money J. and Ehrhardt A. A. (1972) *Man and Woman: Boy and Girl*, Baltimore, Johns Hopkins University Press

Money J. and Russo A. J. (1979) Homosexual outcome of discordant gender identity/role in childhood: Longitudinal follow-up. *Journal of Pediatric Psychology*, 4, 29–41

Money J., Schwartz M. and Lewis V. G. (1984) Adult erotosexual status and fetal hormonal masculinization and demasculinization: 46, XX congenital virilizing adrenal hyperplasia and 46, XY androgen-insensitivity syndrome compared. *Psychoneuroendocrinology*, 9, 405–414

Murphy T. F. (1990) Homosexuality, a philosophical analysis. *Journal of Homosexuality*, 19, 132–137

Neel J. V. and Weiss K. M. (1975) The genetic structure of a tribal population, the Yanomama Indians XIII, Biodemographic studies. *American Journal of Physical Anthropology*, 42, 25–51

Nichols R. C. and Bilbro W. C. (1966) The diagnosis of twin zygosity. *Acta Genetica Statistica Medica*, 16, 265–275

Pai A. C. (1985) *Foundations of Genetics: A Science for Society*, NY, McGraw Hill

Pang S., Lerner A. J., Stoner E. et al. (1985) Late-onset adrenal steroid 3 beta-hydroxysteroid dehydrogenase deficiency. A cause of hirsutism in pubertal and post-pubertal women. *Journal of Clinical Endocrinology and Metabolism*, 60, 428–439

Parker S. T. (1987) A sexual selection model for hominid evolution. *Human Evolution*, 2, 235–253

Parkin D. T. (1979) *An Introduction to Evolutionary Genetics*, London, Edward Arnold

Pattatucci A. M. L. and Hamer D. (1995) Development and familiality of sexual orientation in females. *Behavior Genetics*, 25, 4107–4120

Penrose L. S. (1959) Natural selection in man: Some basic problems. In D. F. Roberts and G. A. Harrison (Eds.) *Natural Selection in Human Populations*, Oxford, Pergamon Press

Peterson N. (1975) Hunter–gatherer territoriality: The perspective from Australia. *American Anthropologist*, 77, 53–68

Petit C. and Ehrman L. (1969) Sexual selection in *Drosophila*. In T. Dobzahansky, M. K. Hetch and W. C. Steere (Eds.) *Evolutionary Biology* (Vol. 3), NY, Appleton-Century-Crofts

Philipp E. E. (1973) Discussion: moral, social, and ethical issues. In G. E. W. Wolstenholme and D. W. Fitzsimmons (Eds.) *Law and Ethics of A.I.D. and*

Embryo Transfer: CIBA Foundation Symposium 17, London, Associated Scientific

Pillard R. C. (1988) Sexual orientation and mental disorder. *Psychiatric Annals*, 18, 52–56

Pillard R. C. (1991) Masculinity and femininity in homosexuality: 'Inversion' revisited. In J. C. Gonzoriek and J. D. Weinrich (Eds.) *Homosexuality: Research Findings for Public Policy*, Newbury Park, CA, Sage

Pillard R. C. and Bailey J. M. (1995) A biologic perspective on sexual orientation. *Psychiatric Clinics of North America*, 18, 71–76

Pillard R. C. and Weinrich J. D. (1986) Evidence of familial nature of male homosexuality. *Archives of General Psychiatry*, 43, 808–812

Pillard R. C. and Weinrich J. D. (1987) The periodic table model of the gender transpositions: I. A theory based on masculinization and defeminization of the brain. *Journal of Sex Research*, 23, 425–434

Plomin R., DeFries J. C. and McClearn G. E. (1980) *Behavioral Genetics: A Primer*, NY, Freeman

Pollard I. (1996) Preconceptual programming and sexual orientation: A hypothesis. *Journal of Theoretical Biology*, 179, 269–273

Pool R. (1993) Evidence for homosexuality gene. *Science*, 261, 291–292

Porter R. H. (1987) Kin recognition: Functions and mediating mechanisms. In C. Crawford, M. Smith and D. Krebs (Eds.) *Sociobiology and Psychology: Ideas, Issues and Applications*, NJ, Lawrence Erlbaum

Prout T. and Eaton N. (1995) How 'bad genes' survive. *Nature*, 376, 128

Rainer J. D., Mesnikoff A., Kolb L. C. and Carr A. (1960) Homosexuality and heterosexuality in identical twins. *Psychosomatic Medicine*, 22, 251–259

Raschka L. B. (1995) On older fathers. *American Journal of Psychiatry*, 152, 1404

Reik W. (1996) Genetic imprinting – the battle of the sexes rages on. *Experimental Physiology*, 81, 161–172

Reite M., Sheeder J., Richardson D. and Teale P. (1995) Cerebral laterality in homosexual males: Preliminary communication using magnetoencephalography. *Archives of Sexual Behavior*, 24, 585–593

Rice W. R. (1984) Sex chromosomes and the evolution of sexual dimorphism. *Evolution*, 38, 735–742

Ricketts W. (1984) Biological research on homosexuality: Ansell's cow or Occam's razor? *Journal of Homosexuality*, 9, 65–93

Ridley M. (1994) *The Red Queen: Sex and the Evolution of Human Nature*, Harmondsworth, Penguin

Roldan E. R., Gomendio M. and Vitullo A. D. (1992) The evolution of eutherian spermatozoa and underlying selective forces: Female selection and sperm competition. *Biological Reviews of the Cambridge Philosophical Society*, 67, 551–593

Rosenberg K. P. (1994) Biology and homosexuality. *Journal of Sex and Marital Therapy*, 20, 147–151

Rosenfield A. (1981) Sociobiology stirs a controversy over limits of science. *Educational Horizons*, 59, 70–74

Ross C. A. and Pearson G. D. (1996) Schizophrenia, the heteromodal association neocortex and development: Potential for a neurogenetic approach. *Trends in Neurosciences*, 19, 171–176

Ross M. W. (1980) Retrospective distortion in homosexual research. *Archives of Sexual Behavior*, 9, 523–531

Ross M. W. (1983) *The Married Homosexual Man: A Psychological Study*, London, Routledge and Kegan Paul

Rothblum E. D. (1994) I only read about myself on bathroom walls – the need for research on the mental health of lesbians and gay men. *Journal of Consulting and Clinical Psychology*, 62, 213–220

Rubin R. T., Reinisch J. M. and Haskett R. F. (1981) Postnatal gonadal steroid effects on human behavior. *Science*, 211, 1318–1324

Ruffie J. (1986) *The Population Alternative: A New Look at Competition and the Species*, Harmondsworth, Penguin

Ruse M. (1979) *Sociobiology: Sense or Nonsense?*, Dordrecht, Reidel

Ruse M. (1981) Are there gay genes? Sociobiology and homosexuality. *Journal of Homosexuality*, 6, 5–34

Ruse M. (1984) Nature/nurture: Reflections on approaches to the study of homosexuality. *Journal of Homosexuality*, 10, 141–151

Ruse M. (1985) *Sociobiology: Sense or Nonsense?*, (2nd Edn), Dordrecht, Reidel

Ruse M. (1986) Evolutionary ethics: A phoenix arisen. Thirty-first Annual Conference of the Institute on Religion in an Age of Science: Recent discoveries in neurobiology – do they matter for religion, the social sciences, and the humanities? (1984, Star Island, New Hampshire). *Zygon Journal of Religion and Science*, 21, 95–112

Ruse M. (1988) *Homosexuality: A Philosophical Enquiry*, Oxford, Basil Blackwell

Salais D. and Fischer R. B. (1995) Sexual preference and altruism. *Journal of Homosexuality*, 28, 185–196

Salmon D., Seger J. and Salmon C. (1980) Expected and observed proportion of subjects excluded from paternity by blood phenotypes of a child and its mother in a sample of 171 families. *American Journal of Human Genetics*, 32, 432–444

Salzano F. M. (Ed.) (1975) *The Role of Natural Selection in Human Evolution*, NY, North-Holland/American Elsevier

Sankaran N. (1995) Homosexuality researchers stoic despite uproar over their work. *The Scientist*, 9, 1–7

Savage M. O., Preece M. A., Jeffcoat S. L. et al. (1980) Familial male pseudohermaphroditism due to deficiency of 5 alpha reductase. *Clinical Endocrinology*, 12, 397–406

Schacht L. E. and Gershowitz H. (1963) Frequency of extra-marital children as determined by blood groups. In L. Gedda (Ed.) *Proceedings of the Second International Congress on Human Genetics*, Rome, G. Mendel

Scruton R. (1986) *Sexual Desire*, London, Weidenfeld

Seaborg D. (1984) Sexual orientation, behavioral plasticity, and evolution. *Journal of Homosexuality*, 10, 153–158

Sell R. L., Wells J. A. and Wypij D. (1995) The prevalence of homosexual behavior and attraction in the United States, the United Kingdom and France: Results of national population-based samples. *Archives of Sexual Behavior*, 24, 235–248

Sharp C. (1995) *Coping with Transitions to 'Being Lesbian' and 'Being Old'*, Unpublished research thesis, Sydney, University of Western Sydney, Macarthur

Sherman P. W. and Holmes W. G. (1985) Kin recognition: Issues and evidence. In B. Holldodler and M. Lindauer (Eds.) *Experimental Behavioral Ecology and Sociobiology: In Memoriam Karl Von Frisch 1886–1982*, Sunderland, Mass, Sinauer

Singh D. (1995) Female judgment of male attractiveness and desirability for relationships – role of waist-to-hip ratio and financial status. *Journal of Personality and Social Psychology*, 69, 1089–1101

Smith R. L. (1984) Human sperm competition. In R. L. Smith (Ed.) *Sperm Competition and the Evolution of Animal Mating Systems*, NY, Academic Press

Sprecher S., Sullivan Q. and Hatfield E. (1994) Mate selection preferences: Gender differences examined in a national sample. *Journal of Personality and Social Psychology*, 66, 1074–1080

Stein E. (1994) The relevance of scientific research about sexual orientation to lesbian and gay rights. *Journal of Homosexuality*, 27, 269–308

Sternberg R. J. and Grigorenko E. (1997) *Intelligence, Heredity and Environment*, NY, Cambridge University Press

Strickland B. R. (1995) Research on sexual orientation and human development: A commentary. *Developmental Psychology*, 31, 137–140

Suarez B. K. and Przybeck T. R. (1980) Sibling sex ratio and male homosexuality. *Archives of Sexual Behavior*, 9, 1–12

Suarez S., Drost M., Redfern K. and Gottlieb W. (1990) Sperm motility in the oviduct. In B. D. Bavister, J. Cummins and E. R. S. Roldan (Eds.) *Fertilization in Mammals, The Serono Symposia*, Norwell

Suppe F. (1994) Explaining homosexuality – philosophical issues, and who cares anyhow. *Journal of Homosexuality*, 27, 223–268

Swaab D. F. and Fliers E. (1985) A sexually dimorphic nucleus in the human brain. *Science*, 228, 1112–1115

Swaab D. F. and Hofman M. A. (1990) An enlarged suprachiasmatic nucleus in homosexual men. *Brain Research*, 537, 141–148

Swaab D. F. and Hofman M. A. (1995) Sexual differentiation of the human hypothalamus in relation to gender and sexual orientation [Review]. *Trends in Neurosciences*, 18, 264–270

Symons D. (1979) *The Evolution of Human Sexuality*, NY, Oxford University Press

Thibaut F., Martinez M., Petit M., Jay M. and Campion D. (1995) Further evidence for anticipation in schizophrenia. *Psychiatric Research*, 59, 25–33

Thornhill R. and Gangestad S. W. (1994) Human fluctuating asymmetry and sexual behavior. *Psychological Science*, 5, 297–302

Thorp J. (1992) The social construction of homosexuality. *Phoenix*, 46, 54–61

Tobach E. and Rosoff B. (Eds.) (1994) *Challenging Racism and Sexism: Alternatives to Genetic Explanations*, NY, City University of New York Press

Trivers R. L. (1971) The evolution of reciprocal altruism. *Quarterly Review of Biology*, 46, 35–57

Trivers R. L. (1972) Parental investment and sexual selection. In B. Campbell (Ed.) *Sexual Selection and the Descent of Man*, London, Aldine

Trivers R. L. (1974) Parent–offspring conflict. *American Zoologist*, 14, 249–264

Trivers R. L. (1985) *Social Evolution*, Menlo Park, Ca, Benjamin-Cummings

Turner W. J. (1994) Comments on discordant monozygotic twinning in homosexuality. *Archives of Sexual Behavior*, 23, 115–119

Turner W. J. (1995) Homosexuality, type 1 – an Xq28 phenomenon. *Archives of Sexual Behavior*, 24, 109–134

Ulrichs K. H. (1975) *Researches on the Riddle of Love Between Men*, NY, Arno Press,

United Nations (1995) *World Annual and Statistical Yearbook 1995*, New York, United Nations

Vanwyk P. H. and Geist C. S. (1995) Biology of bisexuality: Critique and observations. *Journal of Homosexuality*, 28, 357–373

Vincent P. (1946) Le role des familles nombreuses dans les generations. *Population*, 1, 148–154

Vining D. R. (1986) Social versus reproductive success: The central theoretical problem of human sociobiology. *The Behavioral and Brain Sciences*, 9, 167–216

Wallace B. (1968) *Topics in Population Genetics*, NY, Norton

Ward I. L. (1977) Exogenous androgen activates female behavior in noncopulating, prenatally stressed rats. *Journal of Comparative and Physiological Psychology*, 91, 465–471

Ward I. L. (1984) The prenatal stress syndrome: Current status. *Psychoneuroendocrinology*, 9, 3–11

Ward I. L. and Weisz J. (1980) Maternal stress alters plasma testosterone in fetal males. *Science*, 207, 328–239

Weinberg M. S., Williams C. J. and Calhan C. (1994a) Homosexual foot fetishism. *Archives of Sexual Behavior*, 23, 611–626

Weinberg M. S., Williams C. J. and Pryor D. W. (1994b) *Dual Attraction: Understanding Bisexuality*, Oxford, Oxford University Press

Weinrich J. D. (1977) *Human Reproductive Strategy. I Environment Predictability and Reproductive Strategy; Effects of Social Class and Race. II Homosexuality and Non-Reproduction; Some Evolutionary Models.* Unpublished doctoral dissertation, Ann Arbor, Harvard University, University Microfilms International

Weinrich J. D. (1978) Nonreproduction, homosexuality, transsexualism, and intelligence: A systematic literature search. *Journal of Homosexuality*, 3, 275–289

Weinrich J. D. (1987a) *Sexual Landscapes: Why we are What we are, Why we Love Whom we Love*, NY, Charles Scribner

Weinrich J. D. (1987b) A new sociobiological theory of homosexuality applicable to societies with universal marriage. *Ethology and Sociobiology*, 8, 37–47

Weinrich J. D. (1988) The periodic table model of the gender transpositions: II. Limerent and lusty sexual attractions and the nature of bisexuality. *Journal of Sex Research*, 24, 113–129

Weinrich J. D. (1995) Biological research on sexual orientation: A critique of the critics. *Journal of Homosexuality*, 28, 197–213

Whitam F. L. (1977) Childhood indicators of male homosexuality. *Archives of Sexual Behavior*, 6, 89–96

Whitam F. L., Diamond M. and Martin J. (1993) Homosexual orientation in twins: A report on 61 pairs and 3 triplet sets. *Archives of Sexual Behavior*, 22, 187–206

Wiegmann D. D., Real L. A., Capone T. A. and Ellner S. (1996) Some distinguishing features of models of search behavior and mate choice. *American Naturalist*, 147, 188–204

Williams G. C. (1966) *Adaptation and Natural Selection: A Critique of Some Current Evolutionary Thought*, Princeton, Princeton University Press

Wilson E. O. (1975) *Sociobiology: The New Synthesis*, Cambridge, Mass, Harvard University Press

Wilson E. O. (1978) *On Human Nature*, Cambridge, Mass, Harvard University Press

Wingfield W. M. (1995) The riddle of man–manly love – the pioneering work on male homosexuality – Ulrichs, K. H. *Journal of the History of Sexuality*, 5, 469–471

Wright S. (1969) *Evolution and the Genetics of Populations: The Theory of Gene Frequencies* (Vol. 2), Chicago, University of Chicago Press

Yalom I. D., Green R. and Fisk N. (1973) Prenatal exposure to female hormones. *Archives of General Psychiatry*, 28, 554–559

Zhou J. N., Hofman M. A. and Swaab D. F. (1995) No changes in the number of vasoactive intestinal polypeptide (vip)-expressing neurons in the suprachiasmatic nucleus of homosexual men – comparison with vasopressin-expressing neurons. *Brain Research*, 672, 285–288

Zuger B. (1976) Monozygotic twins discordant for homosexuality: Report of a pair and significance of the phenomenon. *Comprehensive Psychiatry*, 17, 661–669

Zuger B. (1988) Is early effeminate behavior in boys early homosexuality? *Comprehensive Psychiatry*, 29, 509–519
Zuger B. (1989) Homosexuality in families of boys with early effeminate behavior: An epidemiological study. *Archives of Sexual Behavior*, 18, 155–166

Author index

Aarskog, D. 29
Adam, B.D. 142
Aiman, J. 26
Alexander, J.E. 41–2, 43
Alexander, R.D. 156, 167, 177
Allen, K.R. 39
Allen, L.S. 40, 41, 43
Allison, A.C. 11
Ames, M.A. 21, 22, 27, 29, 176
Ardill, S. 163, 181
Arnold, A.P. 22
Ashton, G.C. 109

Badcock, C.R. 167
Bailey, J.M. 31, 45, 46, 58, 61, 107, 140;
    twin studies 47–8, 53–4
Baker, R.R. 134, 139, 142, 182;
    bisexuality 150–5; EPCs 108, 109,
    111; sperm competition 92, 93, 94,
    95, 183
Barber, N. 105
Barinaga, M. 39, 40
Barkow, J. 14, 15, 67, 107–8, 108, 128,
    172; evolutionary scenarios 75;
    intelligence and fertility control
    157–8; kin selective altruism 137,
    138
Barnes, M. 106
Barraclough, C.A. 33
Bateson, P. 101
Beach, F.A. 105, 152, 182
Beatty, J. 42
Bell, A.P. 33, 40, 45, 49, 89, 143, 159,
    183; promiscuity 40, 77, 78, 79, 184
Bellis, M.A. 134, 139; bisexuality 150–5;
    EPCs 108, 109, 111; sperm
    competition 92, 94, 95, 183
Berenbaum, S.A. 25

Bermant, G. 79, 83
Bilbro, W.C. 49
Birke, L.I. 28, 33
Blaszczynski, A. 45
Bone, J. 57
Boone, J.L. 148
Brandon, R.N. 74, 75
Breedlove, S.M. 24, 27, 38, 61, 107, 117
Broude, G.E. 109, 112
Buhrich, N. 46
Burley, N. 157–8
Buss, D.M. 79, 83, 97, 108, 129, 143,
    166, 182; paternity certainty 93;
    sexual selection 105, 106
Byne, W. 23, 52, 57, 58, 107, 184

Calhoun, J.B. 165
Campbell, D.T. 16
Chagnon, N.A. 126
Churchill, W. 136
Clarke, B. 67, 98, 100, 101
Cloninger, C.R. 80
Cohen, J. 109
Cooper, E. 106
Copeland, P. 16, 50, 53, 54, 55, 56, 118,
    119, 121, 123, 127
Crawford, C.B. 174
Crow, J.F. 120
Cunningham, M.R. 105

Dahlof, L.G. 30
Daly, M. 156, 157
Darke, R.A. 46
Darwin, C. 14, 67–8, 103–4, 105, 108
Dawkins, R. 157, 180
De Cecco, J.P. 30, 52
Deaux, K. 166
Diamond, M. 48–9

Dickemann, M. 59, 129, 145, 146, 148
Dittmann, R.W. 25
Dobzhansky, T.H. 72
Docke, F. 30
Dorner, G. 26–7, 27, 38, 63, 176;
    maternal stress hypothesis 29–36
Durham, W. 126

Eaton, N. 104
Ebers, G. 57, 58, 63
Eckert, E.D. 46, 50–1
Edwards, J.H. 96, 109
Ehrhardt, A.A. 22, 24, 25, 26, 29
Ehrman, L. 99
Einon, D. 108, 109, 142
Ellis, H. 21
Ellis, L. 21, 22, 27, 29, 176
Erickson, R P. 123
Essock-Vitale, S.M. 150
Estep, K.W. 84, 88, 92–3, 94, 96, 102

Farber, S.L. 46
Fausto-Sterling, A. 168, 181
Feder, H.H. 27
Fiet, J. 32
Fischer, R.B. 129, 136–7
Fisher, R.A. 9, 75, 88, 97–8, 120
Fisk, N. 29
Fliers, E. 39, 43
Ford, C.S. 105, 152, 182
Ford, J.J. 27
Forel, A. 21, 22
Fox, R. 112
Friere-Maia, N. 66, 67, 74, 75
Futuyama, D.J. 128, 130, 146, 168, 169,
    186

Gallup, G.G. 60, 74, 83, 127, 149, 177,
    184; sexual selection 102, 181;
    women's reproductive agendas 183,
    184
Gangestad, S.W. 105
Garrett, L. 143, 154
Gayley, T. 132
Geist, C.S. 166
Gershon, E. 57
Gershowitz, H. 109
Getz, W.M. 67, 97, 102
Gibran, Khalil 1
Gladue, B.A. 34–6
Gomila, J. 84, 85–6
Goodenough, U. 120–1

Gooren, L. 35–6, 38
Gorski, R.A. 33, 39, 40, 41, 43
Gould, S.J. 68, 177
Goy, R.W. 23
Grafen, A. 132, 134
Green, R. 29, 45, 140
Greene, S.J. 109, 112
Grellert, E.A. 140
Gribbin, J. 127, 157, 161
Gribbin, M. 127, 157, 161
Griffin, J.E. 26
Grigorenko, E. 159

Haas, O.A. 123
Haldane, J.B.S. 75
Halperin, D. 1
Hamer, D.H. 16, 50, 88, 102, 123, 127,
    184; hypervariable mutation 121;
    overloving effect 116–19; women's
    desire for men gene 13; Xq28 53–9,
    63, 176
Hamilton, W.D. 128
Hanna, R. 166
Hastie, P. 53
Haynes, J.D. 46, 171
Henderson, N. 159
Henry, G.D. 121, 122
Henze, L.P. 106
Heston, L.L. 46, 47
Hewitt, C. 106, 113, 129, 137, 159
Hinz, G. 27
Hirschfeld, M. 21, 22
Hodson, A. 98, 103, 118, 120
Hofman, M.A. 39
Holmes, W.G. 128
Hooper, C. 41
Hoult, T.F. 29, 33
Howard, J.A. 106
Hrdy, S.B. 111
Hu, N. 53
Hu, S. 53, 56, 57, 184
Hubbard, R. 57, 168, 171, 181
Hudson, J.W. 106
Hughes, D.L. 136
Hull, E.M. 25
Hutchinson, G.E. 11, 12, 76, 86, 102
Huxley, A.F. 125, 126, 159
Huxley, J. 15, 74

Imperato-McGinley, J. 23, 24
Irons, W. 126, 136, 160, 161–2, 167

Jessel, D. 171
Johnson, A.M. 7, 59, 109, 183
Johnson, V.E. 77, 78–80
Johnstone, R.A. 105

Kallmann, F.J. 46, 46–7
Kantor, J.R. 174
Kaplan, G. 168, 181
Kennedy, H.C. 21
Kenrick, D.T. 83, 109–10
King, M. 49–50
King, M.-C. 58
Kinsey, A.C. 5, 6, 58, 60, 79, 109, 183
Kitcher, P. 134, 165, 168, 172
Kite, M.E. 107
Klintworth, G.K. 45, 47
Kraft-Ebbing, R. von 21

Lang, S. 146
Lang, T. 46, 171
Lavrakis, P.J. 105
Lerner, R.M. 171
LeVay, S. 38, 39–40, 43, 61, 176
Lewis, S.E. 123
Lewontin, R.C. 127, 168, 172
Lidz, T. 48, 52
Lumby, M.F. 166
Lumsden, C. 126, 157

MacIntyre, F. 84, 88, 92–3, 94, 96, 102
Macintyre, S. 109
Macke, J.P. 37–8
Maddox, J. 57
Magnuson, V. 53
Maguire, M.T. 150
Malcolm, J. 6, 62
Manning, J.T. 105
Margulis, L. 92
Marshall, E. 57, 58
Martin, J. 48–9
Martin, N.G. 46
Masters, W.H. 77, 78–80
Mayr, E. 176
McConaghy, N. 45
McCormick, C.M. 43
McCreary, D.R. 106
McDonald, E. 49–50
McEwen, B.S. 23
McGuire, T.R. 46, 48, 52, 57, 58, 168
McKnight, J. 106, 174, 176, 184
McPhaul, M.J. 27, 37
Meyer-Bahlburg, H.F.L. 28, 29

Midgley, M. 3
Moir, A. 171
Moller, A.P. 105
Money, J. 22, 24, 25, 26
Murphy, T.F. 165, 170, 171, 180

Neel, J.V. 108–9
Nichols, R.C. 48

Pai, A.C. 72
Pang, S. 32
Parker, D.A. 30, 52
Parker, S.T. 95
Parkin, D.T. 88
Parsons, B. 23, 52, 107, 184
Pattatucci, A.M.L. 53, 57, 184
Pearson, G.D. 80
Penrose, L.S. 84
Peterson, N. 160, 161
Petit, C. 99
Philipp, E.E. 109
Pillard, R.C. 45, 46, 57, 59, 140, 143;
    twin study 47–8
Plomin, R. 16, 49, 67, 98, 99, 100, 159
Pollard, I. 117, 149, 176
Pool, R. 58
Porter, R.H. 139
Prout, T. 104

Rainer, J.D. 47
Reik, W. 117, 123
Reite, M. 42–3
Rice, G. 57, 58, 63
Rice, W.R. 118
Ricketts, W. 180
Ridley, M. 81, 87, 104, 165, 178
Risch, S.J. 128, 130, 146, 168, 169, 186
Rogers, L.J. 168, 181
Roldan, E.R. 94
Rosoff, B. 168
Ross, C.A. 80
Ross, M.W. 6, 62, 140
Rubin, R.T. 24
Ruffie, J. 65, 66, 67, 105, 117
Ruse, M. 3, 106, 146, 160, 165, 168, 177,
    180; kin selection 10, 134, 136, 138,
    140, 141, 143; reductionism 173, 175
Russo, A.J. 25

Sagan, D. 92
Salais, D. 129, 136–7
Salmon, D. 109

Savage, M.O. 24
Schacht, L.E. 109
Scruton, R. 165
Seaborg, D. 169
Sherman, P.W. 128
Shields, J. 46, 47
Singh, D. 105
Smith, R.L. 92, 93–4, 109, 110
Snyder, E. 25
Sooman, A. 109
Sprecher, S. 106, 107
Stein, E. 171
Sternberg, R.J. 159
Stoller, R.J. 45
Strickland, B.R. 106, 159
Suarez, S.D. 60, 74, 83, 127, 149; sexual
   selection 102, 181; sperm selection
   within female tract 94; women's
   reproductive agendas 183, 184
Sufka, K.J. 41, 43
Sun-Sung, T. 95
Sutton, J.E. 106, 174, 176, 184
Swaab, D.F. 39, 43
Symons, D. 18, 83, 108, 142, 156, 167,
   182; male and female reproductive
   agendas 81–2; morality 3, 179;
   proximate explanations 176, 177

Thibaut, F. 123
Thornhill, R. 105
Thorp, J. 1
Tobach, E. 168
Trivers, R.L. 105, 109, 128, 149, 183;
   deception 113, 114, 166–7; kin
   selection 130, 136; parental
   manipulation 145, 146, 147
Trost, M. 83
Turner, W.J. 52, 56, 176; hypervariable
   mutation 121–3

Ulrichs, K.H. 21

Vanwyk, P.H. 166
Vincent, P. 85–6
Vining, D. 156–62

Wald, E. 57, 168, 171, 181
Wallace, B. 67
Ward, I.L. 30
Weinberg, M.S. 33, 143, 155, 159;
   bisexuality 6–7, 60, 89–91;
   promiscuity 40, 77, 78, 79, 184
Weinrich, J.D. 45, 48, 59, 64, 106, 159,
   172; gender nonconformity 113, 140,
   149; kin selection 129, 130, 135, 136,
   141; preference for homosexuality
   141, 142, 144
Weiss, K.M. 108–9
Weisz, J. 30
Wiegmann, D.D. 113
Whitam, F. 48–9, 50, 51, 140
Whitley, B.E. 107
Williams, G.C. 73–4, 182
Wilson, E.O. 89, 106, 112, 124, 157, 160,
   168, 172; balanced superior
   heterozygotic fitness model 12, 86;
   'driven' homosexuality 62;
   explanation 169; kin selection 128,
   129, 135, 135–6; morality of the gene
   180–1; sexual selection 105
Wilson, M. 156, 157
Wingfield, W.M. 21
Witelson, S.F. 43
Wright, S. 98

Yalom, I.D. 29

Zuger, B. 45, 140

Subject index

adaptiveness 19, 64–75, 172, 187; advantage 68–9; hybrid vigour 72–3; meaning 73–5; nature of natural selection 69–72; paradox of polymorphism 65–8; *see also* maladaptiveness

adolescent homosexuality 6–7, 51, 59, 60, 150, 183

adrenocorticotrophic hormone (ACTH) 32

advertisements, contact 184

age 96

alleles 11, 13

altruism: kin selection and genes selected for 135–9; reciprocal 16

anatomical studies 38–43, 63

androgen insensitivity syndrome 26–8

animal analogy 164–7

anterior commissure 40, 41, 43

ascertainment bias 52

autosomal genes 13, 86–7

bad sex 143–4

balance polymorphism 11, 76–115; density and frequency-dependent selection 97–101; frequency-dependent sexual selection 101–15; overloving effect 117–18; social adjustment 150–5; sperm competition 92–7; *see also* balanced superior heterozygotic fitness

balanced (stabilising) natural selection 70–2

balanced superior heterozygotic fitness 11–14, 76–91; autosomal, X-linked or heterotic 86–7; dual attractions 88–91; frequency of homosexuality 87–8; sexual drive 77–86

Batesian mimicry 98–9

behavioural plasticity 5–6, 9, 168–9

behavioural polymorphisms 100–1

biochemistry 165–6

biology 4, 18–63, 185

birth rates, declining 156–7

bisexuality 6–7, 60; balanced superior heterozygotic fitness 88–91; social adjustment 150–5

brain: anatomical difference 38–40; functional differences 41–3; sexual inversion 22–3, 24–5

butterflies 98–9

byproduct, evolutionary 115–16

castration 27

cerebral cortex 42–3

charm 105–8

chorionic gonadotropin 22

competition: female for mates 110; sperm competition 92–7

congenital adrenal hyperplasia (CAH) syndrome 25–6, 31–2

contact advertisements 184

continuously occurring mutation 120–3

contraception: impact of 158

Coolidge Effect 83–4

cryptic ovulation theory 95

cultural evolution 159–60

de-androgenised foetus theories 26–38; androgen insensitivity syndrome 26–8; effect of sex hormones on infants 28–9; maternal stress hypothesis 29–36; receptor site 37–8

deception 113–15, 166–7

demographic transition 156–7

density-dependent selection 97–101

detection of deception 114–15
determinism 177–8
developmental homosexuality 6–7, 51, 59, 60, 150, 183
differentials, reproductive *see* reproductive differentials
dihydrotestosterone (DHT) 24
directed social evolution 16
directional selection 69–70, 72, 87
diversifying (disruptive) natural selection 70, 71–2, 87
dizygotic (DZ) twins 45–6, 46–7, 48, 49, 50–1, 52–3
DNA markers 37, 55–9
DNA sequence variation 37–8
Dominican Republic 23–4
double-matings 93, 95–6, 111; *see also* extra-pair couplings
double standard 93–4
driven, the 61–2
Drosophila (fruit flies) 99–100
dual attractions *see* bisexuality

ecological dimension 161–2
effeminacy 140–1, 149
electroencephalographic (EEG) studies 41–3
environment: novel environments hypothesis 154, 157; social evolution 16–17; twin studies and 52–3; unnatural environments 167
estradiol 27
estrogen feedback effect (EFE) 32–6
euheterosis 72–3
evolutionary byproduct 115–16
experimenters 60
explanation: of homosexuality 8–14, 185; scientific and reductionism 174–7; unnecessary and misguided 168–70
extent of homosexuality 6–7, 87–8, 184
extra-pair couplings (EPCs) 93, 95–6, 108–10, 111–13

facultative polyandry 93
familial studies 44–53, 63
fantasies, sexual 79–80
female bisexuality 152–3
female control of reproduction 157–8, 182–3
female heterosexual desire 13
female homosexuality *see* lesbianism

female inexperience/ineptness 152
female mate choice 99–100, 103–5, 162; *see also* frequency-dependent sexual selection
feminisation hypothesis 38–9, 43
fertility: differentials *see* reproductive differentials; female control of 157–8, 182–3; sperm competition and female 94–5
Fisher's theorem 9
fitness-investment-potential of the recipient 137–9
5–alpha reductase deficiency 23–5
fragile-X gene 121
freedom of enquiry 179–80
frequency-dependent selection 97–101
frequency-dependent sexual selection 99–100, 101–15, 166–7; charm 105–8; deception 113–15; female choice 103–5; parental investment 111–13; reproductive differential 108–11
frequency of homosexuality 6–7, 87–8, 184
fruit flies 99–100
functional differences 41–3
fundamental postulate 159–62
futile sex theory 3–4
futility models 116–23; continuously occurring mutation 120–3; overloving effect 116–19

gender: natural transsexuals 23–4; nonconformity 140–1, 149; parental investment and 148–9
genes 11; morality of 180–1; parliament of 81
genetic load 65–7
genetic selfishness 137
genetic variation 9, 20, 43–59, 63, 187; familial studies 44–53, 63; Xq28 53–9
grand theory 174

heterosis (hybrid vigour) 72–3, 86–7
heterotic balancing selection 71–2
heterozygotes 11–12; *see also* balanced superior heterozygotic fitness
homosexuality: defining 6–7, 155; experience of 7–8; extent of 6–7, 87–8, 184; male compared with female 183–5; typology of 59–62

homosexuality gene 58–9; kin selection
    for 128, 129–35
homozygotes 11–12
homozygous autosomal recessive
    penetrance 23–6
hormonal studies 20, 21–38, 62–3; de-
    androgenised foetus theories 26–38;
    pseudohermaphroditism 23–6
hybrid vigour 72–3, 86–7
hypervariable mutation 121–3
hypervirility 166–7

illness 143
imitation 125–6
inclusive fitness 130–1, 147
infidelity 93, 95–6, 108–10, 111–13
intelligence, human 158, 159
interstitial nuclei of the anterior
    hypothalamus (INAH) dimorphism
    39–40, 43
intrasexual selection 103
inversion, sexual see sexual inversion

K strategy 82, 108, 160
kin selection 9–10, 127–44; for genes
    other than homosexuality 128,
    135–9; for a homosexuality gene
    128, 129–35; and social preference
    for homosexuality 128, 140–4
knowledge: reductionism and 175

lesbianism: compared with male
    homosexuality 183–5; twin studies
    51
Leydig cells 27–8
libido 76–7, 77–86, 142
lifestyle preferences 140–4
linkage analysis 37, 55–9; see also X-
    linkages
luteinising hormone (LH) 22, 33–6
luteinising hormone releasing hormone
    (LHRH) 36

M100 site 42–3
magnetoencephalographic (MEG)
    studies 42–3
maladaptiveness 19, 144, 172, 182
malaria 11–12
male sex characteristics 105; secondary
    sex characteristics 104, 113
manipulation, parental 144–9
matching principle 104, 105

mate-guarding 95
maternal-line effect 13, 53–9, 117–19
maternal male fetal wastage theory
    121–3
maternal stress hypothesis 29–36
matriarchy 181
methylisation 123
mimicry, Batesian 98–9
Minnesota Study of Twins Reared
    Apart 50
monozygotic (MZ) twins 45–7, 48, 49,
    50–1, 51–2, 52–3
morality 171; and normality 3–4, 186;
    sociobiology and 179–81
mutation 88; continuously occurring
    120–3

natural selection 67–8, 180–1;
    ecological dimension 161–2; and
    human evolution 125–7; nature of
    69–72
Nazi experimentation 171, 180
necessity to explain homosexuality
    168–70
normalising (directional) natural
    selection 69–70, 72, 87
normality 3–4, 186
novel environments hypothesis 154,
    157

oestrus concealment 95
optimal type 65–7, 70
orientation, sexual 5–6, 90, 166, 168
overloving effect 116–19
ovulation 94–5

parental investment 127; differential
    147–8; frequency-dependent sexual
    selection 111–13; by gender 148–9
parental manipulation 144–9; selective
    benefit 147–9
parliament of genes 81
partners, sexual 77–8, 79, 90–1, 154,
    183–4
paternal discrepancy rates 108–9
paternity certainty 93
patriarchy 181–3
physical evolution 64–123
plasticity, behavioural 5–6, 9, 168–9
polygenic transmission 80–1
polymorphism: balance see balance
    polymorphism; behavioural

polymorphisms 100–1; paradox of 65–8
poor quality heterosexuals 143–4
'pop sociobiology' 172–3
population genetics 11
potency 78–9
predation cycle 133–4
predisposed, the 61
preference, sexual 5–6, 24, 168, 186; social for homosexuality 128, 140–4
Premarin 34–5
promiscuity 77–8, 79, 183–4
proof, standards of 169–70
prostitution 142
proximate causative theories 176–7
pseudohermaphroditism 23–6
psychology 174, 175; social 176

quality offspring 160–1

R strategy 82, 83, 108–109, 138
race–IQ debate 180
receptor site 37–8
reciprocal altruism 16
reductionism 173–7
relatedness 139
replication studies 57
reproduction: bisexuality and 150–1, 155; female control 157–8, 182–3; kin selection 131–5, 138–9
reproductive differentials 84–6, 156; frequency-dependent sexual selection 108–10
reproductive fitness 10
reproductive strategies 160–1; and sex drive 81–4

safety/security 106, 107
sampling problems 52, 78
San Francisco 78
scientific explanation 174–7
scientific worth 170–3
scorpionflies 114
secondary sex characteristics 104, 113
selfishness, genetic 137
semi-lethal male disorders 121–3
Sertoli cells 28
sex drive 76–7, 77–86, 142
sex hormones 28; effect on infants 28–9; see also hormonal studies
sexism 181–5
sexual fantasies 79–80

sexual inversion 20, 21–38, 143; de-androgenised foetus theories 26–38; pseudohermaphroditism 23–6
sexual orientation 5–6, 90, 166, 168
sexual partners 77–8, 79, 90–1, 154, 183–4
sexual preference see preference
sexual selection 99–100, 181–2; frequency-dependent see frequency dependent sexual selection
sexually transmitted diseases (STDs) 154
shamanists, tribal 129–30
sickle-cell anaemia 11, 11–12, 71–2, 81
similarity 106–7
sissy-boy syndrome 140–1, 149
social adjustment 149–55
social evolution 14–17, 124–62
social preference for homosexuality 128, 140–4
social psychology 176
social sciences 4, 174–7
sociobiology: central theoretical problem 156–62; sins of 163–85
sperm competition 92–7
stabilising (balanced) natural selection 70–2
stress, maternal 29–36
suprachiasmatic nucleus (SCN) 39
swallowtail butterfly 98–9
swingers 60; see also bisexuality
synthetic theory of evolution 9

testosterone 20, 25, 27–8, 34–5; see also dihydrotestosterone
third sex, theory of 21
transsexuals, natural 23–4
tribal shamanists 129–30
trinucleotide repeat sequences 121
triplets 49
triviality 170–3
21-hydroxylase deficiency 25–6, 31–2
twin studies 45–53, 53–4; evaluating 50–3
typology of homosexuality 59–62

ultimate causative theories 176–7
unchosen nature of homosexuality 186
undirected social evolution 16
unnatural environments 167
unwanted, the 61

virility, excessive 166–7

worth, scientific 170–3

X-linkages 53–9, 86–7; overloving
    effect 117–19
Xq28 53–9; fragility 121–3